The Princess Diana Conspiracy

For my beloved wife and soul mate Sally who died at home, and in my arms, at 12.41pm on Friday 19th April 2013. My heart has gone with you; until we meet again.

The Secret enemy who's sleepless eye
Stands sentinel, accuser, judge and spy
Therefore the fool, the jealous and the vain
The envious who but breathe in others pain
Behold the host, delighting to deprave
Who track the steps of glory to the grave,
Watch every fault that daring genius owe
Half to the ardour which its birth bestows
Distort the truth, accommodate the lie
And pile the pyramid of calumny.

Lord Byron (1788-1824)

The Princess Diana Conspiracy

The Evidence of Murder

by

Alan Power

PROBITY PRESS LTD

Copyright © Alan Power 2013
First published in 2013 by Probity Press Ltd
8 St George's Street, Douglas, Isle of Man, IM1 1AH

Distributed by Gardners Books, 1 Whittle Drive, Eastbourne,
East Sussex, BN23 6QH
Tel: +44(0)1323 521555 | Fax: +44(0)1323 521666

www.probitypress.com

British Library Cataloguing in Publication Data
A catalogue record for this book is available from the British Library.

ISBN 978-0-9575738-0-2

Typeset by Amolibros, Milverton, Somerset
e-mail: amolibros@aol.com
www.amolibros.co.uk
This book production has been managed by Amolibros
Printed and bound by T J International Ltd, Padstow, Cornwall, UK

Preface

Diana was murdered by MI6 with military aid and the order came from the palace; I cannot make my views any clearer. I am required to inform you, at the outset, that this book represents my views. But it is also a detailed analysis of proven evidence, so I believe that when you have read the following exposition these views will also become yours.

Legal advice given was that the words I use should be reduced in passion because to express my true feelings could render me liable to prosecution or make the book unpublishable; so forgive the 'economical with the truth', the constant 'in my view', the 'untruths' and the 'I believe that' qualifications I was required to include. I know you will read through the chaff and find the heart. Where you accept that the point is proven then that is self-evident but if you question my reasoning please remember that this is my honest opinion; I must state the obvious for legal reasons.

I am also required to remind you that an investigation was made by the French police with British police involvement (Operation Paget). But it was, in my view, (I need to keep on saying that) extremely flawed if not downright corrupt and I trust that my reasoning will become very apparent; please rationalise this evidence and take your own stance. If you wish to have detailed information on Operation Paget then be my guest but please don't write a book about it; I doubt anyone would want to read it, unless they are students of the inane.

The inquest detail is more informative because, during this six-month period, some men laboured for justice and much of this book's evidence has been extracted from these inquest transcripts.

Essentially, we are dealing with a subject where disclosure of some facts is not welcomed by certain state organisations. For this reason I needed to tread with special care to reveal the truth and to ensure the law cannot be used to silence me. There are, of course other, albeit criminal, means for this purpose at the disposal of those who are permitted to function above the law. But to permit these miscreants their main weapon of controlling the people through fear is to abandon any hope of achieving democracy. The British nation just continues to use the word democracy and hopes all is well but refuse to fear them and their days are numbered.

As the author of this book I have received several attempts to intimidate me. I have had an unmarked khaki helicopter hover 100 feet above my house in North Wales. I waved; they lingered and then flew off. A friend, who was a serving police officer, noted people climbing up a telegraph pole with line of sight to my house; when he checked the car registration number at the 'office' it didn't exist. I also had a message on my mobile/cell phone when they 'challenged me to pursue my idea'. I travelled by ferry to England from my new home on the Isle of Man and was accompanied both there and on the return by two different sets of 'gentlemen' siting one behind me and one to my side. So anyone who thinks MI6 didn't know where Diana was going needs to reconsider. They abuse people's liberties without conscience.

You will find I have repeated various points several times. This is because you will read a great deal of evidence and I sometimes come across a point where a previous one enhances it. This happens when major points arise and I wish to maximise their value and ensure that you also recall the previous point made, or another aspect of it.

To ask that you enjoy reading this book seems inappropriate and I can't really say that I enjoyed writing it; perhaps, it became more of an obsession. But I do believe that you will become enraged as you read it and, like me, demand justice. This not only applies to the British but all decent people throughout the world – to whom this story belongs. Remember, Diana was born in England of aristocratic lineage but her maternal grandfather was Irish and her maternal great grandmother, Frances Work, was American and from the State of Michigan. (By coincidence a large number of my family settled in the USA generations ago; in the State of Michigan – no particular relevance.)

The book was due to be published at the end of August 2012. It was then changed to 1st November 2012. My intended publishers told my agent they were not going ahead with publication, eight weeks before its due release date (it was listed on Amazon for weeks and then declared to be currently unavailable) because lawyers had told the publishers that the book was 'very dangerous'; good, that's why I wrote it. I always knew disclosure of the truth was going to be dangerous. How could the publishers possibly not know (they could have checked before signing the contract)? But at last, after many obstacles, we proceed; I urge that you now deliberate and reach your verdict.

God bless! Now to the pursuit of the truth, democracy and Diana Spencer's victory; even in death.

Contents

Part Three: Key Eyewitnesses   *187*

Rider for paparazzi Rommauld Rat. Gave convincing
evidence that when they reached the Alma Tunnel
the Mercedes had already crashed. There were no
other paparazzi present. The assassins had gone.

Acknowledgments

Books

Thomas Sancton and Scott MacLeod, *Death of a Princess – An Investigation*, 1998
Morton, Andrew, *Diana; Her True Story*, 1992
Cohen, David, *Diana – Death of a Goddess*, 2004
Tim Clayton and Phil Craig, *Diana; Story of a Princess*, 2001
Botham, Noel, *The Assassination of Princess Diana*, 2004
Burrell, Paul, *A Royal Duty*, 2003
Rees-Jones, Trevor, *The Bodyguard's Story*, 2000
Gregory, Martin, *Diana – The Last Days*, 1999
Campbell, Lady Colin, *The Royal Marriages*, 1993
Dimbleby, Jonathan, *The Prince of Wales: A Biography*, 1994

Newspapers

The *Sun*
The *Daily Express*
The *News of the World*
The *Daily Mail*
The *Daily Telegraph*
The *Sunday Mirror*
The *Daily Mirror*

The Official Inquest Transcripts

Use is made of my rights under English law rules of 'Qualified Privilege' and 'Honest Opinion'.

Special mention

Death of a Princess; An Investigation was published in 1998, only a few months after Diana's brutal murder. The two American *Time* magazine reporters that authored the book, Sancton and Macleod, contributed greatly to preventing a successful conclusion to this evil crime, by raising serious questions that have never been answered.

It is hoped that with the benefit of inquest evidence *The Princess Diana Conspiracy* will be the next major contribution towards ensuring this criminal act does not remain swept under the carpet and unpunished. The perpetrators of this vile crime would most probably have succeeded without these two exceptional investigators.

Prologue

During the first hour of Sunday morning, 31st August 1997, Diana, Princess of Wales, was killed in a high-speed car crash in the Pont de l'Alma road tunnel in Paris, together with her lover Dodi Fayed and Henri Paul, their chauffeur for the night. Paul was the acting head of security at the Ritz Hotel. Diana was thirty-six years old. Millions of people all around the world mourned the loss of a woman who had become an icon of our times.

Official investigations into the crash maintained that it was simply a tragic accident caused by Henri Paul's drunken loss of control at the wheel while being chased by hordes of paparazzi photographers. Yet herein I shall expound significant evidence that Diana's death was an assassination by 'The Increment', an SAS/SBS military attachment to the British Security Services (MI6).

Beginning in November 2003, I decided to review this evidence and, in search of the truth, I began on a long, instructive but perilous journey. Ten years later, greatly assisted by evidence from the official inquests, I believe that the truth of what happened on that fateful night in Paris is now uncovered; evidence that would satisfy any honest court in the world.

★

Princess Diana's journey from carefree 'Sloane Ranger' to her tragic death, mourned by millions across the globe, was a long and rocky one. Born in 1961, her aristocratic background and connections with the British royal family made her an obvious choice as a future royal wife. In early 1981, at the tender age of nineteen, she became engaged to the Queen of England's son and heir, Prince Charles, and her life forever changed.

It's well known that Diana felt lonely and betrayed from the very beginning of her marriage to Charles. The 1981 'fairy-tale wedding', celebrated by crowds of 600,000 people in London and watched by over 750 million worldwide, was quickly in trouble. The young and innocent Lady Diana Spencer had no idea that her husband-to-be had already professed an undying love for his mistress, Camilla Parker Bowles (née Shand).

The marriage to Diana was undertaken for the sole purpose of producing offspring for the royal succession and Diana was discarded, literally, within an hour of giving birth to her second son, Prince Harry, in 1984. She said that her husband had wanted a girl and after she gave birth to Harry at London's St Mary's Hospital he visited her, looked at the child and said, 'Oh my God, it's a boy, and he's even got red hair!' He then left. Later, Diana was to note at that point: 'Something inside me closed off – by then I knew he had gone to his lady.'

It was reported that Diana said Charles' father, Prince Philip, told his son at the beginning of his marriage that he could leave Diana within five years to be with his mistress. (What better proof could there be that this marriage was solely for the purpose of producing offspring? Charles seemingly did this right on cue. Diana stated this to the journalist and writer Andrew Morton for his book, *Diana: Her True Story*.) Other royals were aware of Charles' feelings for Camilla before the royal wedding, but no one stepped in to help Diana, who found that she was walking blindly into a nightmare situation.

Diana also knew that Camilla had been on the scene since before her marriage, but after the birth of her children she was terrified of speaking out for fear of losing them. The influence that the royals wielded meant her chances of retaining custody in the event of a divorce were slim, so she defied them by building a dossier of dangerous information to assist her with a potential custody battle. If disclosed, this threatened to bring the monarchy to its knees by revealing many of her husband's indiscretions plus other royal skeletons. In an uneasy truce it was, therefore, agreed that Diana would be allowed to retain control of her children and take them wherever she wished.

This situation continued even after Charles and Diana's inevitable divorce in 1996, right up until 1997, when Diana fell in love with Dodi Fayed, the son of billionaire businessman Mohamed Al Fayed. This heralded a new and dangerous phase for the royal family, in which the monarchy now faced the twin risks that it might lose control of the two young heirs, William and Harry, and also that Diana could produce revelations that might cause irreversible damage to the monarchy. Neither could be permitted by the British Security Services or any other agency that advises the monarch.

★

Dodi Fayed – Diana's soulmate and lover at the time of the crash – was, in contrast to her, relatively unknown before their relationship but this catapulted him onto the world stage. Yet he had also been born into a position of great wealth and privilege. His father, Mohamed Al Fayed, had built an extremely successful business empire largely from dealings in Dubai. His various retail enterprises included the world-famous department store, Harrods in Knightsbridge, London, where he had his corporate offices on the fifth floor.

Emaud Fayed (Dodi) was his cherished, eldest son, whom Diana knew from her family's friendship with the Al Fayeds. Diana's father, Earl Spencer, whom Mohamed Al Fayed called 'Johnnie', was a personal friend, while Diana's stepmother, Raine Spencer, was a director of Harrods so, when the relationship between Diana and Dodi deepened in 1997, they had already shared a long history. Dodi, as the forty-one-year-old unmarried son of a very wealthy businessman, was the ultimate 'eligible bachelor' and he had also found success in his own right as a film producer (he was the executive producer of the BAFTA-winning *Chariots of Fire* movie, among others).

During Diana's last fateful summer, Mohamed Al Fayed offered her a holiday at his St Tropez villa in the South of France. Lost, alone, discarded by her husband and restricted in where she could take the children because of security fears, Diana gladly accepted. On 11th July 1997, a Harrods' helicopter collected Diana and her children from Kensington Palace and flew them to London's Stansted Airport, from where they routed to Nice on board the Harrods' executive jet, a Gulfstream IV. On arrival, they all transferred to the *Jonical*, Al Fayed's luxury yacht, and sailed down the coast to his St Tropez mansion, Castel St Helen, in St Tropez Le Parc – an exclusive park of over 100 mansions set in ten acres, on cliffs above the sea. Diana occupied the guest quarters, the Fisherman's Cottage – an eight-bedroom house close to the mansion with direct access to a private beach.

Just prior to his holiday with Diana in St Tropez, Dodi had been dating – and was rumoured to have considered marrying – Kelly Fisher, a very attractive American actress. Whatever transpired with this relationship, it's clear that he was ready for marriage and had decided to settle down. Would he really have abandoned his relationship with Kelly for just a short summer fling with Diana, as the Establishment later tried to claim? Whatever his initial intentions, on 15th July, Dodi – who was in Paris – gave Kelly a false story of going to London on business for his father and flew down to St Tropez to be with Diana, her boys and his family. Diana returned to London on 20th July, two days later than planned; she had enjoyed her stay and wasn't in a rush to return home.

Only days later, on 24th July, Dodi returned to Paris and then continued on to London, where Diana was already sending thank-you letters to the Al Fayed family after the holiday; she spoke of them in very affectionate terms, saying they were 'hugely special people'. On 25th July, the day after returning to London, Dodi took Diana to Paris for the weekend. Together they stayed in the $10,000-per-night Imperial Suite at the Ritz Hotel but dined at the nearby Ritz-Carlton Restaurant, leaving by the hotel's rear entrance – a ploy that would be used during that fateful visit to Paris just a few weeks later. Returning to London on Sunday, 27th July, they went to Nice the following Thursday, 31st July via Stansted Airport, London for a very private holiday on board Al Fayed's yacht, the *Jonical*, sailing to Corsica and Sardinia.

By this point the affair was already intense and the paparazzi in hot pursuit. One of these photographers, Mario Brenna, located the *Jonical* on 2nd August and followed it to various different locations. On 4th August at Porto Cervo, Sardinia, Brenna took a photograph called 'the Kiss' that was published on 10th August in the British *Sunday Mirror* newspaper. The picture caused a sensation and was widely seen as confirming Diana was in love. Brenna's agent said they had been told where Diana and Dodi would be, implying that Diana had stage-managed the event to prepare the world for changes that were coming in her lifestyle; she had recently stated publicly to the press, 'You will have a big surprise coming soon with the next thing I do.'

On 5th August, immediately after this staged photo shoot, Diana and Dodi went to view an engagement ring from the 'Tell Me Yes' ('Dites-moi Oui') range in Alberto Repossi's store in Monte Carlo, fuelling rumours of an impending engagement. They returned to London on 6th August and the next day spent the evening together at Dodi's apartment at 60 Park Lane, next to the Dorchester Hotel. Diana left at 11.00pm and then travelled to Bosnia on a Landmines Campaign sortie the next morning, returning on 10th August. A few hours after returning, the Harrods' helicopter picked Diana up and took her to Mohamed Al Fayed's house in Oxted, Surrey, where she and Dodi spent the following day relaxing on Al Fayed's 500-acre estate while Al Fayed visited his in-laws in Finland. They went to meet with Diana's clairvoyant, Rita Rogers, near Chesterfield in Derbyshire and then travelled back to Oxted by helicopter. This was significant because Diana set great store by readings from Rogers and Dodi was the first man she had introduced to her.

Diana and Dodi had become inseparable so, in London on the 13th August, they went out for a night on the town and then back to Dodi's apartment at 60 Park Lane (Diana left at 2.00am). The following night, of 14th August, she arrived at 60 Park Lane at 7.43pm and again left in the early hours of the following morning. She then kept a long-standing arrangement with Rosa Monckton (of more later) and departed for a short holiday in the Greek Islands on the following day, 15th August, using Al Fayed's Gulfstream IV. She arrived back in England on 19th August and by 9.00pm that evening was back in

Dodi's arms at 60 Park Lane, leaving at 1.15am the following morning. The very next evening, Diana and Dodi took off for Nice at 6.40pm, where they boarded the *Jonical* for another idyllic cruise around the Mediterranean.

On 14th August, Dodi had a conversation with Frank Klein, president of the Ritz Hotel, Paris and overseer of the Villa Windsor in the Bois de Boulogne (so-called because it was the Duke of Windsor and Mrs Simpson's exile home after the Duke's abdication as King of England), which Al Fayed rents from the City of Paris. Dodi asked when the villa would become available for occupation, telling Klein, 'I've spoken with my father about moving in – my friend doesn't want to stay in England.' He later confirmed, in a further conversation with Klein on 29th August and only hours before the fatal crash, 'We want to move into the villa because we are getting married in October or November, Frank.'

Diana and Dodi's relationship was fast becoming known to the world and people now began to realise this was not just a summer fling: the possibility that Diana might marry Dodi and leave the country was a real one. Diana had already said her sons were always urging her to live abroad to be less in the public eye. However, this was repudiated by Queen Elizabeth, who ordered a new statement be issued, disclaiming this possibility. Having the second and third in line to the throne living abroad, without the level of protection afforded by British Security, was not an idea relished by the British monarchy.

In truth, Diana had unwittingly substituted one impossible situation for another. On the one hand, she had found Dodi, who could give her the love that she had so far been denied, but the paradox was that marriage to him would give her a power she couldn't be allowed to possess. She was about to marry into one of the world's wealthiest families that would enable her to become a continuous, public thorn in the side of the British monarchy. Diana had found the man of her dreams and looked forward to a bright and happy future, but she also held a unique position that ensured both the police and Security Services would be watching her every move. This high-profile relationship posed a unique threat to the monarchy.

However, the fast-developing romance continued apace. It had seemed probable Diana and Dodi would proceed towards marriage from the moment they went into the Alberto Repossi store in Monte Carlo on 5th August to view engagement rings, but when they ordered one on 22nd August 1997, and arranged to collect it in Paris on 30th August, it was certain. Of course they wouldn't set a date before Diana's decree absolute came through on 29th August and she would want to inform her children before making the news public. But all the events of the preceding weeks had clearly been leading up to this point. Diana had faced the daunting task of seeking a new way forward, but her celebrity had made this virtually impossible – having a normal life was not an option for her. She needed a new partner with impressive and precise credentials who must be wealthy, available, good with her children and preferably a soulmate with whom she could share common interests.

When Diana found Dodi, it was like a dream come true – pure heaven for eight blissful weeks, until darkness fell.

Part One

'Genesis'

Fiasco Royale: Diana's Royal World

To understand why the Establishment would opt for such a draconian solution as murder it is essential to understand the risk Diana posed to the royal family and to perceive her relationship with them. But we must also consider the reason why Charles Windsor married Diana and the potential content of her dossier. (Diana constructed this dossier to assist with her anticipated forthcoming custody battle for the retention of her children and to defend her overall position.) Without this background some might accept the authorities' creed that the monarchy had nothing to fear, so there was no motive for murder.

We must also be aware of the background to the British system of governance to witness the nervous and tenuous hold the monarchy has on power. In fact, it's not dissimilar to the Mafia, where there is a 'Godfather' who heads several different factions, each one swearing allegiance to the supreme leader in return for favours.

The British monarchy was born of the same philosophy, whereby nobles (mostly appointed by a monarch to ensure the system's survival) or heads of different clans swore allegiance to the monarch in return for land and titles, plus other special favours and so they propped the leader up with their loyalty. The British King or Queen is similarly at the head of an ancient and colourful pageant that's been in existence for around 1,200 years and has survived much battering.

The treatment of Diana also has much precedent within the current royal family. The incumbent monarch is directly related back to the first German monarch, George I, then George II, the infamous George III and then followed by George IV. This line has continued through to the present day. George I was reputed to have had his wife's lover, Philip Christophe von Konigsmarck murdered for his 'impudence' and his wife, Sophia Dorothea of Brunswick-Luneburg, was incarcerated for the last thirty years of her life in the castle of Ahlen in her native Celle and refused permission ever to see her children again.

When III died his son George IV inherited the throne although he had been acting as Regent for the previous eleven years because of George III's mental incapacity. George IV had entered a sham marriage in 1785, when he was twenty-three, to Maria Fitzherbert, one of his mistresses, but George managed to have that annulled. He was then ordered to marry Caroline of Brunswick (sound familiar?) and did so on 7th April 1795; it lasted one year.

Caroline left Britain for Germany but upon George ascending the throne she returned since she was now the Queen although George refused to recognise her as his Queen. On the evening of George's coronation 21st July 1821 Caroline was taken ill in her bedchamber. She was ill for three weeks before dying of what she claimed was poisoning. On 7th August 1821 her body was taken to her native Brunswick for burial so that the people would more quickly forget.

There have of course been times when the monarchy came close to toppling and even Queen Victoria survived four assassination attempts. In 1649, a non-royal head of state named Oliver Cromwell proclaimed himself Lord Protector of England after a bloody civil war and the subsequent beheading of the king, Charles I. Charles's son, Charles II, returned from exile in France to reclaim the monarchy and so was back in power by 1660, but this wasn't the only occasion when the monarchy has feared for its existence.

In 1689, the Bill of Rights was passed and in 1693, King William III was forced to sign a declaration at Althorp (Diana's family seat) that removed the monarch's status under the 'Divine right of Kings' and replaced it with 'Limited Monarchy', where Parliament (in other words, the people) became the supposed real power in the land. William signed this in exchange for the support of nobles who had fought against King Charles I on the side of Cromwell in the English Civil War; ironically, it was Diana's forebears who were instrumental in obtaining his signature thus, theoretically, stripping the monarch of absolute power.

When Queen Anne died without any surviving children in 1714, the succession required someone of royal blood to inherit the Crown, which meant bringing George I, the Elector of Hanover in Germany, over to England. George spent most of his time in Germany and never did bother to learn the language of his new kingdom. It was his mentally disturbed grandson, George III, who lost England her American colonies by abusing the settlers' rights: his direct descendants still occupy the throne of England.

This family changed its name from Saxe-Coburg Gotha to Windsor during the First World War when the British went to war against their royal family's close relatives in Germany (King George V of England was a first cousin of the German Kaiser, Wilhelm), lest the people began to wonder at the incongruity of pledging allegiance while at war with their monarch's family. During the same period, George V was also advised by the then-Prime Minister, David Lloyd George (1916-22), not to allow another first cousin of his, the Tsar Nicholas of Russia, to come to Britain just prior to the outbreak of the Russian revolution in 1917 – after the king had already indicated that Nicholas would be welcome. The fear was that revolutionary mood could spread if the British people, already at war, identified with the Russians and decided it was also time for them to effect a change. History has recorded the consequence of that decision, with the sad and brutal demise of the Romanov family, but it also indicates the level of concern felt by the British Government concerning the stability of the monarchy, even then.

And thus we come to the present day. To all outward purposes, the institution of the royal family seems an essentially benign one, albeit anachronistic for the modern world. It is difficult for us, for example, to imagine the life of a twenty-first-century palace courtier – we tend to succumb to the period-drama clichés of obsequious types who bow constantly up and down palace corridors wearing seventeenth-century knickerbockers – yet nothing could be further from the truth with regard to the 'grey men', so named by Diana, who ensure the smooth running of the Palace protocol.

There are several grades of courtier and those at the top of the pile are chosen for their unswerving loyalty to the Crown and many are taken from the elite regiments of the British Army. The connection between the Security Services and the Palace is strong, since one can reason that if the courtier's job is to protect the monarch, then ex-Service employees are a natural choice. Certainly, there is a large cohort whose job it is to protect not only the Head of State but also the institution over which he or she presides. Who exactly makes the decisions regarding the perceived level of risk from any particular threat is a matter of conjecture and even if the Head of State is oblivious to the day-to-day activities of these people, some information must filter through to her advisers. It's known the monarch is aware that some of her employees function this way.

The head of the British state is also head of the Church of England and to ensure this doesn't enter into the realms of farce, the position must be filled by someone who is scandal-free and loved, or at least respected by the people over whom he or she would command allegiance. The present incumbent achieves this, but it is interesting to ask what the future will hold.

As for Diana, her family had been entwined with the royals for many generations. Diana's great-grandfather was equerry to Edward VII and arranged the coronation of George V. Her father was equerry to King George VI and also to Queen Elizabeth II, which shows that Diana's family has strong associations with the incumbent royal family from when they first took the English throne. Certainly, as a child and young woman, Diana revered the royal family and everything they stood for. Yet even she came to believe there were fatal flaws in the royal system and that there must be a seismic shift in attitude and major surgery for the monarchy to survive into the twenty-first century.

In the next section, we look at what caused Diana to change her opinion so strongly regarding the family into which she had so willingly married.

Deception: Betrayal and Motive

Diana's early childhood was no fairy tale and ended with the break-up of her parents' marriage when she was just six years old, which resulted in her mother leaving the family home. She recalls a dark cloud descending, which certainly contributed to her well-known feelings on the sanctity of marriage and the effect that any break-up has on the children.

Park House, on the Sandringham estate in Norfolk, where Diana spent these early years, is also the royal family's winter home, where Diana and her brother Charles grew up with the royal children. There was always a possibility that Diana could be chosen as a royal bride and she clearly had aspirations towards marrying the Prince of Wales and becoming the future Queen of England. In those early years, Diana was, arguably, complicit in what was about to befall her and perhaps decreed her own destiny through her rose-tinted ambition. Her family certainly had the aristocratic lineage that gave her a chance at this ultimate prize. When Diana was thirteen, her grandfather died and her father inherited the 13,000-acre Althorp estate that included a 121-room country mansion, together with the title of 8th Earl. In 1975, she moved there with her family.

In the summer of 1972 and nearly ten years before marrying Diana, Charles, Prince of Wales, fell in love with Camilla Shand and although by 1977, Camilla was married to British Army officer Andrew Parker Bowles, Prince Charles now carried a torch for Camilla that would prevent him from loving anyone else. He had missed the proverbial 'boat' as far as marriage with Camilla was concerned and was effectively forced into choosing someone else to marry because of his royal commitment to produce offspring (Charles admitted that he never loved Diana). So there was never any hope that Charles would settle for Diana because there must be a desire for something to work before there can be any hope that it will.

So whom should he choose for the production of offspring? Charles knew that any 'duty wife' must be naïve enough to enable a deception to continue after marriage. Young, virginal, besotted and of good lineage; Diana was the perfect candidate. Charles considered that he could do his duty, keep his nagging family happy and continue his lifestyle just as he wished, even after marriage. Diana would be a silent and obedient incubator who, doing her duty as a mother, would live a quiet life in the country entertaining her husband's mistress and allow Charles to continue living his life in a style from a bygone age.

For her part, Diana had serious doubts about Charles's continuing relationship with Camilla from the outset, so with the benefit of hindsight, it's clear she should not have proceeded with the wedding. It's apparent she was feeling a lot more than the usual pre-marital nerves but once they had become engaged, there was no going back.

Diana's first introduction to Buckingham Palace, just before her wedding, was to be greeted by a servant with a note from Camilla that suggested they should have lunch. It was an extraordinary move: her future husband's mistress, the very cause of her misgivings and ultimately the reason for the end of her marriage and happiness, was the one person to acknowledge her arrival in her new home. It's clear to me that the intent was to keep all surface appearances as smooth as possible to ensure the wedding proceeded so the carefully balanced and adulterous relationship between Camilla and Charles could continue behind closed doors. Diana was believed to be an excellent choice as a potential royal wife and pressure from the royal family was mounting to quickly tie the knot.

When asked at a 1981 interview whether he loved Diana, Charles issued the banal response, 'Whatever "in love" means.' It's interesting to question what his idea of being 'in love' really did mean.

Perhaps it meant meeting a married woman and falling in love with her before asking someone else to marry him? Constantly telephoning this lover while 'courting' his new fiancé? Accepting presents from his mistress, such as cufflinks engraved with both sets of initials that he wore, even when with his new wife? Going out to see his mistress before and during his marriage despite his wife's entreaties; being overheard by his wife on honeymoon speaking on the phone saying he will always love that person no matter what happens; being found carrying photographs of his mistress in his wallet while still on honeymoon; having his mistress move to a new house only eleven miles from his and having her over to his various parties and social gatherings, before and during his marriage? Perhaps this is what 'being in love means'. It was certainly not love that Charles showed to Diana.

It may also seem unbelievable that Charles should have his lover's husband, Andrew Parker Bowles, colonel of the Household Cavalry, leading the guard from Charles and Diana's wedding ceremony, knowing that, within the week, Charles would be telephoning his escort's wife from the royal honeymoon yacht to profess an undying love for her. If the wedding had proceeded with Charles having the intention of making the marriage work, without another person waiting in the wings, then there might be some sympathy with his position but instead the marriage was a farce, undertaken in the most cynical of ways. Diana was unable to stop the juggernaut and said she felt 'like a lamb going to the slaughter'. What life was this for a nineteen-year-old girl who wanted to marry someone who loved her?

It's not surprising that within weeks of marriage Diana's world had fallen apart and she was feeling unwell, suffering from both bulimia and depression. Then, as time went on, she suffered the further indignity of finding herself being portrayed as paranoid by some royal aides. The charge of paranoia against Diana was subtly levied time and again by the Palace as the years went by, to explain to a disbelieving public that Diana's claims concerning her husband's adulterous relationship with Camilla were irrational nonsense. At all costs the Palace was trying not to confront the Camilla issue that they were keeping hidden from the people.

But since Diana was right and the accusations against her known to be false, it makes the charges of paranoia particularly sinister. Such accusations are designed to make the victim question their own reading of a situation and destabilise their confidence. It was hoped this would divert attention from the truth and entice the public into believing that the fault for any 'misunderstanding' was all down to Diana losing the plot.

One of the main proponents of Diana's state of mind, Nicholas Soames, described Diana's reading of Charles's adulterous behaviour as 'paranoid and having lost all reason'. Mr Soames is, of course, one of the closest confidantes of Prince Charles and was in John Major's Tory government, ousted just prior to Diana's murder, serving as Minister of State for the Armed Forces (1994–May 1997). He will know the machinations of the Army and the British Secret Service very well.

Incidentally, Soames was one of the people most loathed by Diana and undoubtedly one of her biggest critics, having commenced the paranoia accusation on British television. (He did apologise for this during the inquest proceedings. One can only speculate as to whether the apology was for saying that Diana was paranoid when he knew very well that she was not and his conscience was troubling him or because it was known that he had made this comment so was unable to deny it.) Diana also accused him of making threatening telephone calls to her when he apparently advised Diana that people can have accidents (having witness support at the inquests but denied by Soames).

Yet if anyone knew the truth about Charles and Camilla it was Nicholas Soames, having made his home available for several of their clandestine meetings. So he must have known that his comments about Diana's supposed paranoia, with reference to Charles's infidelity, were false before making them.

It is interesting to look more closely at these allegations of paranoia. The Palace first claimed there had been no affair between Charles and Camilla until 1992 – that is, after Charles and Diana had separated. When the evidence proved this to be a lie, the Palace corrected the date to 1986. Yet claims regarding Diana's supposed paranoia were made after 1986 by the Palace because they were still trying to maintain the first lie concerning the 1992 date, proving either they had lied to the people or Charles was lying to the Palace. It is certainly hard to believe that the Palace didn't know about Camilla at the time (the Archbishop of Canterbury certainly did; hence his reference to Diana being used as a 'royal incubator').

The principle reason for Diana's state of mind was that she knew that her husband-to-be was an on-going adulterer. It should also be noted that these accusations of paranoia were levied against Diana when the Palace knew they were false and that she suffered from bulimia. It was also known that this condition could worsen due to an increase in stress levels, but still the accusations continued just so long as the Palace preserved their image and prevented the people from learning the truth.

There are two very significant reasons why Charles and his entourage wished for everyone to believe there had been no impropriety before 1992. Firstly, it would be proof that the Palace had lied to the people by denying the affair, and secondly, because the people would then question when Charles had begun his illicit union with Camilla. They would quickly realise that it started before his marriage to Diana and continued thereafter, thus proving his marriage to be a complete sham. (Charles admitted that he never loved Diana and said that his father had bullied him into marriage. This is from Jonathan Dimbleby's book – *The Prince of Wales: A Biography.*) This, of course, is further confirmation that Diana was totally deceived from the very beginning.

Prince Charles eventually admitted to infidelity from 1986 (presumably the earliest time from which it could be proven). This was five years after the wedding – the point at which his father, the Duke of Edinburgh, had said he could break free and the year when Camilla bought her country house, near to Charles in Tewksbury. It is also amazing that the Palace expected people to believe the new date put forward for the commencement of infidelity after the previous one was proven to be a lie.

In a strange echo of history, Charles's great-great-grandfather, King Edward VII, had taken a mistress who, remarkably, happened to be Camilla Parker Bowles's great-grandmother, Alice Keppel. But in contrast to Charles, Edward managed to keep both his wife and his lover 'on the go'. If Diana could be kept 'in her place', be a mother to the future King and the official Queen, who would look pretty and raise the heir and spare, then she would have served Charles's purpose. It appeared Charles believed that as long as he was happy and produced heirs, then nothing much else mattered after all, as Palace footman and later Diana's butler Paul Burrell heard him say, 'He would be king'. But this plan depended on Diana's meek acceptance of the situation and the Palace gravely erred in underestimating her.

Charles and Diana's marital charade continued until 1985, when they agreed to live separate lives but maintain appearances of unity for the sake of the monarchy and their children. Diana had held on, praying her husband's relationship with Camilla Parker Bowles would grow cold, but it was clear that this was a forlorn hope; she had fulfilled the task for which she had been 'contracted' and Charles had no place for someone who received prime attention at every event, making him feel flustered and irrelevant.

On many occasions Charles had been on tour with Diana and was virtually ignored while everyone pressed to see her, so he couldn't wait to be accompanied by someone who wouldn't overshadow him. The marriage simply couldn't continue, for either party.

The arrangement in 1986 was for both to go their separate ways but to maintain some pretence of unity so as not to embarrass or threaten the monarchy. However, this arrangement was doomed to fail and matters were made worse by Diana frequently raising her head to undermine them. The Palace had already started the re-invention of Charles's image and they needed to put the Diana phenomenon behind them; essentially they wanted Diana to leave public life altogether. The propaganda campaign intensified as they attempted to persuade the people that Charles would be a suitable king. In this, they had their work cut out for them, having tried and failed over the previous thirty or so years.

Diana, for her part, had to decide what to do. She still wanted her marriage to work but her hands were tied and so she decided to take on the Palace and beat them at their own game. She would find a way to let the people know the truth; they were on her side. Meanwhile, she must not let Charles, the Palace courtiers and others succeed in denigrating her to prevent the truth from emerging. Diana would be described as having Borderline Personality Disorder, Paranoia, being out of control and a loose cannon – in fact, anything was used to undermine her appeal with the public. Diana had to contend with the 'grey men' at the Palace, who would stop at nothing to win the propaganda war for the monarchy, yet she had stated publically that she would not go down without a fight.

It's apparent to me that Charles viewed Diana merely as a tiresome appendage and did not foresee her becoming a superstar, who would continue to outshine other royals. Yet during the time from 1986 when they had decided to live separate lives, Diana had attracted a ceaseless barrage of media interest because she started enjoying life and was looking for alternative paths, as a battered wife might, with one eye over her shoulder. Press reports were variable but hostility in some sections made Diana feel as though the propaganda war was being lost because she didn't have the resources to match the Palace. The only way to correct this was to establish the truth. To set the record straight, she cooperated with Andrew Morton's book, *Diana: Her True Story* that was published on 7th June 1992.

The prospect of people recognising the sham of her marriage and no longer needing to tolerate the abuse being administered by various sycophants became an enormous lure and so when the opportunity presented itself, she didn't shrink from it. Had she done so, the royals would have continued to run roughshod over her. So, to secure her position, she decided to take the truth to her public and reduce the risk of losing custody of her children.

The book, though written with her cooperation and consent, was handled carefully so that Diana could deny her involvement, maintaining 'deniability' – a practice frequently relied upon by MI6, the British Government and the Palace. Diana knew the furore this would cause; indeed, it was cataclysmic. Finally, the cat was out of the bag, revealing the fairy-tale marriage to be one of royal perfidy and abject humiliation.

After the book's publication, the truth ensured that the relationship between Diana and the Palace inexorably deteriorated and in 1992, the Queen ordered a separation. Living apart as opposed to divorce was attempted at first because the royal family had serious concerns regarding British public opinion, knowing Diana was held in such high regard. Diana also didn't want a divorce.

This arrangement worked for a while but Diana's strength grew and with the Palace no longer in control, there was now the prospect of a dangerous and prolonged conflict between the two sides. Diana showed no sign of leaving the public limelight and the royals misread how her popularity would alter after a split; it made no difference. It was further believed that when the public were informed on 5th September 1995 that Diana was to lose her HRH title and would eventually be out of the royal family, the people would soon lose interest and she would then disappear; again it made no difference and Diana remained as popular as ever

Diana now threw herself into the charity work that was closest to her heart and once again began commanding the headlines. Before she left the royal family, all her foreign trips had to be approved by the Palace. On several occasions the Palace would say they thought it was better if Charles attended a particular function instead of Diana, if they felt it would generate too much favourable publicity for her. The situation quickly descended into a battle for each side to find out who was going where, so each could try to outflank the other. Vitriol between the parties produced exceptionally lurid remarks but it wasn't so much whether anything else of an embarrassing nature would arise but rather whether or not the Palace could keep it hidden, which is why Diana proved so dangerous because she knew a great deal about the Royal skeletons.

Diana's determination to exact revenge for her years of abuse and the endurance of marital unfaithfulness plus her insistence on keeping custody of the children all created a volatile mix that the monarchy would have trouble suppressing. But with rapidly diminishing Palace control and once she had established her relationship with Dodi, the barometric danger level was raised several fold.

Meanwhile, Charles had done a good job of destroying his own image with very little help from Diana. Apart from the 'Camillagate' tapes, in which Charles described himself as a tampon, there was the infamous 'rape tape', where Charles was allegedly accused of being discovered in bed with one of his male servants; one servant even makes accusations of male rape against one of Charles's other servants. This came to light through Diana's friends but was quickly hushed up, with the Palace decreeing there was no need to involve the police. The British courts, as ever impartial in their deliberations concerning the royals, initially restricted the freedom of the press by preventing the reporting of these matters, but eventually the story came out anyway.

The saga of this so-called 'rape tape' is worth considering in more detail. It encompasses a series of events that took place between the years 1995–2003 and started when one of Charles's assistant valets, George Smith, claimed he had been raped by one of Charles's gay servants. The second injunction was then lifted and that allowed the person involved in the alleged rape incident to be named as Michael Fawcett, one of the Prince's closest aides and someone in whom Diana thought Charles had an unhealthy interest.

Just after the initial allegation, according to the former British newspaper, the *News of the World*, Diana had been preparing her defence against the royal onslaught due to engulf her over the custody of her children. The only way she knew of defeating the power that the royals wielded was to make certain it wouldn't be in their interests to try. If Diana could produce a document containing irrefutable evidence of much of the Palace 'sexploits' over the previous fifteen years then the royal family would realise they would risk losing not just the children but the monarchy if they elected to attempt a custody battle.

This dossier was prepared using tapes of George Smith's accusations and included his claim that he was unable to proceed with police assistance because the rapist was 'too powerful'. During Diana's taping of this statement, a further accusation described as 'shocking' came out, involving Charles with another male servant. The timing of all this was between Charles and Diana's decree nisi on 28th August 1996 and the decree absolute due on 29th August

1997, just before Diana was murdered and only hours before she could legally commit to Dodi Fayed, as I believe she clearly intended.

A few years after Diana's death the police deemed it necessary to arrest two of her former butlers: initially, Harold Brown and then Paul Burrell. Brown was arrested in November 2000 on charges of theft that were soon dropped, but not before his home had been thoroughly searched. Were the police looking for 'stolen artefacts', as they claimed, or Diana's secret dossier? Only weeks later, in January 2001, Burrell enjoyed the same treatment. The police began to search for those alleged artefacts that were apparently taken from Diana's collection after her death. Burrell was prosecuted and taken to court but meanwhile, Diana's dossier still couldn't be found and the alleged rape tape was still missing.

After almost two years, in November 2002, literally hours before Burrell was to give a sworn testimony in court regarding the alleged tapes, the Queen fortuitously remembered that Burrell had told her that he took Diana's items for safekeeping. The two years of mental anguish suffered by Burrell and his family didn't receive a mention; once again, the monarchy managed to wriggle out of the situation, its blushes spared.

Soon afterwards, George Smith tried to go public with his claim of the 'shocking incident' concerning Charles and the gay rape, but legal stifling once more initially prevented the truth from being disclosed. In March 2003, a police investigation severely criticised the way Charles's office had handled the rape allegation. Then, in October 2003 Burrell released his book, *A Royal Duty*, and stated during the publicity campaign that Diana had told him of the contents of the tape but he refused ever to reveal this information. Meanwhile George Smith again reiterated his accusations.

On 1 November 2003, Charles's one-time closest aide, Michael Fawcett, obtained an injunction banning another aide from telling a story concerning him and then, on 3 November, Fawcett obtained an injunction against another newspaper. On 6 November, this was successfully challenged and Fawcett was finally named as the servant behind the injunctions. Charles's private secretary, Sir Michael Peat, was allegedly forced to ask Charles whether he was the man referred to as indulging in gay sex with his servants. Charles subsequently denied, on television, that this was true.

Irrespective of the 'rape tape' allegations, it was clear that back in the mid-nineties Diana posed an increasingly serious threat to the royal family and their apparent predilections. The dossier of royal skeletons that she was compiling was powerful stuff that could help her custody battle, but it also directly endangered the monarchy. In addition, she could undermine the monarchy in a more subtle way: by threatening to take her children abroad. This would mean they would grow up without the discipline perceived as necessary by 'the Firm' (Diana's nickname for the royal family) to help them run the monarchy when the time came. It would also make the boys more vulnerable to security threats.

Far from helping the situation, the announcement on 5th September 1995 that, once divorced, Diana would lose her HRH status had simply meant the Palace had even less control over her. This was brought sharply to light on 20th September 1995, when Diana stated on the famous *Panorama* TV interview that she would fight to the end and not go quietly. (The announcement concerning her HRH removal may well have prompted Diana to agree to the interview.) She also expressed the view that Prince Charles was not capable of being king, nor did he believe he was capable, and that her son William should succeed, bypassing his father – a notion not far from the hearts of the British people. She had sworn vengeance for the wrongs done to her and would soon present a serious and continuous threat to the royal family unless something unforeseen happened.

That, as we all know, is exactly what did occur.

★

Diana had three distinct phases to endure in her transition from wronged wife to independent superstar. The first was living the lie of a sham marriage. Second was living apart from her husband but still being a part of the royal family and retaining all pretence of there being some sort of relationship. And the third was being apart from the royal family and trying to reinvent her life. She found the first phase extremely exhausting and hypocritical, especially with all the negative propaganda that she suffered. After she had been provoked into defending her position by breaking the code of secrecy that has surrounded the royals for generations by cooperating with Andrew Morton, she entered the second.

The continuance of this charade became impossible to maintain and hence the official separation but still matters might have ended there. However, the BBC *Panorama* TV interview on 20th November 1995 was then screened in which Diana stated her view that Charles wasn't up to the job of becoming king and stated that it was her intention not to go quietly but fight to the end. The 'Grey men' at the palace, so described by Diana, became alarmed and this induced the final phase that caused the Queen to decide enough was enough.

It ended with the Queen ordering a divorce in 1996, one year before the crash in the Alma tunnel, with the Decree Absolute that would have enabled Diana to re-marry being granted just thirty-six hours before she was murdered.

★

Times have changed significantly of late with perhaps the biggest change being that the people, who used to be subservient to the monarchy years ago, now hold the power and so the monarchy exists for the people. This fact seems not to have yet been appreciated and the people appear unsure of what, if anything, they want from the monarchy. This is because it's easier to retain the status quo and let natural forces apply where change only rears its head upon something significant happening, provoking people into thought – perhaps something like the brutal murder of Diana.

The royals neither envisaged Diana would become the icon she did, nor that she could upset their plans for her to 'disappear', something she herself believed was always the royals' intention once her purpose was served. Diana would never disappear of her own volition: she had suffered too much at the hands of the royal family to go quietly.

Diana's married life was a sham from start to finish. The wedding almost didn't proceed and Diana had already told her sister, Lady Sarah McCorqodale, that she was thinking of pulling out. Lady Sarah told her that now her face was on the tea towels it was too late. The honeymoon was a disaster and the first Christmas and New Year had the new bride cutting her wrists and throwing herself down the stairs of Sandringham House while pregnant with her first child because her husband, Charles, was forever ignoring her and had others with whom he preferred to spend his time.

The duplicity in the royal family concerning the purpose of this 'marriage' wasn't obvious to the world as it was to Diana; it took us a little longer to realise the truth. When Diana learned that Andrew Morton intended writing about the royal family she took a fateful decision that not only knocked the royals' socks off, but also administered the coup de grâce to the Wales's 'relationship'.

It was a watershed in Diana's life that led her into the arms of Dodi Fayed and the thirteenth pillar of the Alma tunnel.

Perfect Scenario: Means and Opportunity

We have briefly considered the background to Princess Diana's precarious situation prior to 31st August 1997 and the reasons why she was viewed as such a threat by the Establishment. Clearly the events preceding this date all indicated that she was becoming a thorn in the side of the monarchy. I firmly believe the evidence shows that Diana's marriage to Dodi was imminent and many issues were quickly coming to a head. It's safe to say that a number of influential figures wanted Diana simply to 'disappear'. In this chapter we will look more closely at the events of that fateful night and ask the question: was the crash just a tragic accident that could have happened to anyone? Or was it a meticulously planned assassination, in which the young princess, newly in love, was executed in cold blood?

Let's first look at the events of 30th/31st August in more detail to establish why there was such a perfect opportunity for murder on that fateful night.

★

Assassinations of this magnitude require good planning, up-to-the-minute intelligence, a suitable location, well-trained agents and control over the subject's activity to ensure the desired path is followed. The Ritz Hotel and its vicinity were the perfect location for events to unfold. We believe it is now proven that the British Security Services (MI6) had hotel staff in their pay, including Henri Paul, deputy head of security at The Paris Ritz and the driver at the time of the fatal crash. Paul would be of immense value to MI6's plan, since there should be an unwitting insider to direct activities.

It was essential that Diana and Dodi dined at the Ritz Hotel on that eventful evening and imperative that the assassins had someone in Dodi's confidence to persuade him to return to his apartment via the Alma tunnel later that night. Mohamed Al Fayed's car, which would normally be used, was a large, strong Mercedes with armoured plating, so its occupants would most probably survive an impact, even at high speed. In addition, the tinted windows would minimise the effect of any strobe gun used to disorientate the driver. The reason proffered for the use of a smaller Mercedes S280, with no bullet-proofing and no tinted windows, was that it would go unnoticed by the paparazzi, blending in with the Paris traffic and so become less visible when Diana and Dodi left from the rear door of the Ritz.

It was also important to persuade Dodi that leaving from the rear of the hotel to return to his apartment was seen as his idea otherwise there could have been a problem with his bodyguards, who might telephone London for countermanding authority. So it was important that Dodi should tell the bodyguards that his father had already approved the plan. Only Paul could achieve this because it was known Dodi would accept his judgment and Dodi did telephone his father. The bodyguards later said that Dodi gave the order to leave by the back door and for Paul to drive but they were not party to the conversation between Dodi and Paul while inside Dodi's Ritz apartment. (It was proven during the inquests that Paul gave the order.)

It was crucial to the assassins that Diana and Dodi took a small detour from the Ritz to Dodi's apartment, where they would stay the night, because the five-metre section of road where death was highly probable is at the entrance to the Alma tunnel, which is where the assault must take place. This is exactly where the first assault did indeed take place.

The length of road from La Place de la Concorde would allow the Mercedes to attain a high speed before reaching the Alma. With the driver blinded at the Alma tunnel's entrance and his path to the right blocked by another car, together with inoperable steering and pursuing assassins posing as paparazzi that forced the Mercedes to maintain a high speed, impact was certain and should prove fatal. The driver and inside man, Henri Paul, had been deceitfully motivated to achieve these perfect circumstances for the assassination and ended up paying the ultimate price.

In all this, the unwitting role of the paparazzi was that of scapegoat. They remained outside the hotel for Diana and Dodi to emerge and so, as part of the plan, Henri Paul volubly encouraged them to remain saying that the couple would be returning to Dodi's apartment and so ensured the paparazzi's unwitting support. Just before Diana and Dodi's departure, Paul had another Mercedes drive to the front of the hotel as decoy, allowing time for a head start from the rear door of the hotel.

The British Secret Service knew by 22nd August, latest, that Dodi and Diana would be at the Ritz on the evening of 30th August when an engagement ring would be collected from Alberto Repossi's store, a few hundred yards from the hotel. They also knew that Diana and Dodi would almost certainly intend staying at Dodi's apartment that night. This was excellent intelligence and provided more than adequate time for any group of professional assassins to plan an attack.

It is also interesting to note that the British Embassy, where MI6 are known to regularly have agents on hand, is only a few hundred yards from the Ritz Hotel and a mile or so from the death scene. The inquests will later prove that MI6 had Diana and Dodi under constant surveillance, but especially during the month of August 1997. According to a former MI6 star operative, Richard Tomlinson, they also had a large number of personnel, including several senior ones, at the British Embassy in Paris that weekend and it was later confirmed they were also at the Salpêtrière Hospital, where Diana was taken after the 'accident'. Whether they arrived before or after the crash is unknown.

When Dodi and Diana flew to Paris-Le Bourget airport from St Tropez on 30th August, the press had already received information 'from an unknown source' that they would arrive in Paris that day, so the paparazzi were already primed to be at the airport and await the couple's arrival. It was therefore guaranteed that the paparazzi would encroach on the hotel and Dodi's apartment for the duration of Diana and Dodi's stay and follow them wherever they went, thus presenting the necessary cover and the hoped-for putative cause of the planned, impending crash.

The couple's luggage was taken to Dodi's apartment directly from the airport, confirming intelligence information of where they intended sleeping and eavesdropping indicated their intention to eat at the Chez Benoît restaurant first, and then return to the apartment. Having precluded them from eating at Chez Benoît by ensuring a paparazzi reception, there was only one other place where they could achieve privacy: the Ritz Hotel. (It was important that they went to the Ritz, where Henri Paul could influence Dodi whereas he would have been unable to do so from the Chez Benoît restaurant.) The fact that the paparazzi were waiting for Diana and Dodi at the Chez Benoît proves others knew where they would eat that evening; MI6 certainly knew. And so the perfect scenario was set.

Owned by Mohamed Al Fayed, the Ritz employed Jean Hocquet as head of security, with Henri Paul as his deputy. In June 1997, Hocquet retired and Henri Paul became the acting head of security, reporting to the hotel manager, Franco Mora, and through him to Frank Klein, the president. Klein was known to appreciate Paul's unswerving loyalty and knowing he wouldn't refuse an order, he made him the effective head of security at the Ritz. He was in this role when the crash took place and Paul's army background made him a perfect choice for the task he was unwittingly about to perform.

Paul's trusted relationship with Dodi made him well placed to persuade on the rear exit move under the guise of establishing greater security and to unknowingly suit the preferred timing of the assassins. Since Diana and Dodi were travelling back to Dodi's apartment later that evening and needed to negotiate their way through a horde of paparazzi, an escape plan was already in Dodi's mind. The photographers had been giving him a hard time and as it was a special evening for them both Paul had no difficulty in persuading Dodi they should prevent the paparazzi from ruining it.

Leaving from the hotel's rear exit was a ruse that had worked only weeks before, on 25th–27th July, when Dodi and Diana had spent the weekend at the Ritz, so it was a tried-and-tested method known to be acceptable and not a notion Dodi was likely to reject. A simple plan for the couple to rid themselves of their tormentors was therefore on course.

The night security officer, François Tendil, telephoned Paul at 9.55pm to inform him that Dodi and Diana had returned to the hotel for their evening meal and had retired to the Imperial Suite due to a lack of privacy in the Ritz restaurant; he also informed Paul there was a problem with the paparazzi. Paul was at the Champmeslé bar near the Ritz, collecting his black Austin Mini that was parked nearby when Tendil's call came through.

Paul returned to the Ritz at 10.08pm, though it's unknown where he was that afternoon between leaving the Ritz at 7.05pm to when he received Tendil's call. He probably went home to his apartment at 33 rue des Petit-Champs since it was noted that he was clean-shaven when he returned to the Ritz and had changed his clothes. This need not have taken him very long, so the bulk of the missing time was available to meet other people.

One senior Ritz official told police that he had seen Paul at 7.30pm in the Bourgogne bar, near to Paul's apartment, but the owner, Myriam Lemaire, said, 'When he'd come in, he'd have one drink, read his paper and then leave. I never saw him come in with anyone else and never take more than one drink.' She added that she hadn't seen him that night. Two bartenders at Harry's Bar, just around the corner from the Ritz, said they saw Paul that night and that he drank two whiskies (the manager said he wasn't there).

When discussing whether or not Paul had been drinking more than he should that night, it's important to keep focused as to its relevance. It is obviously useful in passing the buck with regard to blame but also serves to redirect minds away from more important questions, such as who was driving those vehicles that surrounded the Mercedes at the Alma, and who shone the flashing light in Paul's eyes (as seen by several witnesses) when he was driving at high speed into the Alma tunnel's entrance.

After the 'accident', Mohamed Al Fayed produced a video, taken from the Ritz security cameras, that showed Diana, Dodi, Dodi's bodyguard Trevor Rees-Jones, another bodyguard called Kes Winfield and Henri Paul, right up until ten minutes before the crash, all behaving normally and leaving the hotel by the rear exit. Some of the paparazzi did attest to Henri Paul being euphoric that evening, but the order he had been given excited him – after all, the cash found on Paul after the crash indicated that he was being paid a great deal for that night's work. One of the Ritz barmen also confirmed that Paul had seemed 'excited' but there are other reasons to explain his voluble behaviour other than being drunk: he had been entrusted by the Security Services, as he perceived it, to escort the boss with his princess.

Although not specifically licensed to drive hotel cars, Paul's regular duties included driving VIPs around. However, his driving skills were later illustrated to be exceptional, as demonstrated during the attack on the Mercedes. A police expert later commented, from witness evidence, that Paul showed 'remarkable reflexes' – not the response one might expect from a drunken man.

Paul attended the Mercedes training school annually for four years (from 1988 until at least 1992), where he was proud of the good marks he always attained. He was also a fixed wing pilot with a full current instrument rating that requires a pilot to fly by sole reference to instruments – which takes concentration and skill, requiring control and coordination. Just days before the crash, he had taken his demanding pilot's medical examination. During this evaluation, the medical examiner is required to identify any problem areas such as alcohol dependency that would preclude him from retaining his licence: he passed outright. Paul was a responsible person who enjoyed a drink but even the British policeman Inspector Scotchbrook later confirmed that Paul had taken two drinks that night, and no more.

Both the paparazzi and Paul were prepared well beforehand as scapegoats and some alcohol in Paul's bloodstream was desirable to enable MI6 to claim this to be the cause of the 'accident'. If the hit went wrong, then Paul would save the day; case closed. Yet surely it's likely that Dodi or the bodyguards would have noticed if he was drunk?

Trevor Rees-Jones and Kes Winfield were with Paul in the Hemingway bar at the Ritz that night and said he looked perfectly fine. It was the bodyguard's job to protect their principals and they were experienced in looking for any danger signs – it's what they were paid for. Does anyone believe that either would allow Paul to drive their boss in a drunken state and then accept a place in the front seat of the car he was driving, as Trevor Rees-Jones later did, thereby putting his own life at risk and, in the event, with near death consequences for him?

There are indeed so many issues raised over Paul's blood alcohol samples that, given the rest of the fiasco, it's hard to have confidence that they were simply not switched or, even if they were taken from the correct body, not subsequently contaminated. As we shall see in more detail later on, we know that the assessment of Paul's blood didn't follow the correct procedures (the inquests later made very damming remarks regarding the value of all the blood tests) and so this must be taken into consideration if one wishes to pursue the drunken driver/accident theory. Remember, the police control the laboratories where these samples are taken and so squaring results with staff at the test centre would not have been a problem if that was their intent.

Interestingly, Dr Peter Vanezis, Regius Professor of Forensic Medicine at Glasgow University, was asked by Mohammed Al Fayed to try and confirm the test results so he duly went to Paris, three days after the crash. Yet he wasn't allowed access to Henri Paul's body, which is strange considering all the conspiracy theories that were by now abounding. Here the police were presented with an opportunity for a non-partisan expert to confirm their findings but, although not required to comply with this request by law, here was a missed opportunity to show the world there was nothing to hide; why did they refuse?

Now let us consider Henri Paul's connection with the Secret Services. In his capacity at the Ritz, Paul was very discreet concerning his regular contacts with the police and various Security Services in connection with visiting dignitaries but when police visited his apartment after his death they found contact numbers in his phone book for the DST (the Direction de la Surveillance du Territoire), the Renseignements Généraux (the intelligence-gathering arm of France's national police), the Direction Générale de la Sécurité Extérieure (the DGSE – the French equivalent of the British MI6 or American CIA), and even the Elysée Palace, residence of the French President.

On being approached, the DGSE refused to acknowledge or deny links with Paul, although Yves Bonnet, a former head of the DST, said it would be 'normal procedure for someone in Paul's position to be approached by the Services and asked to provide information on the hotel clientele'.

Former British MI6 officer Richard Tomlinson says that when he was in MI6, he requested to see Henri Paul's file because he was 'intrigued that a Frenchman was prepared to work for the British', which according to him is rare. Tomlinson said he believed that Paul worked for British Intelligence and one of his tasks would be victim surveillance, which entailed placing internal bugging devices in guests' bedrooms. He added that Paul was most likely being briefed by MI6 during the missing hours between 7.00pm and 10.00pm and paid for information given or actions to be undertaken (c. $2,000 in cash was found on Paul's body, post-crash).

It's certainly interesting to note the large number of known MI6 agents, or assets, who were within one mile of the 'accident' while it was taking place, including some of their senior personnel. This is not some unproven conspiracy theory; is it conceivable that these agents were unable to protect Diana, or at least know who murdered her? So why didn't they come forward and assist the police by arresting those who did? Also, why were they in Paris that night?

Consider too which organisation had the manpower and sophistication to orchestrate and synchronise the necessary activity and intelligence for such an attack other than MI6. If not MI6, then one would need to believe that this attack was executed right under their noses and that another organisation of similar size and capability committed it. You would also need to believe this, despite many of the players in this story being known to have associations with MI6, including Henri Paul and James Andanson (owner of a white Fiat Uno, which was to play a big part in that evening's proceedings). So, if not MI6, what large organisation would MI6 feel the need to defend for murdering someone whom they were duty-bound to protect?

An act of murder, as the inquest coroner intimated, could only have been executed by a Security Services organisation. But let us look a little more closely at the role MI6 played that night. Two main sources of information on this are Richard Tomlinson, ex-MI6 (Britain's overseas Security Services), and David Shayler, ex-MI5 (Britain's home Security Services). These men are two of the few British secret service agents known to the public and both have decided that personal integrity and the interests of truth and decency override the risk to their personal liberty.

As we shall see, both men have publicly proffered opinions concerning the probability of events surrounding this crime and both believe it was murder, coordinated by MI6. Small wonder the Security Services prefer to knock their past star operatives, otherwise they would have to answer extremely awkward questions. Yet Tomlinson, who valued integrity more than dishonourable duty, courageously and publicly described his experiences in an extremely frank way, allowing us into the world of MI6 state-sponsored murder that should have gone out with the ark (or, certainly, the end of the Cold War).

Tomlinson, ex-Cambridge and MIT, was a high-flyer in MI6 and was not amused with the behaviour he was expected to countenance, purportedly in the name of the people. A former parachutist and radio operator in the TA's 21 SAS and 23 SAS, he joined MI6 in 1991 and was honoured as the best recruit on his course in training. He served in Sarajevo and Iran, but was then summarily sacked in 1995, with no reason for his dismissal and no access to a union representative. As a result of this deplorable treatment at the hands of his former colleagues, he wrote a book about his time in MI6, *The Big Breach*, and was promptly charged under the Official Secrets Act. He was sent to prison in December 1997, serving six months of a twelve-month sentence.

This was particularly useful timing since Tomlinson, having already tried to give evidence to Judge Stephan, the man in charge of Diana's murder 'investigation', was intending to return to France and try again but was prevented through incarceration. Particularly disturbing are the comments of Tomlinson's trial judge about his imprisonment being in the 'public interest' – it would be interesting to know just whose interests his Honour was referring to.

When Tomlinson emerged from prison he tried once again to speak to Stephan, but was arrested by French Security Services when he arrived in the country, beaten up and had his laptop computer stolen, which was then handed to MI6. He was then to speak on New Zealand television but was arrested by the New Zealand Security Services on arrival and the remainder of his belongings were seized. Three weeks later he saw Judge Stephan at last, despite having been arrested in Paris only one month previously.

After giving his testimony, Tomlinson was invited to speak on NBC's *Today* on American television but when he arrived in New York in September 1998, he was detained by customs and sent straight back to Geneva on the orders of discomfited officials, undoubtedly at the behest of MI6 – he wasn't even allowed to leave the airport. Clearly, he presented a major threat to the tissue of lies being propagated by the authorities.

But another nasty event with remarkably coincidental timing occurred. Tomlinson was booked to return to Geneva on Swissair flight 111 on 2nd September 1998 after his *Today* interview but, because of the intervention by American Custom officials at JFK airport, on the orders of the CIA, he was returned sooner on another flight.

When Swissair Flight 111 departed New York it developed an in-flight fire on take-off and diverted to Canadian airspace where the plane crashed, killing all 229 passengers and crew (including 137 Americans). The Black Box that aircraft carry for such horrendous disasters was unable to give the recorded information for the last six minutes of the flight; apparently due to an electrical failure during that precise period. I cannot make further comment about this issue.

Tomlinson was clearly one of the major threats that MI6 needed to deal with in order to keep the truth from the people. He also confirmed that MI6 were following Diana around for fifteen years before she was murdered. Sometimes MI6 would have three cars waiting outside her home at Kensington palace. When they believed that one car might have been spotted that car would peel off and the second would continue and still be followed by the third. So watch for MI6 and police denials in court about their interest in Diana. This information further enhances our view concerning the veracity of police statements.

So, what knowledge did Tomlinson possess that was causing such a furore? First of all, he made significant comments on the role of other members of MI6 and their unusual numbers in Paris that night, saying, 'Something big was going down.' Furthermore, he states that he personally looked at the file of a Frenchman who was a pilot and who worked at the Ritz Hotel in Paris when he was a serving officer. He confirms that, since Paul was the only pilot working at the Ritz, then it would be Paul who was working with MI6 from 1992 onwards, bugging Ritz Hotel guest rooms when required. He also confirmed the names of two senior MI6 officers, who were working from the British Embassy in Paris that weekend: Nicholas Langman and Richard Spearman.

Spearman he describes as very senior, having been secretary to the then MI6 boss, David Spedding. Spearman took up his Paris post at the end of July, around the same time as it was becoming increasingly obvious that Diana had found a new life and the British monarchy had a new and major crisis looming. Interestingly, Richard Tomlinson tells us that Spearman, whom I believe was Witness I at the inquests, was SAS liaison officer for the MI6 'Increment' team. Witness I's reluctance to give any evidence whatsoever at the inquests would, thus, be explained

The famous 'Kiss' photograph of 7th August, taken on board Al Fayed's yacht that told the world of Diana's new love, was published a few days after Spearman's appointment. MI6 knew what this meant: Diana and Dodi planned to marry and had stage-managed this photo because they wanted the world to know. The whole flow of these events made Diana and Dodi's intentions clear. Photographer Mario Brenna had been tipped off as to the couple's location, almost certainly by Diana and Dodi themselves – Brenna's London agent said they were informed down to the last detail as to where Diana and Dodi were going in Sardinia on that day, though he refused to identify the source. Frank Klein, president of the Ritz Hotel, also said that Dodi had told him that he intended to marry around October or November that year. Diana and Dodi had prepared well for their bombshell announcement to the people via the press on their return to England.

The murderers recorded all these conversations and had a crucial time frame in which to work. Now they had confirmation that they had to take a serious decision about Diana, giving them more than enough time to perfect the detail of a malevolent response for which they were already prepared. They must strike before Sunday's departure since it would be too dangerous afterwards; motive would then be too obvious, so the acceptable level of 'deniability' would have evaporated.

The press had been notified of Diana and Dodi's impending arrival at Paris's Le Bourget Airport on 30th August and they were waiting when the Harrods' jet touched down at 3.20pm. They never left the couple's side, following them from the airport to the Ritz and then, at around 7.00pm, to Dodi's apartment on the rue Arsène Houssaye. The paparazzi knew Diana and Dodi were going to eat at le Chez Benoît when they left their apartment at 9.30pm and then, having harassed them at the restaurant, making it impossible for them to remain, they followed their Mercedes to the Ritz Hotel and camped outside. Everyone knew the Ritz was the only remaining place where they could find privacy and so the scene was set for the evening's programme to commence.

CCTV footage from the Ritz security cameras, collected and later viewed, shows a whole host of unidentified people watching outside the hotel during the course of the evening. There was also a man who owned a white Fiat Uno, who was soon to be hotly pursued by Mohamed Al Fayed's team, reputed to be present. His name was James Andanson, an MI6 asset who was to die a horrible death (officially a suicide), some thirty-three months later by burning himself almost to ash, despite first being shot *twice* in the head.

Others were noted as glancing from side to side as though scanning the area and it was ascertained that they were definitely not paparazzi.

One of the men was challenged by a paparazzo who, when asked which paper or periodical he represented, gave an evasive answer.

Encouraged by Henri Paul's larger-than-life behaviour outside the Ritz, the paparazzi decided to remain and await the couple's exit for the return to their love nest at rue Arsène Houssaye. This was a serious risk to the assassins, since the paparazzi could have decided to leave and remove their cover, but Paul, acting under orders, prevented this by volubly goading them. The main reason from the assassins' viewpoint was that the Mercedes needed a brief head start and so the paparazzi wouldn't catch up by the time it entered the Alma. This gave time for the attack without the paparazzi witnessing the assault vehicles but it ensured they wouldn't be far behind to act as scapegoats.

Let us, for a moment, place ourselves as putative British MI6 agents who wish to murder a high dignitary. It's important that it appears to be an accident because the knowledge of murder alone would provoke a public crisis, whether or not we are caught. So, blowing up a plane or a boat is undesirable because our intent here would be obvious.

We prefer not to use regular agents for the attack because we risk discovery of complicity and some of our staff could be disobliging, so we shall use hit men from the team we hold in reserve for this purpose, who will mount the attack under the direct control of our select MI6 cabal. Ostensibly, they will operate aside from the Service proper in case of discovery. We call this 'hit' team our 'Increment', i.e. an increase in our capability for those times when we need to establish our distance from unsavoury acts. This will help us in our key objective of maintaining 'deniability'.

As secret service agents, we have on-going intelligence of both the scene and subjects, and must plan the route well in advance with everything in place for when we need to go operational. Before the attack is authorised, we need to assess the results of the propaganda campaign we are waging against our subject's lover, Dodi Fayed, during August and hope this will change her thoughts about proceeding towards marriage. We shall quickly know if it has worked because they are now together all the time and during

August, we shall further assess the position – the last chance before the order will be given. This relationship is very dangerous because it gives our subject the power to destroy the monarchy and puts her beyond Palace control.

We know that on 5th August, the subjects visit Alberto Repossi's jeweller's store in Monte Carlo and take away with them a brochure on engagement rings so we know how strong this relationship is. In early August we know for certain that they are an item due to the publication in the press of the 'Kiss' photograph of 10th August and by further eavesdropping.

On 22nd August, our subjects order the engagement ring but it needs customising and so we learn there is an agreement to collect it in Paris on the night of 30th August. We also know that the negative propaganda campaign on Dodi Fayed in the US has failed to change our subject's mind, so marriage is likely to be proposed after the ring has been picked up and announced on Monday, 1st September. Therefore we have at least eight days of knowing our subjects' certain intent of being in Paris to finalise a hit, giving us more than enough time to prepare, especially since our people are already in place.

We know our subjects will be staying at one of two venues on 30th August and we are virtually certain it will be Dodi's apartment on the rue Arsène Houssaye but we need to confirm this by checking where their luggage is taken upon arrival at Paris's Le Bourget Airport. We must be successful in our mission on this night because the risk of taking action after an announcement of their engagement would prove too great.

The earliest that the couple can commit officially to each other is 30th August because our subject's decree absolute is to be finalised on Friday, 29th August, the day before we intend to strike.

We know the roads around Paris and have discovered a few sites where an 'accident' would almost certainly prove fatal. If unsuccessful, we shall ensure the necessary back-up to guarantee success by having agents waiting to administer the coup de grâce. There is one spot at the Alma tunnel, within a five-metre area at its entrance, where the attack must be initiated otherwise the car will have gone past the danger zone and a fatal crash would then be far less probable. This is where we plan to strike.

We have agents resident in Paris and even one who is close to the secondary target, Dodi. His name is Henri Paul and we shall use him as an unwitting participant in the planned sequence of events. His role is to drive the subjects to their love nest and Paul will obey orders since he is unaware of our lethal intent: he will be necessary collateral damage. We know Paul enjoys a drink and lives alone so is an excellent adjunct to our purpose and will also provide cover as a reason for the crash. Paul will spend the afternoon of Saturday, 30th August receiving his final instructions and pep talk and his whereabouts between 7.00pm and 10.00pm that evening will remain unknown.

The scene is set. We have all the plans ready and in place. Now we just have to finalise the detail and await the final order.

★

So, what happened next? According to official reports, this is how the story unfolded.

Around midnight on 30th August, a decoy vehicle drove round to the front of the Ritz to distract the paparazzi from the forthcoming rear exit plan. At around 12.20am, Diana and Dodi left the Ritz by the rear entrance of the hotel to return to Dodi's apartment. The couple were the rear passengers in a black Mercedes S280, driven by Henri Paul. Dodi's bodyguard, Trevor Rees-Jones, sat in the front passenger seat and was the only one wearing a seatbelt that he put on during the journey to the Alma.

The Mercedes managed to overtake all the stationary vehicles at the Place de la Concorde traffic lights and obtain a substantial head start. It then drove parallel to the River Seine towards the Place de l'Alma underpass that was now only seconds away. The only paparazzi pursuers anywhere near to the Mercedes were Rommauld Rat and his rider, Stephane Darmon, and they were at least a minute behind. (The Mercedes passed an inquest witness, Alain Remy, as it sped under the Pont Alexandre III. According to Remy, the Mercedes was travelling at around 87–94mph and there were no other vehicles in sight.)

At about 12.23am, just as the Mercedes entered the tunnel travelling at high speed, a powerful flash of light was noticed by several witnesses. Henri Paul lost control of the vehicle as he collided with a white Fiat Uno near the tunnel's entrance; he was being pursued by motorbikes (definitely not belonging to paparazzi) and cars had been witnessed 'loitering' at the tunnel's entrance.

Inside the tunnel, as the Mercedes struggled to maintain direction, its path to the right was blocked by another 'presence'. The car swerved to the left of the two-lane carriageway and collided head-on with the thirteenth pillar that supported the roof of the underpass. It then spun to hit the stone wall of the tunnel, travelling backwards before eventually coming to a halt, wrecked almost beyond recognition. The driver of the Fiat Uno has never come forward and the vehicle was neither officially identified, nor even officially accepted as existing, until two weeks after the crash despite later proof that the police knew of the Fiat's existence within hours of the crash.

As four people lay dead or bleeding in the wrecked Mercedes, the paparazzi immediately began taking photos on arrival. The loitering attack vehicles had all departed the scene, never to be seen again, except for the Fiat. Diana, who had been sitting in the rear right passenger seat, was still conscious and reportedly murmuring, 'Oh my God!' Dodi Fayed, next to her, and the driver, Henri Paul, were both dead on impact.

The emergency services arrived at the scene and pushed the photographers out of the way. Fire officers attempted to resuscitate Dodi but he was officially pronounced dead by a doctor at 1.32am. Henri Paul was pronounced dead on removal from the wreckage and both men were taken to the Paris mortuary. Still conscious, Rees-Jones had suffered serious multiple facial injuries. He was the only person to survive, though he had been knocked unconscious and later claimed not to remember anything of the crash, although a witness, Karen Mackenzie (see later evidence), reported that he had told her, 'If I remember, they will kill me.'

Diana was reported by a paparazzo to be bleeding from the nose and ears, with her head rested on the back of the front passenger seat immediately after the impact (though later reports state that she had no visible injuries). When medics arrived, she was supplied with oxygen and removed from her car at 1.00am. She was finally removed from the Mercedes and taken to the Pitié-Salpêtrière Hospital at 2.06am, although the ambulance needed to stop twice en route to apply cardiac massage. Despite lengthy resuscitation attempts, she died at 4am. Her death was officially announced at a press conference at 5.30am.

In 1999, an eighteen-month French judicial 'investigation' concluded that the crash was caused by Henri Paul, who had lost control of his car at high speed while drunk. Six years after the crash, on 6th January 2004, the British inquests into the deaths opened in London upon the request of Michael Burgess, coroner of the Queen's household, who asked the Metropolitan Police Commissioner, Lord Stevens, to investigate the increasingly vocal rumours regarding MI6's involvement in the deaths. Dr John Burton, the royal coroner had, by now, stood down.

The 832-page report was finally published nearly three years later, on 14th December 2006, with the inquiry being wound up following the completion of the inquests in April 2008. Its conclusions were emphatic: there was no conspiracy, MI6 were not involved and all the evidence pointed towards a tragic accident caused by Henri Paul, but exacerbated by the actions of the paparazzi.

This is the end of the official story. Yet, for very good reasons, the questions refuse to go away. Let us now look at the alternative version of events.

★

In the official version of events, the paparazzi and Henri Paul, Diana and Dodi's chauffeur for the evening, were to blame. It was Paul's 'drunken' and 'reckless' driving that apparently caused the 'accident'. But now imagine you must drive very fast in your car to stay ahead of other cars that are aggressively pursuing you, as several witnesses described. Then imagine that, as you enter a tunnel, a car hits you at the exact spot where there is a dangerous fault in the road.

Do you think there is a reasonable chance you might crash, drunk or not, blinded or not, able to steer or not? The level of alcohol might determine how well one handles the car in this situation but it's known that Paul showed great skill in preventing a crash when the Mercedes glanced off the Fiat Uno just outside the tunnel. However, he could not recover control when the Fiat struck again further inside the tunnel, following which the Mercedes impacted with the thirteenth pillar.

Based on close inspection of the evidence (shared in court by one police expert), it is my view that the assassin's initial intention was to block the recovery lane at the tunnel entrance and force the Mercedes into the pillars but this attempt failed and so he was forced to try again further into the tunnel. This second impact must have been a rare 'accident' in any country's road history since it required a driver, having hit a car once, to accelerate aggressively and pursue it in order to hit it once again rather than brake and stop. In any event, Paul was later credited with showing tremendous reflexes for any driver that he should be able to escape from the first impact. He would probably have also beaten the second but for this 'presence in the right lane' and his car most probably being disabled. Also, he was blinded at the tunnel entrance by a strobe light, as we shall see later.

Synchronisation of the several elements involved in this attack was crucial since it was necessary the assassins didn't mistime their opportunity. They knew when the Mercedes would arrive at the Alma tunnel through advance intelligence. Witnesses described the Fiat and several other vehicles 'loitering' at the tunnel's entrance that immediately departed the scene post-incident. Using this intelligence, the assassins ensured they could time their run precisely to block the Mercedes' path by using a blinding flash at the tunnel entrance and, very probably, disabling the steering by using a remote device fitted to the car. Witnesses reported 'aggressive motorcycle riders' forcing a greater speed from the Mercedes to increase the probability of death on impact.

In addition, agents were ready to enter the wrecked car after the crash and eliminate the target or execute an alternative plan, had onlookers prevented entry. This required people who were highly trained, ruthless, with enormous resources and advance knowledge of exactly when all the above would take place as well as having a motive. If the only realistic motive for murder is the protection of the monarchy, then which organisation could possibly carry out such an attack of this complexity other than MI6?

It's known that several MI6 agents were in Paris and that the subject's intentions were known beforehand. In fact, the Alma was a perfect attack site and almost en route from the hotel to Dodi's apartment. The Service had control of the Mercedes and influence over its chauffeur, who in turn exercised influence over the target's companion, Dodi. The British Embassy was within the loop, being only a mile away from the attack site and had large doors at the rear enabling vehicles to enter from a quiet, narrow street at 35 rue du Faubourg St Honoré. At that time of night in Paris, and in August (a time when many Parisians traditionally leave the city), the chances of anyone seeing the vehicles enter were exceedingly remote. There was also a convenient escape route from the attack site via la rue Débrousse, allowing vehicles to leave the expressway immediately after emerging from the Alma tunnel. According to witness statements, this is precisely what they did and then headed in the direction of the British Embassy.

What better place to conduct this murder – not on home soil because the British police couldn't be relied on for complete discretion, given Diana's popularity in her own country. It therefore had to be conducted under the auspices of the Secret Services in a country known for having a tight control on political matters, where the odd murder wouldn't present a problem (archaic medical rules would also be helpful). In addition, it would need to be conducted in a country that the subjects were likely to frequent. France was ideal.

The best place would be Paris and the best time during the month of August when the city virtually closes down. As a result there would be fewer potential witnesses and those who did see anything would most probably be tourists and not so familiar with the scene. By far the best of the Paris accident black spots is situated between the Ritz Hotel and Dodi's apartment, and is not far from either, and so, with an MI6 operative at the wheel, it would be simple to direct the route via the Alma tunnel. With surveillance they would know which restaurant the subjects intended using (as was proven) and so it was a simple matter to inform the paparazzi of the couple's movements and guarantee a commotion outside the Chez Benoît restaurant to prevent them from entering.

The plan then was to force Diana and Dodi to the Ritz, which was the only place where they could achieve privacy. Following this, the paparazzi would await the subjects' departure from the hotel and Henri Paul would be tasked with persuading them that the subjects would be leaving the hotel that evening to ensure they waited outside. The subjects had to leave the Ritz by the back door to achieve a head start since it was imperative that the pursuing paparazzi didn't actually witness the attack. However, their arrival would be necessary fairly soon afterwards for scapegoat duties and to add to the confusion.

It was the perfect plan and executed to near perfection, yet a few things still went wrong. Witnesses observed far more detail than the assassins had hoped for, leaving many questions unanswered; the Fiat also left evidence behind. The 'Accident Theory' could not possibly satisfy witness evidence and so the lid was clamped down on detail, the crash site was quickly cleared, agencies were at work raiding homes and stealing photographs to hide any peripheral evidence, stories of who was to blame were fabricated for public consumption and the paparazzi were held responsible for the deaths, with the crash then explained away as an 'accident'.

This chapter has summarised the background, giving an overview of the events of that night. Now we can examine the post-attack detail in the public domain within weeks of the incident and consider those thorny questions that refuse to go away. Let's start by looking at the role the authorities played in the cover-up immediately after the deaths.

Conspiracy: Pre-Inquest Detail

Substantial evidence, strongly suggesting an attack, was available within days of Diana's death. So why didn't the police immediately investigate? In this chapter we show how the authorities prevaricated and misled the people, both immediately after the crash and from then on.

During these inquests, why did the police ignore the most significant eyewitness evidence of 'loitering', 'aggressive', 'hindering' and 'blocking' vehicles near the tunnel? This was information that the chief police investigator declared to be irrelevant despite even the coroner, Lord Justice Scott Baker, admitting that this indicated 'some evidence' of a planned attack. Another central issue concerns the 'Mishcon note'. This was a note that Diana wrote to her lawyer, Lord Mishcon, years before the crash in which she stated that her husband planned to murder her in an ostensible car accident. Diana wrote this as a precaution with the express instruction it was to be handed to the police should the need arise, which of course it did.

The police withheld this valuable evidence for eight years, from both the French authorities and the English coroner, claiming there was no indication of wrongdoing despite also admitting that disclosure was a legal obligation and that 'they cannot rule out murder'. Such was the note's importance that when it was finally released in 2003 – after Paul Burrell, Diana's ex-butler, made public a similar note from her that he had also been given – the authorities were forced to instigate an inquest. (It is my view that if Diana hadn't given a similar note to Burrell as that which she had given to Mishcon, there would never have been disclosure of the Mishcon note and, therefore, no inquest; well done, Diana.) Somewhat timidly, the police state that prior disclosure would have caused much hurt in the royal family, once more putting one family's feelings above all others and ignoring basic justice. But this is a police admission that they broke the law since the royal family are supposed to be subject to the law of the land in 'British Democracy'.

If you are satisfied that numerous suspicious circumstances existed from the outset and an investigation should have immediately commenced then you have to ask whether the delay could have been caused by anything other than some nefarious intent. The officer in charge of this process, Sir David Veness, was police liaison with MI6, but without untainted evidence, cooperative witnesses and unbiased investigators, little can be done to obtain justice.

With Diana's death, disinformation was fed to the media and the deception maintained because the paradox is that once the lies start, they must become the truth: there is no going back. Those responsible for initiating such lies stood to lose everything if the truth ever emerged and so the stakes were very high, not only for those who planned and then carried out this attack, but also for those running the political machinery, who felt the misguided need to suppress the truth in defence of the monarchy.

Much to the chagrin of the assassins, there was no shortage of witnesses, with one of the biggest errors being the Mercedes' collision with the Fiat and disclosure of this knowledge to the public. Keeping such information from the public had been essential if an 'Accident Theory' was to succeed, which is why so much energy was expended in denying the Fiat's existence. But the Fiat proved other vehicles were involved, which complicated matters when it came to justifying the detention of the paparazzi (some were arrested after the crash). But if not paparazzi, then who was driving the other vehicles?

When the Paris Deputy Prosecutor Maud Coujard appointed Criminal Brigade Chief Martine Monteil to investigate the deaths, it's certainly clear to me what this highly professional woman believed when it came to the probability of murder. Why else would such a senior police officer with Paris's finest investigative team, reserved for the most serious criminal matters, be appointed and required onsite for an 'accident' within minutes of the attack?

French political support for the conspiracy could not be sought until a few moments after the attack, so it took a while before the political machinery could intervene. However, this was not before Monteil had issued her first statement, making it clear that the police were pursuing assassins. She was forced to issue another report within minutes, effectively retracting the first, and police later suggested it was laughable that this could be anything other than an accident. Clearly, this denigrates Martine Monteil for saying as much in her first statement – but what made her change it?

In the prosecutor's report of two years later, however, it was acknowledged that 'interfering vehicles' were present at the crash that 'nobody could adequately describe'. This not only proves that the police knew of their existence from the onset but also that they were secreting evidence away from public scrutiny. Certainly, they initially denied that the Fiat or these other vehicles existed, so are these yet more proven lies? (Take note of this point during the inquest proceedings that follow when Sir David Veness, the main representative for the police, attempts to justify ignoring these vehicles despite the coroner, Scott Baker, admitting that there was some evidence of a staged attack.)

It's also known that various witnesses, who corroborated this evidence, were not even contacted by police and some witnesses claimed that some of their statements taken by the police had their signatures forged. Why would experienced officers ignore these vehicles other than because of political intervention? And why would those vehicles be driving in such a 'definitely aggressive manner' so described, among others, by the American businessman witness Brian Anderson when it is known they were not photographers? Why would the police forge witness statements?

By 2.00am, less than two hours after the attack and just before Sir Michael Jay, the British Ambassador, became involved, Chief Monteil drafted her initial report that the Mercedes had been 'pursued and interfered with' since it was obvious from witnesses' reports that they were not paparazzi, but vehicles that had disappeared and whose drivers had not come forward.

These vehicles had been working in tandem: cars were loitering, motorbikes driven aggressively and swerving in front of the Mercedes, flashes of light and collisions at the tunnel entrance were seen, vehicles were slowing down around the wreck and then accelerating away, escaping via the same next exit of the expressway. All these vehicles were never to be seen again except for the Fiat Uno, when discovered by John Macnamara's team in February 1998 (Al Fayed's security chief). How could this be anything other than murder?

The vehicles of all the arrested photographers were found to be free of any collision damage. Indeed, the police had initially excluded them from any involvement. However, since the police knew that information concerning these 'interfering vehicles' would soon become public, it is my belief that they then arrested the paparazzi to facilitate the accident theory. A reversal of Monteil's first statement was immediately required, saying there was no evidence that any vehicles interfered with Diana's car and also pointing to Henri Paul as another scapegoat, to whom they would later revert. What caused Paris's most senior officer to justify this change of view was never explained. Let's look at these two statements in detail, the first being made within a few hours of the attack.

The first statement

> 'According to the first witnesses, the Mercedes, proceeding down this portion of the road at high speed, appears to have swerved because the chauffeur was being pursued and interfered with by vehicles of the journalists who had given chase. The driver must have lost control of his vehicle and failed to recover. Again, according to the first witnesses, the paparazzi who were pursuing the Mercedes hastened to take photos after the incident, neglecting the elementary gestures of assistance to people in danger. Based on these observations, the first policeman on the scene proceeded to take the photographers in for questioning.'

Apart from Monteil's presumption that these 'interfering' vehicles were paparazzi and those taking photographs were the same people that witness evidence later proved had already left the scene, this more logically describes events. Only hours later, however, a second report effectively retracted the first. One is able to surmise this followed political intervention, given that in such a short space of time nothing could have changed the police viewpoint from an evidential perspective.

Second statement

> 'None of the testimony so far received permits us to establish whether a vehicle could have been sufficiently close to the Mercedes to the point of touching it or interfering with its trajectory. Among the elements to consider in explaining this accident, we should note the following: the vehicle was moving at excessive speed; the chauffeur did not regularly drive this type of vehicle (powerful and heavy); the vehicle, according to maintenance records, seems to have been in perfect condition (repairs and tests made in June 1997); the two toxicology analyses on the driver showed a blood alcohol level of 1.87g/l and 1.74g/l).'

You will note that the first statement affords witnesses a lot of credibility and suggests the probability of an attack. The second statement delivered the only plausible explanation if the police were to convince the public of an accident and paparazzi involvement, but still they hadn't dealt with the aggressive vehicles that immediately left the scene, as mentioned in the first report and as described by most witnesses or made any comment about the debris in the tunnel that came from the Fiat Uno. The police just ignored them.

Henri Paul's blood results were produced in record time (a fact remarked on during the inquests) and it's now known these results were not available when this police statement was given to the public. Yet the police still made the case for drunken driving. It was stressed the car was going too fast, there was a dangerous curve at the entrance to the tunnel and that Paul was unused to driving large cars and he was also drunk. The latter two statements are both untrue, as evidenced by his excellent driving school results and later police confirmation that he wasn't drunk. But you must consider also how this second report could say that there was no indication of another vehicle interfering with the Mercedes since, apart from the revelations already mentioned, we were later informed that there was debris all over the tunnel. And it was also proven the police then knew of the Fiat's existence when, for some nefarious reason, they lied.

We have now migrated from having irrefutable evidence that 'interfering vehicles' caused the Mercedes to crash to the theory that Henri Paul's drunkenness caused the 'accident'. In addition, the police hoped that by detaining the paparazzi, they could divert people's minds from these vehicles and pass the blame onto them. If knowledge of the Fiat and other mysterious vehicles could be kept from the public, then a cover-up might succeed – after all, this was not just one vehicle accidentally coming across Diana's car but a number of vehicles working in tandem (confirmed during the inquests) and then leaving the scene together, from the same next exit.

The idea that these events took place randomly is utter nonsense. It's deplorable that those whose testimonies suggested murder had their depositions refused or their testimony challenged before giving any evidence and, according to several witnesses, changed by the police. Also some were later ridiculed when giving their evidence while others, less specific about their observations, or whose depositions nurtured the idea of a possible accident, had their testimony accepted.

Would it be stretching the imagination too much to believe that shortly after the police arrived in the tunnel, the political machinery had swung into action and 'instructions were received' that a plausible 'accident' must emerge from this crime and that the truth of its origins should never be known? It's worth noting that such an order would have to come from the highest echelons of the British Government and the request made to the very top of the French Government, so even if the British Government was oblivious to the planning of this crime, they were certainly instrumental in its cover-up.

★

While reading through this book please consider the following points and decide to which school of thought you belong. Most will agree that there are three options:

(1) The French police fully investigated this whole affair to the best of their ability.
(2) They were instructed to follow set procedures and investigate the murder, but preserve their findings for the eyes of the Establishment only at the behest of those with a vested interest in the truth continuing to remain hidden. Following this, they were then told under strict orders from the Security Services to allow a set of false details to leak, suggesting an accident.
(3) They are irrevocably incompetent.

We submit that points one and three may be immediately discounted since it's improbable the best police officers from the capital city of a major European country could be totally incompetent and there was no proper investigation since the man in charge of the French investigative charade, Jean-Claude Mules, told the people that he discarded everything that didn't fit with his original hypothesis and he wasn't open to new evidence. And so by a process of elimination that leaves point two. This would require the police to give an outward impression of doing their best and proffering titbits of information pointing towards it being a mere road traffic accident, while ensuring all evidence remained secluded. According to our evidence this is exactly what happened.

It might assist us at this point to consider the structure of the police in France to understand how a cover-up would be handled. Otherwise the obvious question is that surely the system would produce someone unprepared to follow the rules necessary to maintain silence? It's the case, however, that the police in France are not structured in the same way as British or American forces but are much more secretive and under the control of relatively few people, so if a cover-up were being sought, it would only require that certain well-chosen people lead and control the 'investigation'.

The then French President, Jacques Chirac, specifically selected Judge Stephan to lead the investigation into Diana's death. This meant sidestepping the duty judge, Devidal, in favour of Stephan, who had previously been chosen by Chirac on another secretive matter. It was only after a great deal of pressure from a very disgruntled Devidal that the unusual step was taken of allowing her to assist Stephan. One may well ask why the President of France saw the need to appoint Stephan in place of Judge Devidal in the first instance; why did he need someone on whom he could rely to exercise absolute discretion when investigating a mere accident?

The two main sub-divisions of authority in France are the Ministries of Defence and the Interior. The gendarmes (La Gendarmerie) are essentially military police, who report to the Ministry of Defence and make up the majority of police, but the other force reports to the Ministry of the Interior. These are further sub-divided into two and are the Direction Centrale Police Judicaire (DCPJ), so-called because they are actually part of the judicial system, and the Directoire de la Sécurité du Territoire (DST), essentially equivalent to US Homeland Security or British MI5.

Then there are the Jugés d'Instructions, who have absolute powers to investigate criminal matters and who lead the investigation, consider the evidence and then direct what should be investigated or ignored before deciding whether or not to proceed. Needless to say, they possess considerable power. Place a suitable Jugé d'Instruction in charge of an investigation and you have complete control over all events. The French police, investigating magistrate and Secret Service all report to the head of the Interior Ministry, who at the time of Diana's death was Monsieur Jean-Pierre Chevènement (he was in the Alma tunnel within the hour of Diana's murder). An overseer was then appointed to release information for public consumption depending on what the higher echelons of power regarded as being acceptable.

The laboratories in France, where samples of Henri Paul's blood were sent, are also under the control of the Police Judicaire so all matters relating to this 'investigation' were under the direct control of the same few people. A cynic might argue that when looking for the best country in which to assassinate Diana, they could do worse than choose France in a populace-denuded Paris during August and by using the Alma tunnel.

Our star turn, crime squad commander Jean-Claude Mules, who was put in charge of the crime scene, was initially adamant that a thorough investigation into the crash was conducted. However, he is also on record as saying that when he investigates a crime, he first establishes what he believes happened and then seeks evidence to support that theory. 'If you start off with an investigation into a traffic accident, one cannot add things which would only complicate the original hypothesis,' said Mules. In other words, one should ignore issues that might prove your original thinking wrong! As a result, he failed deplorably to consider that there could have been another reason for the crash.

How can the police claim they looked at all possibilities when it's apparent, according to the man in charge, they did not? Surely the point of investigating is to assess whether or not one's initial hypothesis is correct and if in doubt, regroup, look at the accumulating evidence and then shift one's hypothesis accordingly? It is arguably redolent of sheer arrogance to proceed in any other way, although we understand that any decent police officer would feel as though his integrity had been impugned by complying with these orders, thus making his professional life a complete sham.

Any police officer will tell you that crime scenes need to be protected until all available evidence has been collected. In this case the Mercedes was removed from the tunnel within hours and traffic allowed to flow again despite the French police chief originally considering this to be a murder investigation (and remember that this was not traffic police but the head of the Criminale brigade). When a 'crime' is degraded to 'an accident' within a few hours and the crime scene hastily cleared, one has to ask why this was ordered and what caused this sudden change of heart. The car was taken away and no one allowed to examine it until public disquiet enforced a sojourn to the UK in 2004, seven years later, but by then it was in pieces and we can be certain that any incriminating evidence would have been removed.

The car's manufacturers, Mercedes-Benz, offered to send experts to do a thorough examination of the Mercedes at the time of the crash and again months later, but each time the French authorities declined. Later, it was also deemed necessary to reconvene the crime scene on two further occasions by taking the Mercedes back to the tunnel and laying it in the position at which it came to rest after the crash. Why, if all procedures had been followed correctly on the night of the crash, was this necessary? Can there be better proof that the car should never have been removed and the forensic evidence properly collected? Who gave the political order for the Mercedes' removal from the tunnel so early and why?

A French police source said that some blood tests were done on Diana and she was pregnant; we will look into this in much more detail later on. But, according to journalist Peter Allen, Sir Michael Jay, who was then the British Ambassador to Paris, requested that the French embalm Diana's body before returning it to England even though it was known that a post mortem would be needed. Some say the order emanated from Prince Charles's office at St James's Palace against normal practice and against French law since no member of Diana's family had given their consent.

Also, Charles had ceased to be Diana's husband, literally just hours before her murder and why would the police be involved in embalming? What possible reason could there be other than to hide something? No sensible explanation as to why Diana's body was embalmed before being returned to England, making an autopsy virtually impossible, was ever given.

It's interesting to note that French law prevents people from gaining access to medical records or allowing Mohamed Al Fayed the opportunity to re-test Henri Paul's blood or to buy the Fiat Uno for 'safety reasons', despite the car having been for sale – yet illegally embalming Diana for no apparent legitimate reason and against French law seems not to cause a problem. Was Jay concerned with what British doctors might find? Perhaps the medical profession could not be squared so easily as the police and that is why no post mortem was carried out in France. There has been no comment from Jay himself on the matter (interestingly, he later became a member of the security community and then head of the British Diplomatic Service).

Mules admitted that Judge Stephan refused the police access to Diana's post-mortem examination results, stating, 'In France there is the secret medical and the police do not have direct access to the medical dossier.' He said this decision was taken by a higher authority before Diana's body was released, adding, 'Even the top police inspectors of the crime squad do not know about these things that take place at a *diplomatic level*.' (My italics.) So he explicitly admitted that the decision to embalm was a political one and not sanitary, as later claimed during the inquests.

Years later, the British police admitted: 'They cannot rule out murder.' This comment was made because they were aware that, with a huge number of people in Britain and around the world believing it was murder from the beginning, they should appear to be on the public's side. Implicit in this statement, however, is an admission that they should have investigated this crime from the outset.

If MI6 had nothing to hide, why did they not issue a public statement and offer their files to the French authorities? Why did the French authorities not demand these files, especially after it was proven that MI6 had been lying to them? Or should we accept Mules's view, the commander in charge of this charade, that 'Secrets are secret and so we could never have pierced the secret'? What did Mules think his job was, if not to pierce secret after secret? Perhaps most French villains come clean after a week or so! But at least he concedes there is a secret to pierce. This is the man who first establishes what happened and then goes all out to prove he was right, and who admitted disregarding evidence that did not support his hypothesis.

The French authorities did not carry out an autopsy on Diana to establish the cause of death. Why not, since this is routine? Crime squad commander Jean-Claude Mules said, 'This was decided after an external examination of the body by Professor Dominique Lecompte, director of the Institut Legal Medical, a coroner. I was there! Imagine that an autopsy is performed which might later discredit the great professors. For two-and-a-half hours the greatest surgeons, doctors and professors in the country had tried to resuscitate her – I cannot really see how they could not know the cause of death.'

If Mules had been committed to an investigation, then he would obviously have realised the possibilities of Diana not having received fatal injuries in the car crash but instead being murdered afterwards while still in the car or somewhere between the crash site and the hospital; perhaps even in the hospital?

Fentanyl, in high doses, is a virtually traceless poison that has been reported to be used by the Security Services (it can be administered via a spray). Had an examination been properly conducted, it might have shown some traces of this or whatever noxious substance had been administered, in addition to discovering pregnancy. It's also known that the French Police received an order, written on one of their files, saying that blood samples of Diana were not to be taken 'on instructions received'. From whom did these instructions come and for what purpose?

Another intriguing irony is that we know Diana was watched by MI6 and it's known that they were there that night in large numbers, so why didn't they do the job paid for by the public purse and come forward to ease concerns by telling us who committed this crime and explaining why they didn't take steps to prevent it? Perhaps they could also explain why they were in Paris and in such large numbers in the first place. We are, presumably, meant to believe their orders were to protect the Princess of Wales, but if so, why did they fail? And if not, why were they watching her? From the evidence we will see it is hard to escape the conclusion that certain of their number should either be sacked for incompetence or hanged for treason.

If evidence concerning the presence of a Fiat Uno had not been available, no doubt the 'accident theorists' would recount how foolish the 'conspiracy theorists' were for believing there was a Fiat or, indeed, any interfering vehicles. In the same vein, the police disregarded copious eyewitness evidence, such as that from Françoise Levistre – corroborated by several other witnesses – of a strong flash of light just before the Mercedes lost control, temporarily blinding Henri Paul and causing the car to crash.

Remarkably, Levistre described this as taking place exactly where it was needed to blind Paul. This wasn't established until after he gave his evidence. (Levistre was also the only witness to initially mention a small white car from the attack scene – how would he know if he hadn't seen it since the police denied its existence for two weeks?) MI6 used the strobe system because there is no residual evidence; the flash went into the ether and the Fiat for repair and thence to a garage, where it was discovered by Al Fayed's team.

There were two main problems for the assassins: residual evidence from the Fiat and an excess number of credible witnesses. Most incriminating debris from the tunnel was removed with alacrity and virtually all photographic evidence seized. Weeks later, the police were forced to admit the existence of the white Fiat because leaked proof from analysis of the paint traces found on the Mercedes, together with witnesses, made continued denial impossible – all despite gargantuan efforts by the police and MI6 to prevent it.

Henri Paul, the Ritz Hotel's much-maligned deputy security manager and doomed chauffeur, received payment in cash that afternoon in the sum of around $2,000. (Approximately $2,000 in cash was found on Paul after the crash.) The police not only failed to investigate this but also took the view that: 'He was entitled to have this on him – perhaps he was going to buy something.' (The inquests were also dismissive.) MI6 almost certainly promised to pay Paul a lot more than his usual fee to ensure this vital human adjunct to murder would perform as planned.

Other enquiries revealed Paul had about £300,000 in thirteen different bank accounts despite his salary being only £20,000 per annum. It was also discovered that several payments totalling tens of thousands of pounds was paid into his bank in the preceding months before the crash. During the inquests, neither Mules nor the coroner chose to explore where the money had come from, despite the coroner stating at the inquests' commencement that this was one of the main eight 'building blocks' he set out to establish during proceedings.

Paul was earmarked as collateral damage after unwittingly helping these assassins and means were devised of persuading him to take the wheel of the Mercedes. The whole scenario would be very intoxicating, accounting for his 'voluble' behaviour that was later reported. However, there was no need for full payment, only an inducement with the promise of more to come. It was a virtual freebie for the Security Services – they knew Paul wasn't coming back!

But Henri Paul wasn't the only man involved who was linked to MI6 and known to be in the tunnel that night. James Andanson, a paparazzo who owned a white Fiat Uno, also had affiliations with the organisation. He later denied even being in Paris on the night in question but was already under investigation by the French Judicial police in connection with an unrelated murder, thus making the revelations about him even more interesting.

Recently retired Scotland Yard Chief Superintendent John Macnamara, who was in charge of the investigation for Al Fayed's team, tracked down Andanson and his Fiat to his hometown of Lignières, Central France, in February 1998. It's hard to believe the entire French police force was incapable of tracing the Fiat after six months of apparent searching unless, of course, they did so and then kept quiet. One wonders why the police did not pursue an investigation post-attack into whether any paparazzi owned a Fiat Uno because when Macnamara did so, his team quickly came up with the name of James Andanson. It's hard not to draw the conclusion that the French did not wish to pursue him for some reason that has never been clarified.

Mules said he subsequently interviewed the owner, James Andanson, whose white Fiat Uno had recently had its left taillight replaced (forensic fragments from the tunnel showed it was the left taillight from a Fiat Uno that had been smashed), but elected not to pursue him further, with no reason being given.

As for Andanson, he 'died' in May 2000 in an extremely bizarre and highly improbable 'suicide', where he was burnt to ash, having first *twice* shot himself in the head. Yet Mules still did not consider any connection with Diana.

Al Fayed's team found that the Fiat had been sold to a dealer in October 1997, just a month or so after Diana's murder. It was for sale in a garage where the rear nearside taillight had been replaced and the bodywork had undergone repair work to the same left rear area where the attack Fiat had been struck by the Mercedes, as proven by forensic evidence. When the French police discovered that Al Fayed's agent had found the car and had been to see it, they threatened him for interfering with police enquiries and told him he could face prosecution if he further 'interfered' with the 'investigation' rather than thanking him for succeeding where they had apparently failed.

On being questioned, the police once more gave evasive information. Commander Mules said that when he viewed the Fiat, it was on blocks and hadn't been driven for a considerable time despite evidence, disputed by the police, that the car had been used by Andanson in the preceding few months and had been repainted. One police report said the car didn't have a battery and had been used for keeping chickens.

It's known that the Fiat was for sale but not as a chicken hutch and friends of Andanson stated that he had been driving the car until a few months before its sale. Why the police presented such a variance in evidence is beyond understanding and their behaviour is only logical if a cover-up had been ordered, in which case all becomes clear. They were under instruction to maintain their position and avoid confronting the obvious truth: Diana had been murdered and Andanson was involved.

Andanson's pursuits are shrouded in secrecy but information concerning his connections and proclivities have leaked, so we are forced to assimilate what we know and draw our own conclusions. Don't you think the police should be interested in the amazing coincidences surrounding this man's activities in relation to Diana's murder? Surely he is an obvious suspect or perhaps Andanson just didn't fit in with Mules's original hypothesis? Most interesting of all, are Andanson's attempts to deny he was in Paris at all. He couldn't decide whether he had been in St Tropez or Corsica and even produced airline tickets to show he had been at Orly Airport (near to Paris), although he was unable to prove he took a plane. Indeed he could have bought the tickets and not flown anywhere, or someone might have bought them for him. Later, his son James said his father had phoned home at around 4.30am on that Sunday morning but he had been led to believe that he was in Bordeaux in the West of France. Meanwhile, Andanson's wife, Elizabeth said her husband was at home with her in Lignières.

Clearly there were obvious reasons to question this man thoroughly, given he could not even decide on his own alibi for the night but the reason that the police admitted to interviewing Andanson was because others knew of the claims concerning his role in the Alma and they didn't have any choice but to maintain appearances.

The reason put forward for not investigating him at first was that the white paint marks on the Mercedes didn't match the Fiat Uno. A leaked report contradicted this view and proved the police were sidestepping certain questions. The paint marks from Diana's Mercedes were in the infrared spectra absorption band of Andanson's Fiat and therefore identical. Scepticism was further increased when analysis of the black polymer tracings taken from the Fiat's wing mirror were also found on the Mercedes and shown to match. The police have never commented on these and numerous other obvious errors or deliberately misleading statements.

Andanson's job gave him a perfect cover for working on assignment for the Services. During the summer of 1997, from July to the end of August, he spent his time pursuing Dodi and Diana; he was in St Tropez while they were there. He would have known that the couple would be in Paris for the evening of 30th August since he had many contacts, including among the police. It was unthinkable that he wouldn't attend the biggest moment of his paparazzi life, especially having recently decided to join the Agence Angeli, the best-known celebrity agency in France.

Everyone knew at this time how close Diana and Dodi were to something special happening – they were the hottest item on the planet! If Andanson were to be involved in their assassination, then he would have been there to take the photo to beat all and make a fortune, in addition to earning his blood money. He took these photographs without the knowledge of MI6 and it would be the combination of bragging to his friends (later reported) and having become too high-profile by promising to make the pictures available that led to his very strange death, just thirty-three months later (much more on this later).

Richard Tomlinson, ex-MI6, and his ex-MI5 colleague, David Shayler, who were both pursued for disappointing their respective services by displaying extreme integrity, confirmed MI6 have used journalists or photographers for years. They can move freely and without suspicion and people expect them to travel from country to country and be involved with, or around, celebrities. James Andanson was not a 'one-off' paparazzi asset but one of several that had been used (and will be again) by the Security Services. Tomlinson confirmed MI6 did have at least one photographer 'on the books' and Andanson had, on several occasions, been 'in the vicinity of' people who had died rather unexpectedly.

Isn't it strange that here was a man who excelled in gaining the photo shot others couldn't, who spent time from June to the end of August following Dodi and Diana, and was said to have been outside the Ritz Hotel earlier on the day of their murder, who subsequently declared he wasn't in Paris and created two conflicting alibis? Even stranger that the police didn't manage to find him or his Fiat (it took Al Fayed's team a short time to do so) and, when the police did interview him, they declared he had no case to answer, maintained total secrecy over the whole affair and kept details from the press. Judge Stephan didn't even mention Andanson in his final report.

Whereas this in itself is disconcerting, the whole affair took on a different hue a few years later. On 4th May 2000, Andanson drove, or was driven, 600km south to a town called Millau and after buying jerry cans of petrol, continued north to le plateau du Larzac, an open space of thousands of hectares used by the military. Here, he supposedly strapped himself into his BMW, fired two bullets into his head and then set fire to his body, fuelling the flames, in death, with more and more fuel until his remains turned to ash.

It was said that for a human body to be burnt to this degree, petrol would have to be constantly added, requiring a corpse to continue its cremation for some considerable time after death, if it was to be suicide. It is fortunate Andanson chose this desolate spot because there was little chance of anyone causing a disturbance while his corpse was burning away. The keys to his BMW car were never found so, having first locked his car door from the outside, he must have used a carrier pigeon to whisk them away to a safe haven – yet verdict: suicide!

There is, of course, an alternative possibility: that it was another state-induced and then suppressed murder. The inquests didn't even allow Christophe Pelât, the Montpelier fireman who discovered Andanson's body and who confirmed two bullet holes in his skull, to attend court even though he explicitly offered to do so.

Andanson had become centre stage in maintaining the tissue of lies and his very existence threatened the thread of 'deniability', essential in ensuring the truth behind that terrible night in Paris never emerged. The only two men who could give the game away for certain, other than some of MI6's own operatives, were Andanson and Trevor Rees-Jones who (fortunately for him) developed amnesia. So it became necessary to remove Andanson, one way or another, because he had become the one person involved in Diana's murder that had been identified and tracked down which meant that, at some time soon, he would let something further slip or be persuaded to talk for a large sum of money.

Indeed, Al Fayed had offered a substantial sum for information on the Paris attack before Andanson's death. Andanson is known to have been indiscreet in mentioning to friends including crime writer Frédéric Dard that he was in the Alma when Diana was murdered, and that he could prove it. People were now around who could offer significant sums of money to persuade a man driven by a strong desire for wealth that in exchange for information he might become wealthier still and beyond his wildest dreams; unless it was ensured that he could dream no more.

There is significant evidence that MI5, Britain's Secret Service home division, raided the home of London-based Sipa agency photographer, Lionel Cherruault, in Kilburn at around 3.30am on 1 September 2007, twenty-seven hours after Diana's death. They stole computer hard disks together with credit cards and cash from Mrs Christine Cherruault's purse in the hope that this would offer cover as to the true purpose of the break-in. All other electronic equipment was left untouched as they loaded their goodies into Christine's car before driving off into the night. When the police arrived soon after the break-in, fingerprint checks were made but none were found.

Later, the next morning another detective arrived and made a startling statement: 'I must tell you something,' he began. 'I've just read this report and have to confirm to you that you were not burgled.' A flabbergasted Cherruault said, 'You mean they were grey men?' (meaning MI5/MI6), to which the detective responded, 'Call them what you like, you were not burgled.' The commandeered car was found twenty-four hours later and held no clues; all fingerprints had been wiped clean. MI6 believed that photographs of the Fiat Uno that would show the white marks on the Mercedes and offer proof of the collision had been sent from LS Presse director, Laurent Sola, in Paris in the early hours of Sunday, 31st August, to Mr Cherruault at his home and they wished to continue to deny its existence.

Remember, this happened the day after the Paris incident and at this point, there was no known proof in the public domain that the Fiat existed; MI6 were trying hard to keep it that way. On 16th June 2000, only weeks after Andanson's bizarre death, the Sipa agency in Paris also enjoyed a raid from armed, hooded thugs, who once more stole hard discs, shot a guard in the foot and this time succeeded in gaining information on Andanson. It's irrefutable that the search that took place in Andanson's office was for the photos of Diana's last moments that he had been bragging about to friends but the police did nothing in either case.

Five weeks after Andanson's death, the famous crime writer Frédéric Dard, also died from an apparent heart attack. It's known that he and Andanson had been friends and in discussion about writing a book on Diana's murder (later evidence from the inquests). These raids and indeed the murder of Andanson would not have been ordered for an insignificant matter, so something seriously threatened the authorities' tissue of lies. In addition to the paint marks, MI6 also needed to seize all photographs taken from around the Ritz, or in the tunnel, that might identify certain people. Why, unless for the obvious reason?

The facts in this chapter were drawn from the period before the inquests commenced and are included for background and to illustrate why we question the behaviour of the authorities by showing what information had been in the public domain for a decade and still they did nothing. In the following chapter, we refer to details taken from the official transcripts that should satisfy even the most ardent of 'accident theorists'. The issue isn't who murdered Diana, Dodi and Henri Paul but to obtain proof that they were murdered and that alone will bring the curtain down. We believe this is clearly illustrated but again, it is for you to decide.

In the US Grand Jury system the people decide whether a crime has been committed and in both the US and British courts, a judge may accept a majority verdict, where only ten of the twelve jurors agree, producing a majority of circa 83 per cent (nine from eleven jurors at this inquest). In this case, huge numbers of the world's populace gave their judgment that they believed this was murder years ago, so where was the criminal investigation? The Establishment try to maintain 'deniability' because once the mask slips, their lies will become apparent and they will have to explain to furious nations, the British in particular, why they lied. No doubt they will say that they did so to protect the people and prevent a crisis, but this excuse won't wash. An even bigger crisis has been created by the lie itself; one that can no longer be ignored if the British people are to expiate their shame.

Part Two

'Protagonists'

The Authorities

I believe this book illustrates an abundance of evidence to show Princess Diana was murdered and so there was no excuse for forbidding a verdict of 'unlawful killing by persons unknown'. The authorities suppressed the truth to prevent both the monarchy and British Government from collapsing into turmoil and the possible swelling of the people's rage onto the streets. We now aspire to prove that Diana was brutally murdered by following a process used by courts throughout the world, where juries convict on the basis of 'beyond any reasonable doubt'.

We show that MI6 do kill people and are even issued with handouts on the subject, thus removing a central denial they utilised from the outset. But we also prove that they are quite prepared to engage in the criminal activity of perverting the course of justice in a court of law.

We also note that during these inquests the court didn't apply any sanction against MI6 or require that they answer questions they preferred not to answer. Would MI6 take these risks, under full public gaze, without grave need? They did so because their non-attendance would guarantee that this matter remained a festering wound for both MI6 and the monarchy.

In this chapter, we also show that both MI6 and the police pursued Diana for several years prior to the Paris attack and were abusing her civil liberties even then. It is also my belief that, in addition, we illustrate that the police attempted to defeat justice during the inquests by deceiving the court. So we now examine the available evidence that incriminates both the police and MI6.

The hypothetical purpose of these inquests was to determine whether MI6 was responsible for planning and executing the attack on Diana in Paris on instruction from the Palace. This was as a result of the Surrey coroner, Michael Burgess, who took over from the royal coroner John Burton, asking Lord Stevens, the then Scotland Yard chief, to look into murmurings of MI6 involvement. But the coroner, Lord Scott-Baker, made the presumptions from the outset that MI6 could not have been responsible but for 'the possibility of rogue officers' and also that there was no need for the royals to attend. So what was the point of the hearing?

Sir Richard Dearlove was MI6 Operations Director at the time of Diana's murder and became Chief (so-called 'C') during 1999–2004; he now gave his 'evidence'. His spontaneous opinion was that it couldn't have been rogue officers 'without the knowledge of the Service; that was impossible'.

And so we were told by a former MI6 boss that even if so-called 'rogue officers' were responsible, the Service hierarchy would still be aware of their actions. Following this logic, then this cabal was still comprised of serving MI6 officers and would still require the nod from someone at the pinnacle of power. Here is the reason why the judiciary could not permit the option of finding for murder because such a verdict would be the de facto conviction of MI6. This point is enhanced by the coroner's comment, during the inquests, that if this was an attack then it could only have been carried out by a Security Services organisation.

But Dearlove then effectively reversed his 'evidence'. By saying that it couldn't possibly be rogue officers he had, of course, placed MI6 in grave danger since, if it couldn't be rogue officers and the jury became convinced that this was murder then MI6, as the only possible culprits, were guilty of murder. He now stated that it would be *difficult but possible* for agents to act without the knowledge of the MI6 hierarchy'.

This ridiculous and banal reversal of 'evidence' assisted MI6 by offering them an escape route. But there was a large contingent of senior MI6 in Paris that weekend, including Dearlove and Richard Spearman who was the MI6 SAS liaison officer, according to the ex SAS and MI6 officer, Richard Tomlinson. Also include Tomlinson's statement that 'something big was going down' and credulity swiftly evaporates. Let us consider, for a moment, the logic of 'rogue' officers being responsible.

If this was possible, the world would obviously expect a judge to demand that MI6 assist with discovery of their identity. Although without an 'unlawful killing by persons unknown' verdict being available to the jury, denied by Lord Justice Scott Baker, then it was impossible to deliver justice even if they were shown to be responsible for this evil act and identified since the jury didn't have this option available.

But the court didn't pursue rogue officers at all. Instead, and despite being set up to finally settle this matter, the court expressed its gratitude to MI6 for their attendance and exculpated them before the inquests even began. In addition, and in the same breath, the court then admitted that this putative rogue cabal from within MI6 could have been responsible for the crime. So, in this convoluted eventuality, these rogue officers were permitted to commit this crime without even being considered by the court and you might ask why, if justice was being sought.

Also, since MI6 acts of its own volition and without government oversight, then if a rogue element existed, this illicit cabal would operate within an undemocratic organisation that does as it pleases and then, in turn, this cabal also does as it pleases. If this reasoning isn't nonsense, then the people should be seriously alarmed.

Continuing for the moment with the logic that these putative rogue officers were responsible then it would be automatic for Dearlove to investigate them, if he really sought justice and so, if Lord Justice Scott Baker truly believed Dearlove's new 'evidence' that it could be rogue officers, why didn't he pursue Dearlove over what action he had taken to seek their identity?

Scott Baker expressed the rogue officers' option several times and even used them to defend MI6 during his summation, so we presume that he believed this was a possibility. It was therefore an obvious question for him to ask Dearlove. You might wonder why Dearlove was never asked this question. As mentioned before, you can't have it both ways. The court should have realised that if evidence is to be changed then the people expect that so should the attendant logic or suitable explanation given.

Dearlove had no reason to investigate rogue officers because as he had stated, this was impossible, but he now says it was difficult but possible. So in this eventuality, and if he wasn't lying to the court, he should have immediately investigated them if he was truly seeking justice. Since he didn't investigate, I suggest that it follows he is either complicit in the crime or was not seeking justice and his changed 'evidence' was a convenient position to adopt. But, if not complicit, then you need to ask why he wasn't seeking justice and what other reason could there possibly be? Why, also, didn't Scott Baker demand an explanation for this ridiculous and effective reversal of 'evidence'?

It is apparent to me that Dearlove's reversal of evidence was his attempt to protect MI6. But the rogue officer reasoning needed to be pursued to the end of the hearing because, although the jury would most likely harbour serious concerns about MI6 being responsible, they also needed definitive proof that it was MI6 to condemn them. So, if the concept of alternative, possible culprits to MI6 could be introduced, this further shielded MI6.

(The jury needed to be satisfied that these 'rogue' elements could operate without the knowledge of the Service if MI6 were to stay out of harm's way and the Service also needed to maintain their 'deniability', so claiming a rogue element was a useful ruse. But remember, Dearlove's change of 'evidence' was despite his autonomic response that this was 'impossible'. Also, part of the permitted verdicts included 'the following vehicles' – consider; this applies perfectly well to assassins as well as paparazzi. The court didn't qualify which of these applied.)

Did Scott Baker realise the conundrum he had created? If he genuinely believed it could have been rogue officers, with the meaning that most people would apply, rather than a specific MI6 bolt hole, contrived to assist their 'deniability', why didn't he bother to pursue these rogue officers with Dearlove? He certainly still used the rogue officer reasoning until the end of the hearing and during his summation. Or does this show, as I believe it does, that the court knew this was nonsense and there was never any intention of delivering justice? You might be forgiven for believing these inquests were a total sham.

Now let us proceed to the detail that emerged from the inquests. As you will see, the main thrust of this narrative rests on two issues that we illustrate by reference to the official transcripts, from which much of this book is taken:

(1) That Henri Paul was not drunk and that the medical evidence submitted to incriminate him should have been declared inadmissible, and

(2) That the vehicles witnessed escaping the death scene at high speed after the crash were not 'following paparazzi', but had lain in wait for the Mercedes en route. These vehicles were already at the Alma, loitering and awaiting the Mercedes' arrival. The paparazzi arrived soon afterwards.

I believe that both these crucial points illustrate a murderous conclusion, not an accident. But again it is up to you, the reader, to be the jury.

The British Security Services (MI6)

MI6 is supposed to serve the interests of their people and, like the CIA, is responsible for supplying their government with foreign intelligence, amongst other activities. It works out of headquarters at Vauxhall on the South Bank of the River Thames in London. The organisation's activities are surrounded by mystique, ostensibly necessary for the people's security, but in reality for their own protection; until 1994, its very existence was not even officially acknowledged. Clearly, this is an organisation that does not like public scrutiny, which is why it was no surprise when it attempted to have Diana's inquest illegally heard behind closed doors by members of the royal household. But what other serious matters could induce MI6 to take the risk of committing perjury with the world watching?

As it happened, an inquest was avoided for several years until Paul Burrell released a note to the press that was given to him by Diana and of similar nuance to the Mishcon note. The next day Diana's lawyer, Lord Mishcon, went to the police concerning this note that he had given them six years earlier. Within days this forced the subsequent disclosure of this 'Mishcon note' that had been illegally kept secluded by the British police. Both notes describe Diana's fears that she would die in a car crash staged to look like an accident. It was these notes that confounded the authority's attempts to avoid further public scrutiny and forced the opening of the inquests only a few months later.

MI6 were pursued throughout the inquests by brilliant, undaunted lawyers, who sought to liberate the truth but extracting revelations from such an organisation as MI6, one that effectively functions above the law, turned out to be a painfully laborious task. However, we ask that you carefully consider the points herein raised and determine whether or not you believe MI6 'evidence'.

So, after ten long years, these inquests were finally upon us due to the authorities having no other option. This was after three other coroners had either resigned or stood down. John Burton, the royal coroner, stood down and Michael Burgess, the coroner before Dame Elizabeth Butler-Sloss assumed the role, also resigned. It was reported that he considered the whole affair highly suspicious but resigned on the grounds that he was too busy.

Baroness Butler-Sloss, a high court judge and friend of the royal family, was the penultimate coroner. She tried to organise an illegal jury consisting of members from the royal household. After this was challenged successfully by Mohamed Al Fayed she stood down when the Law Lords ruled that her attempt to sit without a jury, or to use one made up from members of the royal household, was illegal. At least this affords some hope for the integrity of the British judiciary.

The inquests began on 27th September 2007, ten years after Diana's murder, and ended with the coroner's summation on 2nd April 2008. They were held in the imposing Royal Courts of Justice (RCJ) in the Strand, the last Gothic building to be built in London. Officially opened by Queen Victoria in 1882, it is full of oak panelling, with three miles of seemingly never-ending corridors, where one can easily become lost. Designed by George Edmund Street, it boasts more than 1,000 rooms and the interior is every bit as impressive as the exterior.

The coroner, Lord Robert Scott Baker, was appointed a high court judge in 1988, becoming Mr Justice Scott Baker and he received the customary knighthood prior to joining the Supreme Court as Lord Scott Baker. Numerous lawyers were involved. Mohamed Al Fayed was represented by Michael Mansfield QC – a prominent, quick-witted and endearing lawyer, with a bohemian hairstyle, who penetrated the tenebrous world of MI6 and, to their acute discomfort, revealed a great deal. The Chief of London Police was represented by Richard

Horwell QC, Mr Croxford QC represented the Ritz Hotel, Mr Ian Burnett QC was counsel for the coroner, Mr Tam QC acted for the Security Services, Mr Keen QC acted on behalf of Henri Paul's parents, Mr Hough QC acted for the court and Mr Macleod QC represented the Chief of the Metropolitan Police.

After jury selection, the newly appointed jurors were sworn in on 2nd October 2007 and then travelled to France to become familiar with the whole scene. They visited the Ritz Hotel and went from there to the Pont de l'Alma tunnel and then to the Pitié Salpêtrière Hospital, where Diana was taken after the fatal crash. Video footage of various key events during that night in Paris was scrutinised, together with CCTV footage of the evening's activities. The jurors were then introduced to police 3D computer modelling software that creates supposed scenarios of what the police believe happened. A cynic could argue that here was an opportunity for jury inculcation.

On 10th October 2007, witnesses started to be called and most of those whose testimony was crucial to a murder verdict appeared in the first month of proceedings during the October. These included statements from David Laurent, the Blanchards, François Levistre and his wife Valerie, who were all among the most powerful voices that propounded murder. Whatever the reasoning this testimony would have dimmed for the jury five months later when the opinions of more temperate voices would hold sway (although the jurors will have taken notes and have had the benefit of the coroner's final summation).

Mohamed Al Fayed, without whom these inquests would never have taken place, attended and twice gave evidence. Also Sarah, Duchess of York, the Queen's other former daughter-in-law, gave evidence together, with a whole list of well-known figures from Diana's previous world. These included Nicholas Soames, whom Diana loathed and had accused of making threatening calls to her only seven months before she was murdered. There were past police and Security Services chiefs, together with some police officers who were acting on behalf of the British police and Security Services.

Many of the witnesses didn't attend court. Some submitted a written affidavit, while others gave evidence over a video link from

France. Written evidence cannot, of course, be challenged and video links do not permit the jury sight of a witness's response to the questions asked by lawyers so please take note of the nature of the evidence given by those who did not attend court.

The police were seen after the Christmas break in January and the Security Services towards the end of February, when there was only about six weeks of evidence remaining. The evidence of Richard Tomlinson, the former MI6 agent whose testimony caused the service such trauma, was heard before MI6 gave testimony. MI6 didn't therefore need to tolerate more scrutiny of their testimony, other than for the lawyers' interrogation, since Tomlinson could have taken issue with more MI6 'evidence', had he heard it before giving his own. He would have had much MI6 'evidence' to question.

There was a palpable air of tension when MI6 witnesses were questioned; it is certainly remarkable to me what bad memories they all seem to have, especially considering they are mostly recruited from Cambridge University and are supposedly chosen for their intellect. Some of these agents were finally forced into admitting they were at the British Embassy in Paris that night, but we are required to believe they didn't know about Diana's death until late on the Sunday and they also couldn't remember where they were, what they were doing or which other agents were present.

During the course of MI6 'testimony', all agents except those already known to the public, such as Sir Richard Dearlove, retained their anonymity by using letters or numerals for identification. Dearlove was operations director for MI6 during the Paris incident and became chief, otherwise known as 'C', in 1999 after the sudden death of Sir David Spedding, on whose watch Diana was murdered.

Spedding died from cancer on 13th June 2001 – almost exactly one year after James Andanson committed 'suicide'. Spedding's secretary, Richard Spearman (I believe he was the witness known as H/SECT-Witness 'I'), the SAS liaison officer for the MI6 'Increment' team, was posted to Paris two weeks prior to Diana's murder. During the inquests, Dearlove and other MI6 officers gave unintentional insights into the supposed criteria by which MI6 operates and posed a disquieting view of their shadowy behaviour.

Dearlove completed the customary five years as head of MI6 in 2004 but was still, during these inquests, master of Pembroke College, Cambridge – a well-known recruiting ground for MI6 agents. As operations director for MI6 during this period, he will know the truth about the Alma incident, whether or not he himself was personally involved in its execution. But the coroner, Lord Justice Scott Baker, determined from the outset that neither MI6 nor the Palace could have been involved in such a crime and the only way MI6 officers could be involved was if they were rogue agents.

Dearlove disagreed; he took this book's view that 'it couldn't have been rogue elements without the approval of the Service; that was impossible'. He later suggested under examination, however, that it would be 'difficult but possible' for agents to act without knowledge of the Service hierarchy – what a contradiction. But it was established that in these circumstances hypothetical rogue officers remain serving officers, so the Service was responsible, irrespective of from where, within its command structure, the order for Diana's murder emanated.

If, therefore, you are prepared to accept the view that an ex-boss of MI6 is more likely to know the extent of their capabilities than a judge, then this removes any justification for Scott Baker's initial stance on the exculpation of MI6. Also, if they should have been under greater scrutiny, then it follows that so should the royal family, who have a known relationship with MI6 and around whom this whole affair turns.

Yet it was always unlikely that the organisation's role in the deaths would be examined properly in court. Until 1994, MI6 wasn't even controlled by statute with one famous description of them being that they are 'a bunch of meddlers with a public school education [meaning 'private' in the UK] and a free supply of plastic explosives'. Even Dearlove confirmed that MI6 agents are encouraged to run free with creative and laterally thought through ideas.

A central issue was whether MI6 have a remit to kill people when it is considered apposite – and, if so, who makes that call and by which criteria? One of Dearlove's first questionable statements at the inquests was delivered when he stated that MI6 don't kill people. He then later admitted that there are occasions when Section 7 of the

ISB (Intelligence Services Bill) 1994 needed to be invoked but that 'all these proposals' (which clearly refers to more than one intended assassination) went through him as operations director during the period which covers 1997.

Section 7 is now confirmed by Dearlove as where lethal force is allowed but this apparently requires the approval of either the British Foreign Secretary (a post held by a man of principle at this time, Robin Cook, who was also MI6's political boss. Cook mysteriously died at the age of fifty-eight on 15th May 2006, not long before the inquests began, on land owned by a Ministry of Defence official) or another minister, such as for example, the Minister of State for the Armed Services (a post held until May 1997 by Nicholas Soames – Sir Winston Churchill's grandson, a close personal friend of the Prince of Wales – who severely criticised Diana on British television and whom Diana accused of making threatening calls to her at Kensington Palace, with witness support at the inquests).

Further examination of Dearlove revealed that Section 7 is only invoked when 'great damage could be done to Britain or her citizens'. This book endeavours to show that the principal reason Diana was murdered was because she was about to attack the monarchy, specifically Charles, Prince of Wales, and would be enabled once married to Dodi. So in effect we have confirmation from a former MI6 boss of both a reason for murdering Diana, and the fact that it's permissible under their code. Following Dearlove's confirmation that any such attack could only have been carried out by serving agents, whether or not they were acting independently, he then refused to comment on whether MI6 use a team known as 'The Increment'; no denial of their existence.

This secret paramilitary organisation comprises troops from the SAS and SBS military for the purposes of carrying out lethal operations, as described by Richard Tomlinson. Dearlove denied specific knowledge of this group (is this even possible?) but stated that MI6 use 'other capabilities about which we know nothing' (not as bad as the Increment/worse; who knows), adding that he *didn't think* (my italics) that the Service's capability had anything to do with Diana. He was operations director and in Paris at the time of

Diana's death but doesn't know whether or not MI6 were involved? Surely this beggars belief?

Dearlove was then asked whether any MI6 officer had deliberately lied to a court of law, thus perverting the course of justice. 'Not that I am aware,' he replied. He was then confronted with evidence regarding a money laundering trial in the Cayman Islands in 2002, known as the 'Euro Bank Case'. This trial took place while Dearlove was still 'C', chief of MI6 so responsible for their activities. Four former bank employees were accused of money laundering, but the trial collapsed when it came to light that an MI6 agent had infiltrated the bank to gather intelligence and had subsequently been ordered to destroy evidence to cover up the agency's link with the investigation.

The final judgment from the Chief Justice of the Cayman Islands criticised MI6 for even considering putting together an operation that 'relied upon a plan that depended on the court being misled'. This so-called 'London Plan', it transpired, had been specifically conceived to *pervert the course of justice*. Put on the spot, Dearlove immediately spluttered, 'That was a one-off.' This acknowledgement clearly shows what MI6 are capable of, and reveals how even a former MI6 boss is prepared to behave in a court of law; his memory certainly didn't need jogging when confronted with this truth.

Embarrassed by this line of questioning, Dearlove responded that the lawyers 'have dug this one out', adding that he 'would have liked a little warning'. What right did he think he had to expect a little warning to tell the truth in the people's court and why didn't he, as a public servant, volunteer this information freely in the first instance if he was truly seeking justice? Why else was he at the hearing and what else did he fail to disclose? You might reasonably ask how the court responded to this behaviour; the answer is that there was no response.

You either take the view that this public servant deliberately lied to a court of the people's justice or that he had forgotten about the event. But, since he was the boss of MI6 at this time, how could he forget unless there was so much corruption going on that he couldn't keep track. But we must question why the court didn't even question Dearlove over this act, let alone apply any sanctions against him. So are the people supposed to find this demonstrable disdain acceptable? What reason should they apply to tolerate this atrocious act? Perhaps the coroner could explain? Remember, these inquests were to satisfy people that Diana was not murdered and that MI6 are not criminals.

When questioned about general operating procedures within MI6, Dearlove divulged some of his insights. He said that he knew all the intricacies of MI6 and confirmed they can operate without the knowledge of the Foreign Secretary (unless, of course, the Foreign Secretary should inadvertently discover some unpalatable truths), adding that MI6 stations abroad often operate from British Embassies and that control was possible without reference to London. He further added that HQ was 'usually' kept informed on 'any significant proposal', thus confirming MI6's ability to murder Diana; they just needed to decide that she wasn't significant. (This would have been essential with Robin Cook as Foreign Secretary – but did Cook know the truth for he would never have tolerated such behaviour? It was most convenient for some that he died unexpectedly prior to these inquests.)

Dearlove denied that MI6 had training manuals on assassination (no mention of the assassination handouts that were later inadvertently admitted to by Witness 'X'). Perhaps Dearlove had forgotten again! The inquests then turned their attention to an extremely incriminating allegation, made by former MI6 agent Richard Tomlinson, that MI6 had plotted to murder the Serbian leader, Slobodan Milosevic, in a staged car accident in a tunnel in 1992, some five years before Diana's 'accident'.

Evidence from Tomlinson, specifically concerning Witness 'A', was a central source of evidence used by lawyers for the attack on MI6. They wished to prove that MI6 were eminently capable of carrying out such a violent and murderous attack on Diana. Following this evidence, it's proven that Witness 'A' had definitely submitted a file for the assassination of Slobodan Milosevic to the MI6 hierarchy, despite his continued denial.

Tomlinson described a two-page document seen while working with Witness 'A' detailing three alternative plans to assassinate Milosevic. The first proposed method was to use a Serb opposition paramilitary group (the most 'deniable' method); the second involved using 'The Increment' to kill him using a bomb or sniper ambush. Finally, the third method was to use a strobe light to blind Milosevic's chauffeur as he passed through a motorway tunnel in Geneva. The central pillars of that tunnel were also described as being essential to increase the probability of death.

At first the questioning focused on how 'official' this proposal was and whether Dearlove was aware of it. He said that when he heard one of his agents (Witness 'A' during the inquest) had put forward this assassination plan, he 'believed' that he had interviewed him about it. This was later denied by Witness 'A' during his cross-examination when he said he wasn't interviewed but had, in fact, been encouraged to write the proposal down by Witness 'E', who also in turn initially denied encouraging him, or even seeing the proposal but was later forced into admitting he must have seen it after all. (It is my contention that Dearlove misled the court on this point because he was trying to maintain that Witness 'A's plan for Slobodan Milosevic was just an ephemeral document and not official – inadvertently proven to be untrue by Witness 'X'.)

Witness 'A' wasn't even interviewed by police until after Richard Tomlinson, the ex-MI6 agent and former colleague of Witness 'A', had forced public disclosure. (You will also note how MI6 obfuscated their answers throughout their testimony in the hope of confusing the jury but I am trying hard not to confuse you.) Tomlinson said this proposal was submitted to Witness 'E', head of the MI6 Balkan section, by Witness 'A'.

Witness 'A' was extremely ambitious according to Tomlinson; he was the deputy head of the Balkan target team and 'unlikely to submit ideas that would jeopardise his promotional aspirations'. When ready to submit his proposal, he bypassed his immediate boss 'H' and went straight to 'E', head of the controllerate, believing he would receive a more favourable response. This he did, as 'E' told him to put his plan on paper. 'A' 'clearly intended this proposal should be taken seriously', as Tomlinson stated higher officials in MI6 ('E' in this case) were supportive and clearly carrying out their normal duties by accepting this proposal.

'A' was asked how he envisaged his plan should work. Had he considered using Serb dissidents in Switzerland to assassinate Slobodan Milosevic on one of his visits to Geneva, or was he considering military options? 'A' now admitted 'military options' thus confirming Tomlinson's previous description for the Milosevic attack (Since military options were to be considered, and they were clearly not considering an invasion of Serbia, what other than SAS/SBS troops could possibly be used? This action must be covert otherwise there would be no deniability if caught so I suggest this is an inadvertent description of the Increment that most certainly exists – I have been personally assured, from a reliable source, that it does.)

'A' was then asked, if this idea was against MI6 ethos, how could he have considered putting it forward to the big boss and how did it find its way to the policy-making tenth floor? At this point he let slip that in exceptional cases they could reconsider it, again confirming that it was an official document.

But why would MI6 reconsider something regarded as abhorrent and that Dearlove, the boss, apparently needed to interview Witness 'A' over? Also, do you think Diana could be classed as an 'exceptional case'? How many supposed errant princesses are there around?

'A' went on to describe this system of pink and white stationery used for memos or proposals respectively. Memos are pink on A5 paper and are for the 'ephemeral file' (used for internal notes) that can be destroyed, but white on A4 paper cannot since these are formal documents and will have a tag attached. 'A' then tried to alter his previous evidence by saying that his proposal concerning Slobodan Milosevic was an internal note on pink memo paper but he was forced to recant when it was proven that the memo was on white official paper with an attached minute board, contrary to his initial claim, so it couldn't be shredded.

Confronted with this lie, Witness 'A' gave the banal response that his proposal was considered 'white, treat as pink' but this was later proven to be yet another lie when Witness 'X' confirmed it was indeed an official white document with a tag attached and so was being actively considered by MI6. For what target, you might ask?

This 'evidence' also proved yet more of Dearlove's equivocation when he pathetically tried to suggest that he believed he interviewed Witness 'A' concerning this plan to murder Slobodan Milosevic. It is now shown there was no reason for Dearlove to interview him since it was clearly a normal proposal that he would have expected from Witness 'A'.

I believe I can say, hand on heart, that nobody reading this book will believe a word of what these MI6 witnesses were saying but because most were only identified by numerals or letters they cannot be held to account (not that they would be in any event). This means these people were deceiving the court and there can only be one reason for this perversion of justice; ten years after Diana's brutal murder.

The fact remains that during the inquests Dearlove was clearly asked whether MI6 permits murder and he repeated, unequivocally, that it does not, but he was then forced to confess that all Section 7 proposals seeking authorisation for murdering people went through him as operations director. So, in other words here we have evidence that MI6 admit that they are authorised to kill people but only under 'special circumstances', thus confirming Diana as a potential target.

During continued questioning, 'A' was asked the same question of whether he was made aware, during his training, of a team called 'The Increment' and was he required to consider this team during periods of 'lateral thinking'? He answered that he 'was aware of a variety of capabilities', so no denial. Following this, he was challenged that he was required to 'think outside the box' where a threat was perceived to the stability or security of the United Kingdom, to which he answered, 'Only within certain parameters, but yes.'

At this point in the inquests 'A' decided he didn't want to discuss MI6 military capabilities any further (you will note that in this court of law, MI6 possessed the option not to answer any questions they didn't like). 'A's immediate boss 'H' added that MI6 couldn't be seen to be considering the proposal – not that they shouldn't consider these dreadful acts but that they might be caught. Proceedings were becoming so heated by now that the coroner, Lord Justice Scott Baker, decided to bring the session to a close.

The British Secret Service's consequent convoluted explanations for their behaviour were a revelation, with contradictions coming thick and fast as they tried in vain to defend their position. A crucial issue was now whether the Slobodan Milosevic's murder proposal from 'A' was an official document or merely an enthusiastic officer getting carried away with far-fetched ideas.

Dearlove delivered a tortuous explanation where he now admitted, later maintained by other MI6 witnesses, that there was a person due for extermination but it wasn't Milosevic. It was another Serbian leader hell-bent on ethnic cleansing and wiping out much of the Moslem population of Serbia, thereby effectively suggesting that they were really the good guys, doing everyone a favour. But at least it is now established that they do murder people to achieve some political aims.

But Dearlove was now talking of murdering people as though it was a matter of routine. (Milosevic was sent to the war crimes tribunal in The Hague and died in prison when his trial was not going the way that the West wanted. It was reported that Milosevic hadn't taken his heart tablets for a while and, like so many convenient deaths with these sordid people, he also died of a heart attack.) We are not permitted to know which leader they were due to murder so you must decide whether you accept this assertion or was MI6 easing away from yet another embarrassing truth?

On 13 February 2008, Richard Tomlinson gave evidence at the inquests, taking lawyers' questions directly from Marseilles over a video link. Evidence from his time in the Secret Service is a major reason why MI6 didn't come out unscathed when it came to Diana's murder. Tomlinson was the greatest threat MI6 needed to defend against so the lawyers spent much of their time concentrating on his revelations. He described the occasion when his former colleague, Witness 'A', 'tossed over' the document entitled 'The Need to Assassinate President Milosevic of Serbia' – no ambiguity over the target.

He then described the options for assassination that were considered. The most relevant proposal for this hearing's purpose was the tunnel attack, using a strobe light to disorientate the driver, forcing him to crash at night and thus reducing the chance of witnesses. The concrete pillars would also increase the probability of a fatal crash, eerily foreshadowing exactly what happened to Diana in the Parisian tunnel. Tomlinson also, crucially, identified Richard Spearman as one of the MI6 men in Paris that weekend and described him as 'H/SECT', the personal assistant to the then boss of MI6, David Spedding. Spearman's role was liaison with the SAS 'Increment Team'. The MI6 station manager, based in Paris, denied being in Paris at all, so conveniently didn't have to confirm whether Spearman was there.

Several witnesses said they saw a bright white strobe light just as Diana's Mercedes entered the tunnel. It was suggested in court that these were lights from excursion boats (Bateaux Mouches) instead of an assassin's handheld light used to blind Henri Paul but several witnesses observed this flash from a position where the light could not have emanated from the river. It was also very difficult to explain away a loud bang that witnesses described as coming a split second after this violent flash just prior to the Mercedes sliding into the thirteenth pillar.

A British secretary, Brenda Wells, witnessed the crash and observed the flash coming from within the tunnel; she didn't give evidence in court because she has completely disappeared off the map. Then witnesses Benoît Boura and Gaëlle l'Hostis observed this very violent flash of light as they descended into the tunnel from its other end, driving towards the Mercedes so they wouldn't have been able to see lights from excursion boats.

Partouche, Gooroovadoo, Petel, Souad, Brian Andersen and François Levistre all saw this very bright flash. Levistre was inside and at the other end of the tunnel, while Souad had overtaken the Fiat and was just in front of it so was nearer to the tunnel's entrance. The Fiat was, in turn, just in front of the Mercedes so none of these witnesses could have seen lights coming from the river either.

Tomlinson now confirmed that the use of a portable strobe light was part of the MI6 armoury. It was demonstrated to him when at the SBS (Special Boat Service) headquarters in Poole, Dorset, on his initial training course. The determination of this evidence was crucial because, other than river boats, there was no explanation for a violent flash of light just prior to the Mercedes losing control other than a murderous attack, so much effort was spent in trying to blame the boats.

Tomlinson also said that the Paris Ritz Hotel was used by MI6 for meetings. He confirmed that when he was in MI6 he had used the Ritz during a time that they were planning to smuggle items out of Russia and, during proceedings, two MI6 officers later admitted using the Ritz for covert operations. Tomlinson added that the security manager of a large hotel is one of the first people new MI6 officers are encouraged to recruit because 'MI6 cannot spend an inordinate amount of time scrutinising hotels', thus establishing that Henri Paul was certainly approached by MI6 to work for them.

Tomlinson further added that MI6 frequently ask friendly secret service agencies, such as the CIA, to place members of the royal family (especially Diana) under close surveillance when abroad, ostensibly for their own protection. He confirmed that 'The Increment' is a special cell of SAS and SBS troops who are specially trained to carry out covert operations for MI6 abroad, where lethal force is required. And he added that when MI6 consider information is in the national interest, they regard it as permissible to deceive, which I believe we have shown, includes perverting the course of justice in a court of law.

Tomlinson was told that his ex-colleague, Witness 'A', claimed his proposal was only an idea and against MI6 ethos (it had been shredded so he was unable to show the court a copy). Tomlinson replied that that was impossible: it was against MI6 rules and would have been 'a hanging offence'. The proposal had a high distribution list and minute board attached so couldn't have been destroyed unless, of course, surreptitiously.

Tomlinson believed Diana's assassination was carried out by a cabal of MI6 officers using their 'Increment' team. Bear in mind this would require the order to come from some high alternative source if done without approval of the Prime Minister, such as a senior member of the royal family, or one of their sycophants, who had strong ties with the Security Services. It is therefore reasonable again to ask how

Richard Dearlove, the operations director and next 'C', boss of MI6, was in Paris with the SAS liaison officer at the time of the 'accident' yet Dearlove claimed to know nothing of it.

The lawyer for MI6, Mr Tam, tried to counter these accusations. He said that Tomlinson's description of the tunnel attack method was 'out of the films – he had written this for dramatic effect.' Tomlinson retorted that if it was out of films, then why did MI6 shred the document? Tam replied that this proposal came from Witness 'A' alone and not the Service, to which Tomlinson said, 'The description of these events came from a senior member of the MI6 team who was acting on behalf of the Service and clearly not doing this for his own amusement or need.' He further added that there was no need to shred the document because the police couldn't get anywhere near MI6 unless, of course, there were imminent inquests and some files were to be examined by Scotland Yard.

Tomlinson believed that Witness 'A' was coached in what to say at the inquests. I believe it's certain that all MI6 witnesses were coached and synchronised and is the reason Tomlinson was called as a witness before MI6 gave 'testimony' so that his revelations could be subsequently countered and neutralised by MI6 and to prevent him from being able to further question MI6 'testimony' in court.

Witness 'X' was the next agent to be questioned. She began her career in MI6 as a personal assistant, rising to 'middle management' over the course of the next twenty-five years. Presented as an expert on MI6 systems, she was grilled over the deliberately complicated system of white versus pink paper, which seemed designed to create an impregnable shield of 'deniability'. She was challenged to track the paperwork of the Witness 'A' proposal and show the court where this document had come from, who was responsible for its distribution and who in MI6 had seen it before it was, apparently, shredded.

Witness 'X' reiterated Dearlove's testimony that the proposal of Witness 'A' was 'strangled at birth' (despite Witness 'A' saying they might need to go back to it). She was asked who had handed her this proposal and, although stating it was unusual, said she couldn't remember and 'didn't realise its significance.' This clearly illustrates she was used to receiving assassination proposals otherwise she would certainly have remembered if it was the only one; would you ever forget?

Asked whether MI6 records would show evidence on Henri Paul or James Andanson she said neither were recorded but then, under further examination, admitted it was possible a file could have existed and still not show on the records. That comment confirms the futility of relying on MI6 documentation in the case of Diana's death because once you accept they could erase any connection with a crime, and admitted erasing much, you can be sure there will be no records to implicate them. She said that only two people in MI6 were able to destroy documents; officially (But remember the Eurobank Case where MI6 are proven in court to have attempted the destruction of evidence).

'X' was the official contact for Lord Stephens and the Scotland Yard inquiry team so, in order to facilitate access to whatever Stephens wanted to see, she was granted 'God's access' to all files within the Service. Clearly, she was well regarded by MI6 and at a very senior level so was she being modest by saying that she was 'middle management'?

Questioned over whether she denied Lord Stephens any information for which he had asked, she answered no. It would be interesting to learn, however, what else she didn't offer that Stephens didn't know existed. What about, for example, the confidential write-up of 'A's' assassination proposal report, which she claimed not to remember? As the existence of this document was only revealed during Dearlove's interrogation the previous week, here was proof of another crucial piece of evidence that would never have seen the light of day but for cross-examination in court. This begs the question of what other invaluable evidence remained hidden and why MI6 didn't offer this evidence to the court if they were truly seeking justice.

Another interesting point with regard to this particular report is that 'X' said the reason she didn't make this available to police was because she 'didn't want to lead police in certain directions'. But she had just given evidence that she couldn't remember this file. How, therefore, could she have consciously decided not to lead the police by giving it to them; she can't remember it?

But the lies or 'deniability' didn't end there. Conveniently, the minute book was only retained in MI6 records from 1998, the year after Diana's murder, and documents the court needed were all 'ephemeral documents' so didn't come under the normal rules for white A5 official documents and had all been shredded. Whenever difficult questions arose, the goalposts moved accordingly.

'X' believes that a plan to murder Diana would have been in MI6 files and that 'this would have been available to the court'; this is grotesquely insulting to anyone's intelligence and in light of the previous revelations, can anyone believe this would really be the case? Extraordinarily, she then slipped that there were no training manuals on assassination; only handouts!

She further admits that when the French police approached the British Embassy with questions regarding Witness 'A's' proposal (following Richard Tomlinson's disclosure to Judge Stephan that a plan similarly describing events in the Alma tunnel had indeed been prepared by MI6 for another victim) that the French officers were deliberately misled (so who else did they mislead in court). 'X' answered that they were trying to play down any risk to public order and 'knew there was no truth in it' although the lawyers in this court now proved that there was.

The word 'deniability' crops up several times during MI6 cross-examination with reference to the shredding of files and the excuses used for explaining their destruction. During these inquests MI6 used a description that well illustrates their thinking; 'ephemeral is deletable and deletable is deniable' – an excellent way of describing their tenebrous world. They do whatever they please and use an act of Parliament to give them greater protection; they keep records, unless they don't wish to, and then only from a time when they cannot serve any purpose in assisting those who might later seek justice. In all, they had ten years to destroy evidence or 'assist' crucial witness's memories – is it any wonder the lawyers needed to fight hard to irrevocably show MI6 involvement?

'X' was asked how Sir Richard Dearlove could have been wrong about interviewing Witness 'A' over the assassination proposal and again she slipped, 'he must have been thinking of the damage assessments conducted following Richard Tomlinson's *revelations'*. (My italics.) But the court had tried to claim that Tomlinson's comments were not revelations but fantasy. We see yet another slip in MI6 evidence where they now accept that Tomlinson's evidence did produce revelations, not fantasy, as the police lawyer had tried to maintain throughout these inquests. Dearlove wouldn't be concerned with fantasy.

An attempt was made to try and dismiss Richard Tomlinson's evidence because it was almost impossible for MI6 to defend their position against it. But consider this: Witness 'X' didn't dispute that Tomlinson was telling the truth but only tried to offer excuses for his revelations so why did the judge suggest that Tomlinson was telling lies because he was disgruntled with his former employers. Why didn't the coroner correct this 'oversight' and inform the jury of this truth?

So it follows that we may now accept all Tomlinson's evidence including that of the planned attack on President Milosevic of Serbia, strobe lights, Henri Paul as an MI6 asset, that MI6 do kill people using a team called 'The Increment' consisting of SAS troops. Also that Diana was murdered by this team since that is also Tomlinson's opinion. Perhaps 'X' is no longer senior management, or even employed.

Witness 'F' was then brought in to add weight to the claim that the name on the proposal wasn't Milosevic. Her 'evidence' was only submitted in writing, so no examination was possible but it was a clear attempt at damage limitation. No doubt her evidence was hurriedly re-written and resubmitted after proof was forthcoming earlier in court that this proposal was written on white A5 paper, which she now affirmed had a tag attached. This had already been established so nothing was lost there, but isn't it remarkable how a person in MI6 of much lower rank apparently knew the truth immediately whereas the entire senior contingent denied it until the truth was 'dug out of them'? But this also puts the testimony of Witness 'A' to the sword since he had said this file was 'White treat as Pink'.

Witness 'F' reiterated that the name on the proposal wasn't Slobodan Milosevic in an attempt to support other MI6 testimony and therefore minimise the damage that this revelation could cause, especially knowing Milosevic did in fact die while in custody. She disingenuously continued to claim how much furore the proposal had caused when presented in her MI6 section but didn't explain the contradiction of why it was therefore sent to the policy-making tenth floor in the first place, or the comment from Witness 'H' that it was retained because 'they might need to go back to it'.

What we are looking for here, apart from new revelations, is contradictions in testimony and we were not to be disappointed. Next up was 'A's' boss, Witness 'H'. He confirmed that he was 'A's' line manager during the early 1990s and initially said that 'A' had sent him this proposal before it went elsewhere but now believed he must have been incorrect in believing that he hadn't seen it (altogether now; he had forgotten).

'H' was then asked whether he was ordered by 'E' to destroy the proposal. 'H' answered that he 'thought so' but then claimed not to remember anything from the barrage of questions that followed. One point was why had 'E' encouraged 'A' to write the proposal down, especially since such ideas are never countenanced by MI6; why was it also addressed to 'E for action' and why had 'E' given guidance to 'A' on the proposal? On all these points, 'H's' recollection was hazy.

'H' then described the whole affair as 'an extremely minor matter', which again is surprising given that 'F' had said it had caused such a furore. When asked why 'A' kept a copy of his proposal, apparently having been told to destroy it, 'H' said 'we might have gone back to it'.

But how could MI6 re-visit an illegal idea that had 'been strangled at birth', especially if it was considered so abhorrent? Why would 'H' expect people to keep a document if it had really caused such a furore and it had been 'strangled at birth'? Also, why would he keep it if MI6 don't murder people?

'H' slipped again by saying that he was told to remove the proposal from the archive. Only formal correspondence is put into the archive, thus here he involuntarily affirmed that this proposal was official while simultaneously trying to claim it was an 'ephemeral document'. 'H' was then asked whether he would have told 'A' to destroy the proposal, had he known he was keeping a copy and he replied that he was 'too busy'. Clearly, these people treat human life with perfunctory disdain.

Witness 'E' then entered into the fray. He confirmed that he was controller within MI6 of the Central and Eastern European Controllerate when Richard Tomlinson was a serving agent and admitted seeing the assassination proposal. At first, in common with much MI6 testimony, he denied having seen it, but then had to concede when more evidence prevented his continued denial. Surprise, surprise; he confirmed *his memory must have failed him* (my italics), despite the proposal being entitled 'The Need to Assassinate President Milosevic of Serbia', and it was proven that he discussed it for two whole minutes with 'A'.

It is difficult to escape the logic that this was no unusual proposal but daily routine for MI6 officers of a certain station and rank – either that or he was committing perjury for some nefarious purpose. Challenged over this point, 'E' said that he 'couldn't give an answer to that'.

The evidence suggested that 'E' gave the order to shred this proposal and this should have been recorded; it wasn't. 'E' then admitted that MI6 have a document called 'The Order Book', which describes intended targets and MI6 capabilities for engaging in violent actions abroad, including the use of SAS and SBS troops 'in addition to other methods'.

Lawyers pursued him on whether it was the duty of MI6 officers to seek solutions to threats against the UK and could a tactic have been considered to frighten and not kill? 'E' agreed, saying he would need to see the proposal but 'the devil is in the detail'. This despite adding that he 'didn't want to give anybody in the room the idea that they could have a licence to kill' (it's a bit late for that). But 'E' also admitted that he would not dismiss this proposal out of hand. From this it is no big leap to suggest that MI6 were more than capable of murdering a major public figure if, under certain circumstances, they considered it their duty.

Witness 'I' then took the stand; he made a brief appearance and again demonstrated a dreadful memory. He had no recollection of seeing 'A's' assassination proposal or even having heard of it, though it's known to have travelled to the tenth policy floor, where he was a very senior officer. Were there so many assassination proposals he couldn't keep track? 'I' restated the official position that 'A's' proposal was 'stifled at birth' – interesting, given that he claimed not to be aware of it; so, how did he know?

Remarkably, he then added that he had never heard of an 'ephemeral' folder, despite many agents of lower rank having already described this as normal MI6 procedure. He clearly didn't intend saying much, nor was he required by the court to do so. I believe this man could be Richard Spearman who, according to Richard Tomlinson, was in Paris when Diana was attacked and whose responsibility was to act as liaison for MI6 with their SAS 'Increment' team.

Other officers of lesser rank in MI6 were then trooped in to add support to what the more senior ones were saying. From this point on witnesses were described by numerals rather than letters to give their 'evidence' for the Paris-based MI6 station. The first was Witness '1', who didn't attend court but whose statement was read out. This 'lady' was in Paris on the weekend that Diana was murdered and said she was at a restaurant on the Friday evening and, because her diary is blank, she was probably at home with her husband on the Saturday evening; note only 'probably'. Surely it's somewhat surprising that she wasn't more certain of her whereabouts that night when one of the most newsworthy events in recent history had taken place within metres of where she was residing and she worked in an organisation that was to quickly come under enormous scrutiny from the world's media? I shall never forget where I was.

Witness '5' added that he too was in Paris but *couldn't remember* where he had been during the day; he had probably gone shopping with his wife. Later, he went to a restaurant called Thoumieux in rue St Dominique and left around 10.00pm. He then said that he believed he was the only officer at the Paris station that weekend, which was in complete contradiction to other evidence from his colleagues. He had only once made covert use of the Ritz Hotel when he didn't make himself known to any of the staff, thereby providing a further admission of using the Ritz in support of Tomlinson's testimony and against some of his colleagues' denials.

Witness '4' was head of the Paris station in August 1997 and confirmed that Witnesses '1' and '5' were both in Paris that weekend, as was Witness '6' (a central policy-making member of MI6), together with duty officers, duty personnel and duty support staff. By any standards, this is rather a large group of people (and directly contradicted Witness '5's' statement).

Witness '4' said he wasn't in Paris that weekend so was unable to comment on why MI6 staff all originally denied being present to the French police. He also confirmed MI6 have an interest in the Paris Ritz Hotel and, when it was put to him that a logical way for MI6 to obtain information from hotels is to have the head of security working for them, he answered, 'I think that might lead me into an area where I would find it difficult to answer.' Note, he wasn't required to elucidate.

Next up was Witness '6'. He was also at dinner with his wife that night, at Le Bistro d'a Cote, and was able to provide credit card evidence that he had amazingly retained after nearly eleven years. This man didn't want to discuss whether Henri Paul would be of interest to MI6 either, using the same excuse of operational reasons, but he was forced into admission because Witness 'X' had already conceded the point. He now said that the French DGSE (CIA/MI6 equivalent) could well have had an interest in Henri Paul and added that if MI6 had been working on a joint project with the French, then any relevant information would have been passed on to MI6.

Witness '6' confirmed that records kept at an overseas station would be duplicated in London on anything considered significant, which once more showed that MI6 have substantial discretion. If they chose to determine that their imminent action wasn't 'significant' then it seems there was no need to inform London. Witness '6' was then challenged as to whether anything not within the ethos of MI6 was simply omitted from the records. He could not deny this, merely saying, 'That is not my experience of it.'

Further evidence emerged that during the mid-nineties MI6 didn't have any controls in place and were undergoing a radical overhaul of their operating procedures, necessary because MI6 would soon become known to the public. This occurred in 1994 and not long before the Paris attack.

Witness '6' was asked why the French had been deceived by MI6 when an opinion on the evidence submitted by Tomlinson was requested. He replied that there was a fine line to tread between assisting the French and causing public concern, so tacitly admitted deceiving them. Following this, he was also asked whether he knew about James Andanson, which he denied, but was then forced to admit he had seen press cuttings about him.

The British Government Communications Headquarters (known as GCHQ) collects intelligence on behalf of MI6. Sir John Adye, who was at its head from 1989–96, was next to give evidence on their role. Adye was grilled over the interception of Diana's telephone calls during the 'Squigygate' affair that involved Diana and one of her male friends, James Gilby, together with the bugging that she had endured at Kensington Palace. Adye said he couldn't believe that the accusations of royal bugging by his organisation were true.

He then added that he was 'in due course able to satisfy himself that GCHQ were not responsible'. From this it's apparent that the then boss of this establishment at first thought they could be responsible; he needed to check and we need to believe this is true. Adye admitted he was not aware of any warrant for royal interceptions but it was then revealed that the Home Secretary had prevented any investigation by either the police or Security Services into who was responsible. This leads to the somewhat inescapable conclusion that it was one of these organisations.

It is clear from what we have seen in this chapter that there was a continuous flow of prevarication and side-stepping by MI6 and a huge number of discrepancies in the 'evidence' from their agents. For MI6, this was a very dangerous time: they displayed a nervous disposition in court and were clearly not enjoying their exposure.

They denied murdering people while at the same time admitting it, thus showing a justification for murdering Diana 'within their code'. They had also lied to the French Government and the British people and then required the police to support this corruption. In a previous court of law, they perverted the course of justice and, in my view, repeated the felony on several occasions in this particular court. They developed a strategy to avoid answering questions by using an absurdly complicated system of white and pink paper, which nonetheless permits us to suggest that MI6 officers were committing perjury in court; the only alternative reason is they were confused or had extremely bad memories. What reason did MI6 have for obfuscating their answers after ten years?

In addition, why did the court make the absurd comment that 'no longer can people say that there is an impenetrable steel wall' with regard to MI6? The only revelations made by MI6 were inadvertent and forced from them under duress through the lawyers' skills. They desperately tried to hide most of the important detail from the lawyers and nothing was volunteered except a flurry of untruths. The court also seemed content to disregard the apparent lies told by MI6 officers.

Following Diana's accusations regarding MI6 intrusions into her private life, years before her death, there had been much disquiet and many murmurings in government circles. The court was reminded of Lord Jenkins' speech in the House of Lords (the Upper Chamber at the Palace of Westminster) during the early nineties regarding the behaviour of the Security Services when he criticised MI6 behaviour. He had stated that if GCHQ were able to intercept calls freely then what was the point of having a warrant system?

Responses from other peers had followed, with Earl Ferrers adding that it wouldn't be appropriate to delve into how GCHQ operates, thus protecting the enclave of those who function above the law. Lord Annan asked whether a GCHQ officer could have intercepted calls in some rogue manner without the knowledge of their superiors, citing Peter Wright – a notorious British MI5 agent whom Dame Stella Rimington, an ex-boss of MI5, described as 'a man with an obsession, and was regarded by many as quite mad and certainly dangerous'. No conclusion was forthcoming.

After MI6 inquest 'testimony', Diana's lawyer demanded the records of any police investigation or activity concerning her surveillance at any time preceding the crash in Paris but it was declared there were none. He repeated there must be records of when the investigation into Diana's illegal tapping began, when it finished and who was involved. At this point it was reiterated that no information is available.

It is hard to avoid the conclusion that there was a major cover-up in MI6 of all operations relating to Diana's life or death, and from there the next logical step is to wonder why, if they had nothing to hide. Perhaps after all this disingenuous testimony, we can see why Scott Baker made his summation comment, with reference to some witness testimony, that 'people tell lies for different reasons'. Perhaps this thought should be extended to others that gave evidence and whose salaries are paid by the British taxpayer.

The British Police

We all know that the duty of police in democracies is to keep the peace and maintain the law on behalf of the people. It is only in totalitarian states where the prime role of the police is to secure a head of state or dictator's position regardless of any laws they might break, without any requirement to consider the people's will.

So, where do the British Police stand? As we will see, it's a forlorn hope they will ever question decisions of the Security Services that clearly hold sway. In addition, despite not being a democratically elected body, it seems that MI6 take major decisions without the British Government's knowledge, as propounded by the court. The only possible alternative is that the British Government were aware of MI6's intentions to murder Diana and were therefore party to this crime.

We have heard how Lord Justice Scott Baker considered that Diana might have been murdered by rogue MI6 officers aside from the MI6 hierarchy but let us first remind ourselves that so called rogue officers would still be serving agents and therefore still the government's responsibility.

So, if this is the case, where is British democracy? Are the people supposed to accept that an illegal offshoot of an already unelected body with a dubious record, putting it in the kindest terms, may take decisions on behalf of the people and even without the government being aware? If this is true, should it continue and is justice in this matter to go unrequited?

During this chapter we shall see 'evidence' from three of the then most senior police personnel in the UK – Lord Condon, Lord Stevens and Sir David Veness – who were responsible for sustaining the notion that Diana, Dodi and Henri Paul died in an accident. Through this we understand the pressures they faced and their perceived consequences of failure, should the truth ever emerge? (I must point out that all three men sustained their view throughout the inquests that Diana's death was due to an accident. I also add that I believe their views are seriously flawed but their actions helped to preserve the status quo and defend the monarchy. It is my intention to show you evidence of this.)

Having proven that MI6 committed perjury and were continuously equivocal at the inquests plus, as you will soon read, the police were 'getting their stories straight' ten years after the event, one can understand the strength of their purpose. As far as they were concerned, Diana's death was a fait accompli and whereas faults with the security system could, hopefully, be rectified, disclosure of the truth would cause a loss of confidence in the entire British system; including a possible demand for the removal of the monarchy. The way they saw it, therefore, was that this dreadful affair must be swept under the carpet.

I am required to point out that the 'investigation', quite properly in the circumstances, took place on French soil because the British police have no jurisdiction over there. I also point out, however, that I believe that this is one of the main reasons Diana was murdered outside British jurisdiction; to escape the people's fury and enable a more controlled response, especially if the attack didn't go to plan. The assassins also knew this would greatly assist in any cover-up, which it did.

Sir David Veness, the main police player in this debacle, was liaison with the Security Service and had also worked closely with the royal family since he was Scotland Yard Commander with responsibility for the royalty and Diplomatic Protection Group from 1987–90. From 1994, he was assistant commissioner for specialist operations with a broader responsibility encompassing security protection and counter-terrorism. He retired in January 2005 and, in the same month, was appointed under-secretary general for safety and security at the United Nations by the Secretary General of the United Nations, Kofi Annan.

On 24th June 2008, only weeks after the inquests' April conclusion, Veness resigned from the UN after his department was heavily criticised by an internal investigation. This coincided with the publication of an inquiry into their security systems, where it was found that the bombing of the UN office in Algiers on 11th December 2007 came after numerous internal UN warnings of an impending attack. During the attack Veness was preoccupied at the Royal Courts of Justice, London, although he would not give evidence there until 15 January 2008.

An interesting aside is that Sir David Veness was a board member of the International Centre for Political Violence and Terrorism Research, a think tank set up by Rohan Gunaratna. One of Veness's colleagues on this board was Sir Richard Dearlove, formerly 'C' of MI6.

Lord Condon was Metropolitan Police Commissioner from 1993–2000, the top job in the British Police, which he held during the time of the Paris attack. He had frequent meetings with the Home Secretary and Prime Minister, so was well placed to receive political diktats from the British Government. As Commissioner at the time of Diana's murder, Lord Condon carries a heavy burden. He owned ultimate responsibility for the entire 'investigation' on behalf of the people: whatever deception or criminal activity might have been suggested by the Security Services during this period was his to sanction or condemn.

Lord Stevens, who was Condon's deputy for eighteen months before he inherited the mantle, maintained the same position as Condon and Veness during his entire term of office from 2000. He headed the 'Paget Inquiry' from 2004, ostensibly set up to look into the Paris incident and continued in this role after retiring from the police in 2005. Remember, it was as a retired ex-police officer that he interviewed Prince Charles about Diana's letter to Lord Mishcon where she stated her belief that Charles intended having her murdered in an ostensible car accident.

In this section we focus on the main issues for which the police were primarily criticised. First of all, why didn't they investigate

Diana's claims that she was being bugged by the Security Services for many years before Paris? Second, after she had described the manner of her husband's intentions to murder her in a car 'accident' in writing and given this to her lawyer, Lord Mishcon, why was the 'Mishcon note' not handed to the English and French authorities after the Paris incident despite the police accepting there was a 'legal duty to disclose' and that 'they cannot rule out murder'?

Thirdly, witnesses at the Alma tunnel described 'escaping', 'loitering', 'aggressive', 'hindering' and 'blocking' vehicles that all left well before the paparazzi arrived – why was such information considered irrelevant by police? (Veness, who was in charge of the British 'investigation' in France, refused to accept there was any relevance to this evidence despite Scott Baker later admitting in court that there 'was some evidence of a staged attack'. It was clearly obvious to Scott Baker that evidence of an attack was quite strong.)

Also, how could the police blame Henri Paul for this incident since it has been proven that the results of his blood alcohol levels were not yet available to them when they proclaimed to the world that he was inebriated? Lord Stevens' confirmation to Henri Paul's parents that their son hadn't drunk too much is also considered.

Lawyers at the inquests ran through numerous incidents where the police had reason to investigate Diana's concerns over the abuse of her privacy, many years before Paris. What these suggest is that the police, even at the highest level, failed to support a member of the royal family when threatened because MI6 had a surveillance strategy in place.

Veness was asked why this illicit activity wasn't investigated but, although accepting that it took place, he was unable to remember why he had ignored this intrusion into Diana's private life. One of the most notable incidents was the so-called 'Squidgy Tapes', in which a telephone call between Diana and her friend James Gilby was intercepted and recorded from a landline at Sandringham House, one of the monarch's homes, on New Year's Eve, 1989.

Veness conceded that this conversation was deliberately put out on air. The lawyer asked him: 'Somebody had monitored this call originally, recorded it, and then transmitted that recording on more than one occasion so that radio hams could pick it up. Were you aware of that?' Veness responded, 'I was aware.' Questioned further, he went on to say, 'I cannot recall what action, if any, was taken.'

That leaves us to wonder why the police wouldn't take any action. Certainly it seems either the Security Service or police had established a stratagem to paint Diana as a salacious woman and destroy her standing with the public, thereby diverting attention away from the real problem: Prince Charles's affair with Camilla Parker Bowles.

Telephone bugging requires a professional unit to enter a house furtively and only the Security Services, police or professional criminals would have the capability to carry out such an act. The police didn't dispute that an interception took place but denied responsibility, which leaves MI6 or criminals but of course it cannot be MI6 as no documentation is available.

As the lawyer stated, 'If it isn't the police doing it and if it isn't the Security Service then it's somebody else, isn't it?' But can we really believe that criminals managed to break into one of the Queen's residences and that the police didn't bother to investigate it? Or is it simply the case that the police were again lying, presumably to cover-up MI6's involvement (as they would have no reason to protect criminals, would they? – or we really do have a problem!).

Condon was asked to enquire of the Paget team (Lord Steven's inquiry into the Paris deaths) whether there was any documentation on this and return to court to clarify matters. Perhaps unsurprisingly, clarification didn't materialise. You will also recall the problem with MI6 documentation concerning Diana – none was available there either.

Yet it is worth reminding ourselves here that we are referring to an intrusion into a private home of the Head of State, in which illegal tape recordings are made of private conversations. Imagine someone is discovered to be intercepting calls from the private quarters of the President of the United States at the White House and that neither the heads of the CIA, FBI nor the Homeland Security do anything and don't even bother to keep a record. It is totally unbelievable.

Lawyers pursued the question of what documentation should exist if the police had taken the complaint seriously but an answer was avoided and instead the same response was merely repeated: there is no documentation. Condon was then asked if there wasn't an investigation then why not? 'Because it was presumably deemed not necessary at the time,' was his sardonic reply. He claimed to be unsure, but what legitimate reason could the police have for 'deeming it unnecessary' to do their job?

For his part, Sir David Veness remembered the general incident but couldn't recall what he did about it – and this was while Deputy Assistant Commissioner Specialist Operations and Diana was still a member of the royal family. Even when the full tape became public knowledge in August 1992 and he should have been forced into acting, he admitted, 'I cannot recall any precise action.' When asked, 'Did you realise that in fact the Security Service were monitoring her calls and that is why nobody bothered [to investigate]?' he replied, 'No, *I don't think* [my italics] that is the case.'

How disingenuous since he had privileged knowledge of Security Services activity. This is akin to ex-MI6 chief Dearlove saying he didn't think that the Security Service had anything to do with Diana's murder despite being their operations director at the time – and in Paris.

Asked again if a sweep was done of Diana's rooms and vehicle to see whether her fears were well founded, Veness once more said, 'I am not aware.' Surely by any reasonable standards this police response is totally unacceptable and from the evidence here it's clear that Diana was targeted years before she was murdered because she refused to go quietly, as she stated on television. Veness was challenged as to how he would behave if told of a similar plot against the Queen; he agreed that he would act differently but without clarifying why he behaved the way he did towards Diana.

Lord Condon said Sir David Veness had assured him that the police weren't responsible for bugging Diana but it doesn't instil much confidence that Condon needed to ask his MI6 liaison officer (who happened to be responsible for leading the French 'investigation') whether there was any truth in these accusations. Perhaps, more significantly, no reassurance was given that it wasn't MI6 who were bugging Diana, which is what she believed and most accept.

Condon was also asked why there wasn't an investigation and

the excuse given was that Diana was uncooperative with the police. However, the lawyer showed that Diana had a meeting in October 1994 with David Meynell, a deputy assistant commissioner serving in Royalty Protection, during which he had offered Diana a debugging service, according to his report. That alone suggests he must have thought there was a possibility she might be right. Meynell added that she was bright and cheerful so there was no indication that Diana refused to be cooperative, as Condon had claimed.

Veness also confirmed that Meynell 'was of the view that it was being suggested that the official sources had conducted the bugging', but when asked whether he had bothered to check with the Security Services to ascertain whether this was true, Veness says, 'I am not aware that we did, no.' Once again, what possible reason could the police have for not even asking this question of MI6 other than they already knew the answer?

Why there was no police investigation into this illegal intrusion was again put to Condon. He reiterated that after David Meynell had met with Diana in October 1994 concerning these fears, he – Condon – had briefed the Home Secretary about it on 21st October 1994. Diana believed that her rooms had been bugged by MI6 and said, 'Even when no one knows where I am going in my car, there are people waiting for me at the other end.' She knew her telephones were being tapped and was certain the same applied to her vehicle.

Diana said she had many enemies but also lots of friends, some in high-up places who were privy to confidential information and had been told 'without any doubt, that five people from an organisation had been assigned full time' to 'oversee' her activities, including listening to her private telephone conversations. From the same source she had also heard 'that two people from the same organisation performed a similar function in respect of Parliament'.

Diana's friends had informed her that these people were tasked with keeping an eye on where she was going, and who she was meeting. Condon conceded she wasn't referring to the police; the ex-Chief of Police agreed that Diana believed either MI5 or MI6 were bugging her on his watch, with one of his very senior officers concurring, yet he did nothing.

Diana added that she 'couldn't help further without disclosing the identities of her friends'. This she was not prepared to do 'because they could lose their jobs' (or worse). Was this the 'uncooperativeness' to which Condon referred? If so, one cannot blame her for refusing to reveal her sources and it remains unacceptable that there was no investigation done and no record kept of any complaint.

The police always resolutely denied having any interest in Diana's activities because they would have a serious problem in justifying such an interest, especially after the Paris incident, but the cracks were starting to appear. David Davies was a police chief superintendent with about thirty years' service in 1997 who worked with the Royalty Protection group as OCU Commander (Operational Command Unit). He submitted to court that in 1997 he had 'become aware through another protection group officer that Diana intended taking up Al Fayed's offer of a holiday in the South of France and was taking the two princes.

> *Having validated that intelligence* [my italics], I informed DAC (Deputy Assistant Commissioner) Fry, who was then acting assistant commissioner, who informed the Commissioner Lord Condon. I went to see the head of the Scotland Yard Organised Crime Group, who gave me a briefing as to the nature of the Inquiry in respect of Mr Al Fayed for allegations I believe appertaining to the Tiny Rowland affair [Al Fayed's adversary when bidding for Harrods]. Following that, I was directed by the Commissioner [Condon] to inform Her Majesty the Queen via her private secretary, Sir Robert Fellowes [Diana's brother-in-law], who I remember telephoning the next day. I was informed by him that her Majesty was aware. I repeated the advice as I was not sure that he had fully understood me but his reply was the same. *I should clarify that the collective wisdom of the Commissioner and myself of the advice that should be given to the Queen, that it was unwise for the intended holiday to take place at all* [my italics].

Condon denies that these comments on Intelligence relating to Diana were made to him but Davies telephoned Sir Robert Fellowes and informed him that Diana was going to St Tropez with Al Fayed and said that Condon knew of this call.

Davies says in other recorded evidence, 'It was decided, having spoken to you [Condon], that I would contact Sir Robert Fellowes. I telephoned him at Balmoral early in the morning.' He further says, 'I explained what I knew of the trip to St Tropez. I asked if he and Her Majesty knew that the Princess of Wales and her two boys would be in Mr Fayed's transport, including being in his helicopter at the same time as well as staying in his accommodation. I am sure that I mentioned the fact that Mr Fayed is under investigation.' Fellowes replied, 'I am sure Her Majesty is aware, thank you, Mr Davies.'

Now this thought follows: why did Condon try and disown this evidence and, since it was proven that the Queen knew of Diana's intentions before being told by the police then who else, other than MI6, could have informed her? Of course we also know Veness worked closely with MI6, so perhaps it's obvious who informed the Queen?

Lord Condon doesn't remember this advice or of being aware that Diana was going on holiday to St Tropez despite Davies talking of 'collective wisdom' that can only refer to the police hierarchy of which Condon was at the head. Condon meekly claimed Davies must be wrong and denied being party to any action to try and prevent Diana travelling to France, or of having her movements watched while there but here is substantive evidence that the police and MI6 were keen to observe Diana's relationship with Dodi during that summer, despite their denials.

To accept that Davies is wrong you would need to believe that this report, from an officer of some thirty years' untarnished service, is fabricated. This is the same response received by Richard Tomlinson, the ex-MI6 officer who also displayed too much integrity to be acceptable to MI6. An interesting insight is that Mr Wharfe, Princess Diana's police protection officer, gave evidence that Diana said the Queen had ordered the Security Services to investigate her phone tapping. This confirms that not only did the Queen know about the intrusion but that she also wields the power to seek MI6 intervention.

Add to this that Prince Philip, the Queen's husband, chaired a committee called 'The Way Ahead Group', where it is known that MI6 give prepared talks and one sees the influence that the royals have on life in Britain. This is not supposed to be the role of a monarch or their family in British 'democracy'. The monarch is stationed as a mere figurehead and should not be taking executive decisions yet it is beyond doubt that the royals have direct access to MI6 for discussion on issues that cause them concern.

Veness was asked why he needed to inform the Chief of Police about Diana holidaying with Al Fayed, thus revealing that several senior officers were taking a serious interest in this vacation. He tried to sidestep this but had to admit, 'That would appear to be the position, yes.'

This acceptance shows that both the police and Security Services were keeping an eye on Diana and also on the Al Fayed family, who would enable her to become an enormous threat to the royals if a lasting relationship developed with Dodi. So the police saying that they had no interest in Diana, during the period prior to her murder, were now shown to be a fabrication.

(Isn't it strange that Veness showed little or no interest in Diana when in 1992 it was his duty to guard her as a member of the royal family, but now he was extremely interested in early 1997 when she was no longer part of them and therefore not his responsibility?)

When asked for records of police meetings on the French Inquiry, Veness merely replied, 'I am not aware of any such...' He was again asked whether any records of actions taken could be produced and he replied, 'I assume so, yes.' Yet predictably, of course, there are no records and this despite Veness admitting that records were routinely kept by Scotland Yard. The lawyer confirmed that following requests for these documents from Scotland Yard, none have been forthcoming.

David Veness had been put in charge of reporting the detail surrounding Diana's death from the repatriation of Diana and Dodi's bodies to the apparent British 'investigation' and liaison with the French police. He held a meeting at Buckingham Gate, on the morning of the Paris incident at the Royalty Protection Group's main office, near to Buckingham Palace. He said it was to ensure all matters ran smoothly for the successful repatriation of Diana and Dodi's bodies and *'the post-mortem requirements needed* [my italics] when they returned', plus other matters.

Veness informed the court that arrangements were being made to conduct a post mortem on Diana and Dodi in the UK and forensic issues should also be dealt with, adding: 'There should be appropriate arrangements made at the post mortem in order that *all appropriate samples and forensic exhibits should be properly collated and recorded.'* (My italics.) Veness was then challenged as to why he appointed Acting Chief Detective Superintendent Jeffrey Rees to act as liaison for the British Police from 31st August 1997, despite Rees previously being involved in an obscure investigation into Mohamed Al Fayed. Rees wasn't on duty at the time – Veness was forced to send a helicopter to collect him from his holiday home – and considering the nature of the new appointment, this was extremely insensitive, unless there was a compelling reason.

Rees had been involved in an Al Fayed investigation that collapsed within weeks without Al Fayed being charged. Veness somewhat disingenuously conceded that he erred in appointing Rees after being criticised by Lord Scott Baker but I believe that Rees's appointment is reminiscent of the French President establishing control over the Paris incident by choosing Judge Stephan instead of the Duty Judge, Devidal – someone he knew he could rely on.

Veness said that the reason for appointing Rees was because he was a very able officer and in order to conduct the post mortems, there was *'the need for a very experienced officer to marshal the various exhibits, to arrange for the attendance of the key technical specialists, including exhibit officers, to ensure that the optimum forensic samples are recovered subject to the directions of the pathologist'* and that *'we needed to initiate what potentially would be very significant post mortems with the assistance of the best officer I could find available in the notice to hand.'* (My italics.)

Again, this equates with a previous disclosure when John Macnamara, Al Fayed's security chief, was informed during questioning that it was *obvious* (my italics) there would be the need for post mortems in England under English law. So, if the authorities knew there would be the need for post mortems and how important they were, and the main player for the police was controlling this process, why did they embalm Diana in France for the sake of a matter of hours?

What reason other than to mask a pregnancy and/or the presence of noxious substances? Since there was an immediate outcry of foul play from France then no police officer would risk sinister allegations concerning their actions without good reason.

An interesting thought occurs. After embalming, these 'significant post mortems' were now impossible since forensic samples had been destroyed so there was nothing remaining to properly 'collate and record'. Veness didn't need Rees's services merely to collate information: it is my contention that he needed him, knowing that he could rely on him to keep all facts gleaned from Paris for his attention only and so the reason he gave for appointing him was, in my view, shown to be completely bogus.

The British police frantically tried to pretend they were only responsible for liaison with the French because if their role was proven to be investigative and in support of the coroners, by whatever means, then they were guilty of illegally withholding crucial evidence – which would raise some dangerous questions. Veness clearly chose specific people who were prepared to comply with his orders. Remember, Rees was the main contact for Veness with the British police in France and responsible for all emergent detail.

Veness agreed that Jeffrey Rees's terms of reference were: 'to liaise closely with the French authorities, providing them with all assistance and also to facilitate any enquiries they might wish carried out in the UK'. Remember, Rees was kept ignorant of the Mishcon note (Diana's note to her lawyer in which she stated that her husband intended killing her in a fake car accident; more later) and so was unable to assess this evidence while dealing with the coroners. So one wonders why Veness appears not to have trusted Rees with this truth.

Veness was involved in what was known as 'Operation Paris' before it became 'Operation Paget'. This group met for the first time on 1st September, the day after the Paris incident. Jeffrey Rees explained: 'On Sunday, 31 August 1997, whilst I was acting OCG commander, I was directed by Assistant Commissioner Specialist Operations

[Veness] to act as senior investigating officer in respect of the British *investigations* (my italics) into the deaths.' In addition, it is determined that Rees's role was to assist the French and also the coroner, as he further explained: '[the] *OCG role* [was] *to be that of gathering evidence and facts on behalf of the coroners.* [My italics]' (Further evidence that there was no justification for Diana's embalming and that this act was clearly surreptitious. Also note Rees' acceptance that he considered he had been instructed to investigate and not liaise. This is further evidence that police excuses to justify retention of the Mishcon note were false).

Yet despite being required to consider all possibilities and pass any potentially relevant information onto the coroner, we know that Condon and Veness still retained the Mishcon note. So much for the police denying they were involved in an investigation. I find it hard to understand what reason there could be for such behaviour other than, perhaps, they were trying to ensure that incriminating evidence remained hidden; one wonders what else could be hidden.

Veness chaired another meeting six years later in August 2003, saying that, 'The purpose of this meeting was a stock-take to ensure that everything that should be done was being done and in particular that the allegations that had been conveyed by Mr Mohamed Al Fayed's solicitors were in the hands of the French authorities and that they had the opportunity to consider their own actions on the basis of those allegations.'

This is, of course, still minus the Mishcon note and Tomlinson's disclosure that MI6 lied to the French authorities regarding the assassination plot for Milosevic. The lawyer then asked why Mohamed Al Fayed's fears were investigated and not Diana's. Veness didn't know but, if Diana's fears had been considered, there was no excuse for keeping the Mishcon note hidden since this was the mainstay of her position. He added that they were keeping the note secluded until the police considered it 'relevant to disclose' but he didn't accept that any damage was done to the 'investigation'.

Furthermore, Veness didn't even accept that James Andanson, owner of a white Fiat Uno, was relevant and claimed he didn't know who he was. 'That name means nothing to me,' he said. He waffled that he understood this 'in general terms' but, if so, then why didn't he investigate Andanson since by this tacit admission he clearly understood that Andanson was accused of being the driver of the Fiat Uno involved in an attack on Diana's car? Anyone seeking justice would need to investigate this possibility before rejecting it out of hand.

In my view, for Veness to state he didn't know of Andanson is beyond comprehension. One questions whether this shows a serious dereliction of duty, at the very least.

James Andanson's role in the crash was one of the main lines of inquiry that was supposed to have been considered by the French and was 'given' to them by Mr Nicholas Gargan, another senior British policeman who also works closely with the Security Services (later appointed Assistant Chief Constable of Leicestershire, England). Gargan was an attachment to the British Embassy in France, liaising with Rees and MI6 and so there was a considerable presence for the British authorities to determine how the 'investigation' was progressing under the control of the same few people.

Veness was challenged that he must have received regular updates on progress and would surely know all nuances of any discovery, such as the flashing lights in the tunnel, the 'loitering', 'blocking' and 'escaping' vehicles and the witnesses that gave evidence eminently suited to a murder scenario. But to everyone's amazement he didn't believe any of this was relevant. He clearly chose to ignore all emergent evidence from France and had no intention of releasing the Mishcon note unless compelled to do so.

(Of course it was necessary for the police to pretend Andanson wasn't relevant, or even on their radar, if they were to prevent him from being considered a suspect during the inquests since that would have raised the temperature with the jury and been impossible to circumvent. A bizarre situation during the inquests was that James Andanson's wife and son gave evidence, as did their close friends, the Dard family, but the court ruled that the consideration of James Andanson was 'not appropriate to these proceedings', despite his proclivities being examined at length.)

The lawyer continued to put Veness on the spot: 'I suggest to you that you really weren't kept very well informed, were you?' Veness ignored this and repeated that 'had there been significant suspicion, indeed suspicion of any ilk that indicated the French investigation was disclosing that this was anything other than a tragic vehicle accident then we would have reviewed this material again.' (My view is this more likely meant that if anything of substance emerged they would need to see how they could also neutralise that evidence.)

But he had just said that he didn't accept any of the details from France were relevant and had already ignored this evidence of an attack considered highly significant by many others. He added that, 'There was no suggestion at all of suspicious circumstances' – despite the fact that even the coroner, Scott Baker, made the comment, 'There is some evidence, albeit of dubious quality, that the crash was staged,' with reference to the same evidence that Veness had just said he ignored.

As linchpin between the police and MI6, Veness was never likely to denounce his colleagues' corruption by revealing the Mishcon note or any evidence that might incriminate them. The evidence suggests that the police only sought excuses for keeping the note hidden, knowing that the consequences of disclosure would mean that an inquest would be demanded. I, therefore, suggest that Veness's attempts to convince the court that the police behaved properly by illegally retaining the Mishcon note were shown to be inane.

Police excuses that they were not investigating are true: they treated Diana as they did in life, abusing her civil liberties for the benefit of the royal family. It is hard for me to escape the obvious conclusion that they already knew the truth, so needed only to go through the motions.

As the lawyer said, we must now consider the main point everyone was waiting for and that the police had to defend against: the contents of the Mishcon note itself and why the police kept it hidden. Everybody in court knew the significance of this note and that the police would have a torrid time in defending their position, which was clearly illegal. Scott Baker quipped that it didn't need Sherlock Holmes to determine that, but the lawyer retorted, with reference to Veness, 'Well, in this case, maybe it did.'

Lord Mishcon attended a meeting with police on 18th September

1997, a few weeks after the Paris attack, to present his note to them. Veness admitted that he considered it 'potentially relevant' at that time. Lord Mishcon, from the London firm of Mishcon de Reya, was Diana's lawyer and she gave him this note on 30th October 1995 at a meeting in Kensington Palace, which he attended with two of his partners: Maggie Rae and Sandra Davies. Patrick Jephson, Diana's private secretary, was also present. At this meeting, Diana made it abundantly clear her life was in danger from the royal family. Previously, she had said that if a box she was keeping secure went astray, it would be MI5 or MI6 – so we know she was nervous of these people and believed them to be a danger to her life.

Lord Mishcon wrote, 'Because of the serious statements made by HRH in the course of this meeting I decided, unusually, to write this entry and to give instructions it should be securely held.' (Lord Mishcon determined that he would hold the note secure and release it to the police should anything untoward happen to his client in the future.) Consider Lord Mishcon's word, 'unusually' – this emphasises his concern over the contents of the note and the strength of his sincerely held view.

The police continued to defend their curious decision to suppress this note that was only forced into the public eye, as indeed were the inquests, by Diana's butler, Paul Burrell, when he disclosed a note of similar nuance to the Mishcon note. Diana had passed this onto him as a failsafe, knowing the authorities would cover their tracks. Burrell released the note to the press on 20th October 2003 and the next day Lord Mishcon telephoned the police. Clearly, he was concerned whether the note that he had given to the police on 18th September 1997 would ever see the light of day.

Following a meeting between Veness and his 'protection' team on the same day, 21st October 2003, the Mishcon note appeared in the press on 23rd October 2003. The inquests were then opened in January 2004 (so the British police were not dependent on the French 'investigation' finishing before becoming involved, as they always claimed and it's clear from the timing that they were forced into holding the inquests).

It's interesting that the police regarded this note as 'unnecessary to disclose' for six years and yet within weeks of its enforced release, the inquests are opened; even to the most ardent of 'accident theorists' the significance is apparent. This note would not have seen the light of day but for Burrell so, without Mishcon's note and Al Fayed's perseverance, a public inquest would never have transpired. Veness denied the lawyer's suggestion that the Mishcon note would never have been released but for the Burrell note and delivered a somewhat predictable response: *'I don't think that is the position.'* (My italics.)

The lawyer accused Veness, saying that he, 'quite improperly sat on information that should have been handed over because you were aware something improper had happened in Paris'. Veness in turn replied, 'I unequivocally reject that.' The police had been using the excuse that release of the note would have caused the royal family unprecedented pain and suffering and – remarkably – would have risked tarnishing Diana's reputation and added that they also needed Lord Mishcon's permission.

Considering the abuse Diana suffered from the royals, this does stretch one's patience. As for gaining Mishcon's permission, it was suggested that Veness only had to ask Lord Mishcon if it was acceptable to give the note to the French authorities and the coroner, and then ask them to keep it hidden. Lord Mishcon would undoubtedly have agreed and so another excuse for the note's retention bites the dust.

Veness was challenged that: 'You knew full well – is this possible – that the Security Service or agents of the British State, maverick or otherwise, had been involved and you didn't want this investigated.' Predictably, Veness rejected that suggestion but let us follow the logic since so many anomalies and contradictions exist from his 'evidence'.

Since Veness was not conducting this 'inquiry' then unless he was party to everything that arose daily, he could never properly determine the relevance of any evidence he might receive. Also, since so many flaws were shown in his knowledge, he could never make a proper assessment as to its relevance. So, how could he decide whether to keep certain evidence secluded or to disclose it? And this is even if he had been seeking justice. Veness slipped that he didn't *think* MI6 was involved in the Paris attack and then later emphatically denied it. But how could he be so adamant. Surely this indicates he believes they might have been. He admitted there was no investigation to determine the truth of this, but working closely with MI6 as he did, he would scarcely be permitted to continue in this role unless MI6 could rely on his full cooperation and silence.

It was suggested to Veness that the Mishcon note was telling him that back in 1995 (when Diana wrote the note) that 'agents of the state were considering whether to put her away' (murder her). He tried to pass this off, stressing only the French authorities were investigating but this note was written two years before the attack in Paris, when the French were not involved and illustrated a growing malevolent intent towards Diana even then.

The lawyer continued to berate Veness as to how he could know MI6 wasn't involved without investigating them, suggesting surely he would have investigated immediately if he didn't know MI6 was involved. Veness prevaricated that this had never been put to him and he hadn't seen any material to suggest they might have been involved. But why he needed someone to suggest the obvious is yet another mystery. (This was the principle reason for the inquests.)

Veness must have been the only person who didn't consider MI6 involvement and he wouldn't find anything if he wasn't looking. This was despite two notes from Diana via Mishcon and Burrell having entered the public domain, describing how state agents were intending to execute this very act. MI6 were in the dock and Veness represented the police as MI6 liaison and controlled all evidence emerging from France. I believe you should now consider whether the logic put forward for these decisions stands scrutiny and also decide why Veness was chosen to deal with this whole charade.

Michael Burgess became coroner to both Diana and Dodi when the coronial courts, responsible for Diana and Dodi, were conveniently coalesced and so when he learned that Paul Burrell had a note in his possession that could be germane to these inquests, he wrote to him in the following terms:

As I am sure you are aware, there is a common-law duty to

provide to the coroner all and any information relevant to a death which you may have in your possession or is within your knowledge, even without the coroner specifically seeking this from you. Ultimately it is up to me as the coroner to determine whether a document or matter is relevant to the inquests. The letter and/or other documents may need to be examined forensically.

It is interesting to note that the Chief of Police didn't appear to appreciate that this was both the legal and common sense position that he should have adopted regarding the Mishcon note. So the investigation was denied the opportunity of testing the note's substance or considering whether forensic examination was appropriate because the document was being illegally withheld. Not only was the British Police's excuse for the note's retention absurd, but revealing the note would mean the inquests would have been held much sooner, when memories would have been much brighter. As it was, withholding it meant any subsequent murder inquiry would be seriously compromised.

If the police had investigated the Mishcon note, they would have found there were several others who supported Diana's fears. These were not irrational people. For example, Lord Mishcon had spoken with Patrick Jephson, Diana's private secretary, who half-shared her views regarding the note's essence. So since the police knew of Jephson's opinion, why didn't they ask him what reason he had for believing something might be amiss? The lawyer asked Veness whether he checked on the note's veracity, saying, 'It doesn't need a threshold of suspicion beyond the document already held.' He added in the absence of a police investigation the only reason for lack of action was that there was another agenda.

Scott Baker then asked whether, 'it's of any relevance that the Burrell note was in the public domain whereas the Mishcon note wasn't', and, 'If you had had the Burrell note at the time of the meeting with regard to the Mishcon note on the 18th September (1997), is that likely to have made any difference to your approach?' Veness prevaricated that had they known of the Burrell note, it would have changed their minds with regard to the Mishcon note's release. However, as a police officer, he knew that the reason any evidence must be considered by interested parties as soon as it is available is because other parts of the jigsaw could then emerge – as would have happened here.

Veness refused to admit, when he learned of the Burrell note in October 2003, that he should have then conceded he was wrong by retaining Mishcon's note and he didn't seem to understand that he had just made a de facto admission of damaging an investigation through his, and Condon's, decision. The lawyer sardonically quipped that he found it strange that 'a police investigation depends on having the same information twice'.

When asked why he thought Lord Mishcon took the note to the police, Veness answered: 'For safe keeping.' This was immediately rejected by the lawyer, who added that jewellery might have been brought for safe keeping but the note was obviously handed over to ensure full consideration would be given to Diana's fears should a future need arise (remember the word Lord Mishcon used, 'unusually', when referring to his decision to take steps to record his client's concern).

And so Veness stumbled on with the notion that keeping this note secluded was a perfectly acceptable 'option', only disclosing it if he considered it necessary, and again the usual excuse was that it would cause serious upset to the princes and others in the royal family (as, presumably, did Diana's death). Veness then tried to suggest that Lord Mishcon agreed with police 'tactics' by not releasing the note.

It is fatuous to expect us to believe that Lord Mishcon was more concerned about the hurt to one family than to see justice done regarding the murder of his client. Mishcon may well have initially supported the police position because he would have had no reason to mistrust them and will not have known that they intended to keep the note permanently secluded when he handed it to them on 18th September 1997. It was following release of the Burrell note that will have forced him to demand his own note's release and, very likely, he had to insist that the police made it available to the public or he would do it for them.

The lawyer reminded Veness that it wasn't an option to disclose the note to the coroners and the French authorities but it was, in fact, a legal obligation. Condon also agreed that the Mishcon note was 'potentially relevant' but still withheld it with the pathetic reasoning that none of the other points mentioned in the note had come to fruition (such as the Queen abdicating, or Charles taking the throne). Again he proffered the usual excuses that it would cause great harm and distress to the royal family and that they had a duty to obtain Lord Mishcon's agreement before releasing it.

But this continuous and disturbing 'defence' by the police is deplorable: they are fully aware that the royals are bound by British law and here they are suggesting that they actively denied justice to a murder victim because of the hurt it would cause to that one particular family. This is especially nauseous when for years, that same family had abused the murder victim and was entirely responsible for her predicament. Had the police been more concerned for the people's feelings and done their duty, they would have realised that we are more interested in achieving justice for Diana, as indeed her sons, the Princes William and Harry, must also be.

It is irrelevant whether or not other events mentioned in the Mishcon note took place because the issue is that this particular 'accident' did occur. It was the withholding of the note after the attack in Paris that we criticise, not keeping it hidden beforehand. It's the reason why Diana took the note to Lord Mishcon in the first instance: as a safeguard should the beast descend so that justice could be done.

The lawyer then offered the following anecdote: 'If a member of the public or a police officer finds that there is a woman dead at the bottom of a cliff, then she may be dead for a number of reasons: it may be she dropped dead while running along the beach, may have been pushed off the cliff, may have committed suicide. If a police officer produces a note written by the woman two years earlier suggesting firmly that she feels she is going to be pushed over the cliff on one of her Sunday afternoon walks, would you just hang onto the note and do nothing about it?' Condon replied, 'It depends.' That perfunctory answer, surely, is enough for you to understand why I believe that he is complicit in the cover-up surrounding Diana's death.

Stevens, Veness and Condon were all keen to establish that Lord

Mishcon would still have been reluctant to permit the disclosure of Diana's note even when the Burrell note had been revealed, so Lord Stevens continued on this theme: 'He was a very, very honourable man and did not want to disclose things he had taken in confidence from her. He more or less agreed but he still had reservations about the confidentiality he had with his client.'

What abject nonsense! All possible excuses were mustered by the police in their defence so that having kept the note hidden, in order to thwart justice, they now try to pass the responsibility onto Lord Mishcon. (Lord Mishcon is, conveniently for the police, deceased. He died just before the inquest, on 28th January 2006 from a heart attack.) It's not disputed that Mishcon was entrusted with the safe keeping of Diana's note because she knew he would do as requested and ensure the authorities took action should the need arise, which it did.

Diana took the trouble to write this note and give it to Lord Mishcon to ensure her wishes would be carried out in these precise circumstances. Confidentiality might be relevant if Diana expressed concerns about her note's disclosure but she unambiguously asked Lord Mishcon to keep this note secluded but to reveal it, should anything happen to her; this was the reason she gave the note to him. So in fact the opposite is true: Lord Mishcon would have known, as we all know, that Diana would have wanted it made public.

Lord Mishcon's 'honourable' duty towards his client was clear: if anything happened and looked suspicious (and let's face it, it couldn't look more suspicious), then he was to ensure the note was disclosed and fulfil his obligation. To develop unexpectedly a concern for the hurt that could be caused to the royal family that would require Mishcon to disavow his client's wishes and fret over Diana's reputation, despite knowing of the accusations of paranoia levied against her by the royals, was an utter nonsense. The note's publication couldn't affect her, even when alive, and one is expected to believe there was now concern for her memory.

Another point is that, since the note's retention was against the law under a 'duty to disclose', then Lord Mishcon as a noted – and as Lord Stevens said, 'very, very honourable' lawyer' – would need to be persuaded by the police to break the law as well as dishonour a promise to his client; for what purported reason? The police propounded confidentiality in a perverse attempt to divert responsibility; the only concerns Lord Mishcon had were to fulfil his promise, produce the note intact and survive long enough to assist in procuring justice.

Veness was also confirmed by Lord Stevens to be the man with special reporting duties, whom the police ostensibly relied on to watch and identify any issues from France that might provoke a change of heart regarding the Mishcon note. You will recall that Veness didn't even think the flashing lights in the tunnel nor indeed the hindering, blocking, loitering and escaping vehicles that all departed before the paparazzi arrived were of any relevance. Nor did he believe James Andanson to be of any importance despite much evidence linking him to the Paris attack. But despite this pathetic reasoning, Stevens merely confirmed, 'Dave Veness has the overall responsibility of liaising so I *suppose* (my italics), at the end of the day, in the back of his mind he would have been reviewing it as to when it should be disclosed.'

Veness had sole charge over all decisions, yet note Stevens' use of the word 'suppose' that confirms he wasn't even sure whether Veness bothered to review any details. Stevens was again asked where the notes/records of reviews/meetings were with regard to the events in France. There weren't any, of course. He was then asked why not, and once more we have the answer that Veness alone conducted any necessary reviews and he had already confirmed there were no records of meetings or reviews. The police relied on their MI6 liaison to determine the need for any action, so how confident do you feel that Veness did anything other than ensure all pertinent detail remained hidden for the benefit of MI6 and the royal family?

A Commission Rogatoire (French fact-finding group) was also sent to seek information from England to assist the French in their investigation and, as the lawyer says, they were asking, 'Can you help us?' This group specifically sought evidence such as the Mishcon note but nothing was forthcoming.

The lawyer asked: 'Why it didn't seem prudent – if this was all a genuine position being adopted, why somebody didn't go and say, "Look, I hope it's all right, but we are not going to take action on this at the moment." That's perfectly proper, isn't it, for you to do?' It was logical that senior people such as the Home Secretary or the Lord Chancellor should be consulted. Veness repeated: 'Yes, but that consideration was not given.' One must ask; why wasn't it given?

Condon said that he briefed the Home Secretary on 21st October 1994 concerning the bugging of Sandringham House because he thought it necessary to keep him in the loop. But this doesn't explain his reason for not briefing him on the Mishcon note (presumably because withholding the note from the authorities was against the law, as he had already conceded). The reason for non-disclosure needed explaining to the Home Secretary so that he would be kept in the loop with Condon's actions.

Condon said that the police took this decision alone but in order to succeed, a deception of this magnitude would require political support, so isn't it far more likely that the Home Secretary was consulted concerning this subterfuge. However, politicians would, of course, also require 'deniability' so Condon could not admit to briefing him on the true position. All in all, police actions regarding the Mishcon note strongly support our view that the British Government played an active part in a cover-up.

Lawyers continued to question the police's denial that their presence in France was an inquiry/investigation but the police continued to stand firm that it was a liaison despite much evidence to the contrary. Yet it was shown that police actions amounted to that of an inquiry since other police officers, including Jeffrey Rees, had already confirmed it and the police had been spending time making video trips around Paris and seeking other information on behalf of the British coroner. (It is my view that the police role was to seek out any incriminating evidence and ensure that it remained secluded, in similar manner to when MI6 admitted deceiving the French authorities about Richard Tomlinson's revelations, saying it was a fine line to tread between lying to the French and risking panic or serious concern in Britain.)

Lord Stevens and his colleagues tried to distance the police from this because once it was proven that they were conducting investigations, withholding the note took on a new significance. If they were only liaising then the responsibility for action could be considered to rest with the French investigating authorities. But if the British police were found to be investigating then retention of any evidence becomes a criminal offence and cannot be justified.

The British police were also forced into the admission that they were acting on behalf of the coroner as 'coroner's officers', having initially tried to deny it, which means that since the Mishcon note was retained in the UK and not revealed to either the British coroner or the French authorities, they failed under their 'duty to disclose' obligation and so broke the law.

Stevens was then asked why they didn't give the note to the French and the British coroners, requesting them to use the knowledge of its existence but keep its contents confidential from the public, since that would have prevented any 'pain' being caused to the royals. Stevens replied: 'No one did it – it was not done at that stage.' The truth is that it wasn't done at any stage.

Veness had stated that the two main conditions for determining whether to release the Mishcon note were:

(1) There must first be some relevant suspicion concerning the deaths, and
(2) That authority must be sought from Lord Mishcon or his firm.

We shall not insult people's intelligence by further considering suspicion and as for asking Lord Mishcon's permission, this was answered by Stevens: 'No one did it – it was not done at that stage.' Surely this illustrates that Veness's purported reasons for inaction were again bogus. So, once more we ask, why didn't the police ask Lord Mishcon's permission? Or do you believe, as do I, that there was never any intention of asking Mishcon's permission because they never intended releasing the note or indeed holding an inquest.

Is it a remarkable coincidence that Lord Mishcon visited the police on 21st October when both Burrell's and Mishcon's notes then appeared in the press on 23rd October and the inquests opened in January 2004? So Mishcon clearly wasn't attempting to keep the notes secluded. More likely, he was furious that they hadn't been released sooner.

Lord Stevens was then asked to describe what happened after Burrell's note had been released. By now commissioner of police, he contacted Lord Condon and Lord Mishcon to decide what to do. Lord Stevens continued, 'Well, we had a meeting with our senior solicitors, took legal advice, obviously opened the note and I handed that note. I got Mr Veness up and handed that note to our solicitors' department for legal advice.'

When asked why he didn't take legal advice before the Burrell note was published, Stevens replied: 'Because I didn't think there was any need at that stage [In my view hoping there would be no need for an inquest].' But Veness had accepted in his evidence that the Mishcon note took on a new significance with the release of the Burrell note, saying: 'The contents of an article that reported the possession by Mr Paul Burrell of a note which appeared to be analogous in some form to the issues that were dealt with within – if I can describe it, the Mishcon note – that was worthy of consideration and review.'

Stevens also made much of taking legal advice on the Mishcon note just prior to its disclosure but the police obviously didn't need advice to determine whether they could release the note and comply with the law: they needed only to understand the consequences of continued retention. Stevens reiterated his chief concern regarding 'Lord Mishcon's permission that we had to get before doing it – those were the issues that were uppermost in my mind.' This despite the court having shown that permission was not sought at any time.

Towards the end of his 'evidence', Stevens repeated there was no need to disclose the note until an inquest was imminent (conveniently ignoring the point that there wouldn't have been a public inquest without the release of Mishcon note so there was a Catch-22 situation controlled by the police until the Burrell note came to light). The lawyers soon put this to rights but it follows that the publication of Paul Burrell's note was responsible for eliciting the appearance of the Mishcon note when both notes then triggered the inquests' commencement.

Stevens went on to say, 'I did not think it would need to be disclosed until the need came to disclose it' – arrogant confirmation to me that the police were controlling activities in France, though not, I believe, in the interests of justice. One might consider this to be further de facto proof that both the Mishcon and Burrell notes enforced the inquests' opening and that otherwise the police would have continued to prevaricate. Stevens then added, 'Providing Lord Mishcon's confidentiality issue, I have always said that there was a duty to disclose.' So here he admitted there was a duty to disclose, subject to the consideration just given. If, however, you accept our reasoning that the issue of 'confidentiality' after Diana's death is drivel, then this further supports my belief that the police were guilty of deliberately misleading the public and breaking the law.

Interestingly, Stevens travelled to Paris for a meeting with Henri Paul's parents in 2006, accompanied by Sergeant Easton and Detective Inspector Scotchbrook. Both Scotchbrook and Madame Paul took contemporaneous notes and Madame Paul sent hers to her lawyer. There is a most interesting discrepancy and an amazing admission.

Stevens is noted by Madame Paul as having said during this meeting that, 'If this were an assassination, the repercussions in England would be great and incalculable.' This explains all the police shenanigans and also shows the police believed it was, at the very least, possible that someone murdered the Princess of Wales – and this from the very top of the force. Stevens later denied saying this, of course, but the evidence doesn't support him.

It's pointed out that Madame Paul gave unchallenged testimony when questioned by the police lawyer so the court presumed it was accepted; Stevens now found it expedient to disagree when he realised the significance of this remark. He claimed the comment to be made by Sergeant Easton to Claude Garrec (Henri Paul's best friend), who he said was not present at the meeting with Madame Paul. But as the lawyer said, with reference to Madame Paul: 'It is rather odd for her to invent something which apparently you now say did occur on a different occasion, involving different people.'

At this point, Stevens became flustered and began talking of the Pauls in disparaging terms, calling them 'frail people' in an attempt to circumvent Madame Paul's revelation. The lawyer continued: 'How would she [Madame Paul] know what had passed between Sergeant Easton and Claude Garrec on a different occasion and then record it in a near-contemporaneous note of her meeting with you, Lord Stevens?' Stevens had no answer and told the lawyer that he would have to ask Sergeant Easton, whom he claimed made this comment.

Stevens was then asked when he last saw Sergeant Easton. He replied that it was four weeks ago and then said: 'I discussed it with him about five days ago to reinforce that we get this right, because obviously it is something that is not quite right and it conflicts with Madame Paul's evidence.'

The lawyer was not happy:

'Do you not think that, as a senior police officer, that in order to try and get things right, it would be better that the jury should hear your unvarnished evidence on oath, rather than what is the product of a discussion between you and other police officers in advance of giving your evidence on oath, Lord Stevens?'

Stevens nervously answered:

'I can only give the evidence and tell the jury what has taken place.'

The lawyer still wasn't happy:

'Why were you having discussions four days ago with Sergeant Easton with regard to your evidence?'

Now clearly in trouble, Stevens proffered this banal response:

'Because I said that I would expect him to come to court, if that is what you want to happen. That is a matter for the coroner.'

Like a dog with a bone, the lawyer continued:

'Is it usual, in your experience, Lord Stevens, for police officers to discuss in advance what evidence they are going to give on oath in court? What you actually said was that you had these discussions "to reinforce that we get this right". To get *what* right, Lord Stevens?'

By now an extremely flustered Stevens blurted out: 'There is no conspiracy here!'

'*You* mentioned conspiracy,' retorted the lawyer, but then comes Stevens' magical interjection: 'There is no record of my saying those things about great repercussions in England, if this were an assassination.'

So, we now know that Stevens had obviously checked whether there was any evidence that he made this remark. But if he knew he hadn't made it, why did he need to check?

We now move on to the fourth issue for which the police were forced to defend their actions at the inquests: the anomalies found in the reports of Henri Paul's blood-alcohol levels.

Unchallenged testimony from Detective Inspector Scotchbrook, who wrote a contemporaneous note of what the police told the Pauls at the Paris meeting, included the statement: 'Operation Paget would be saying that he [the late Henri Paul] had consumed two alcoholic drinks on the night of the incident', and no more.

This official Paget report is clearly different from that of the French toxicologists and Lord Stevens, but remember that the French told the world that this was a road traffic accident only hours after the crash and it was proven in court that they didn't have Henri Paul's blood results when they declared he had been drinking to excess and was drunk.

Even the British police pathologist, Professor Robert Forrest, proffered the opinion that there was no basis for the results given to the world's media in the early hours after the crash so one wonders why the French police lied. What pressure were they under and from whom? Professor Forrest also spent considerable time checking the results of Dr Pepin and Professor Lecompte, and the point was made that the British police paid quite substantial sums to Pepin for his cooperation, to hold meetings with Forrest and produce material.

Stevens objected to the word 'cooperation' but he had no answer when the lawyer reminded him that neither doctors Pepin nor Lecompte saw fit to attend court and give evidence. The British police reported that Paul's tests revealed three times the French legal limit and twice the British limit for drink driving, so for the official French figures to be accurate, he must have consumed a further four or six doubles (in other words, eight to twelve measures).

(The French authorities could have required their doctors to give evidence but didn't and the doctors certainly didn't volunteer. If one sees the evidence that the paparazzi were prevented from attending court through *political intervention*, it doesn't stretch one's imagination too far to see that all witnesses who could offer evidence that would be difficult to refute would also be kept away from court by the same process-much more later.)

Berating Veness, the lawyer said: 'It isn't very common to put the conclusion of an investigation out before you have done the investigating, is it?' At this, Veness had no choice but to agree, then fumbled his way towards another excuse: 'No, but I am not suggesting – rather I am – I would disagree with you that one leaps from that statement to the fact that the French investigation is to be written off as less than painstaking.'

The 'evidence' that the police gave out on Paul's alcoholic state when they had no idea what he had been drinking proves that they deceived and lied to the people. One might be forgiven for wondering why, especially at that particular juncture. Later in the book, we shall look closely at the detailed issues surrounding whether or not Henri Paul was drunk but for now, suffice to say the police's actions remained deeply suspicious immediately after the deaths and highly questionable during the entire 'investigation'.

Mohamed Al Fayed's People

John Macnamara

Mohamed Al Fayed's security chief, John Macnamara, headed up his employer's private investigation into Diana and Dodi's deaths. Macnamara left Scotland Yard as a senior and well-respected police officer with twenty-six years' service, having conducted many murder inquiries and so he was no layperson 'interfering' with the pursuit of justice. In 2004, he was asked to submit his findings to the belated Scotland Yard 'Paget' Inquiry, set up seven years after the murder.

On hearing of the Paris crash, Macnamara's first recollection was that he considered it to be a terrible accident and only when the political machinations commenced did he become suspicious and so begin his investigation. An investigation that ought to have been performed by the British and French police and, naturally, Macnamara didn't expect to experience obstruction from the French.

Throughout this sorry tale, those who had evidence to impart that imperilled a suitable verdict were either vilified or ignored. John Macnamara was in this category alongside Hunter, Pelât and Tomlinson. Even eyewitnesses, whose evidence did not suit the desired conclusion and whose testimony implied a murderous attack, were ignored or ridiculed. Levistre, Anderson, Benoît, Medjhadi and Souad are all examples of this, as we shall see.

As for Macnamara, he was the man who found the Fiat Uno,

together with its owner, James Andanson, when the French police and British Security Services were trying hard to deny its existence. This discovery was a key reason that the authorities' subsequent deception failed: but for John Macnamara, no one would have ever heard of James Andanson or the Fiat. In return, he experienced a brutal cross-examination with the court intimating that his testimony was fabricated, in common with all those who had proffered evidence supporting murder. Let us review his experience in court, starting with what he heard immediately after the crash.

Macnamara was telephoned early on the Sunday morning, soon after the Paris crash by Paul Handley-Greaves, who is also a former Scotland Yard policeman and in charge of Mohamed Al Fayed's personal protection team. After being informed that Dodi Fayed was dead and Princess Diana had been badly hurt in a car crash, Macnamara's first thought was of the need to repatriate Dodi's body and so he attended at Al Fayed's main offices in Harrods on the Sunday of the attack and within hours of receiving the news.

The repatriation proved to be more difficult than envisaged because the French authorities initially decided that they couldn't return Dodi's body to the UK due to the 'circumstances' surrounding his death. Precious hours went by while they discussed whether it was possible for the Islamic rites of completing the burial before sunset on the day of death to take place: this meant that Dodi needed to be buried before 10.00pm on the Sunday evening, 31st August.

Macnamara spoke with the Surrey Coroner Michael Burgess three or four times during Sunday with regard to Dodi's repatriation time constraints and Burgess telephoned him back, saying, 'almost apologetically', that there would be a delay because Scotland Yard had called to say the 'deaths were suspicious'. Burgess doubted whether it would be possible to bury Dodi by sunset. As one might expect, having been a senior Scotland Yard officer, Macnamara then asked: 'Was other detail given?' to which Burgess replied: 'No, there was not.'

Macnamara realised that this call to Burgess, purportedly from Scotland Yard, could have been a crank call and later said so in court. But Burgess later denied saying he had been telephoned by Scotland Yard or *that he had called Macnamara.* So Macnamara now knew there was something amiss. Macnamara said: 'He knows he made the call to me – he knows it happened.'

Macnamara then telephoned Frank Klein, President of the Ritz Hotel, and asked whether he had heard anything in Paris. Klein then saw the forensic pathologist, Dominique Lecompte, who in turn spoke with Patrick Riou, Director of Judicial Police, and the Minister of the Interior, Jean-Pierre Chevènement. It was decided Dodi's body couldn't leave, so it is possible the repatriation was delayed by about an hour because of this phone call.

Macnamara then telephoned the Gold Command Centre at Scotland Yard (created to deal with motorcycle escorts and general support in this case) and asked the man in charge whom he knew personally – Commander Messenger – whether he had made the call to Burgess. Messenger denied it.

Harrods' lawyers subsequently approached Scotland Yard to ask whether they could meet with Commander Messenger, but Miss Laura Hyams from the Directorate of Legal Services for the Metropolitan Police wrote back, refusing permission for him to be interviewed. The police solicitor later confirmed during a telephone conversation with Macnamara that, 'In any event, he will deny the conversation.'

Macnamara later added: 'I still believed this could have been a crank call and unfortunately, it resulted in a delay in the body – in fact, we never buried Dodi until 10.30 o'clock at night. But it was only afterwards when these phone calls were denied that it made me wonder what is behind it.' Why would both of these men deny making a call that they obviously did make? The lawyer at the investigation simply said, 'Well, I will move on from that.'

The court questioned whether Burgess and Messenger would both deny having a conversation with Macnamara concerning suspicious deaths. But this of course depends on what pressure was applied to both these public servants. Also, would Macnamara cause a delay in Dodi's repatriation without good reason; a task he was specifically entrusted with? And doesn't this rather prove he must have been told there were suspicious circumstances to the deaths, or why else would he call Paris on this issue since he at first believed that he was dealing with a tragic accident? He was unable even to obtain papers from the mortuary to explain why Dodi's body wasn't released earlier and this is inexplicable considering the bureaucratic manner with which the French generally conduct their business.

The court then suggested there was nothing sinister about Burgess calling the deaths suspicious since the paparazzi had been arrested; it was accepted that this wasn't a normal road traffic accident. But both Messenger and Burgess had denied saying to Macnamara that the deaths were suspicious. The issue here is whether these two people lied about making calls to Macnamara. The court cannot circumvent this position by saying well, OK, but the deaths were suspicious. So why did the court, in common with MI6 witnesses, not pursue this point?

Burgess then wrote to Mohamed Al Fayed's solicitors on 23rd August 2003 and denied saying the deaths were suspicious but later he again wrote stating that he was not prepared to enter into any further discussion about his telephone conversation, adding, 'There was never any suggestion made to me by either police force that the deaths were suspicious in the sense that the deceased were deliberately killed.' Macnamara says he never suggested that they were; he had merely asked for confirmation from Burgess that he had received information the deaths were suspicious, which is why Dodi's remains were late in being repatriated.

I believe that Michael Burgess's qualified response indicates he had some concerns – all enhanced by another written comment from him, saying he 'fears that both Lewis Silkin [Al Fayed's lawyers] and Mr Macnamara are reading too much into whatever exchanges may have taken place'. This is no denial that he had spoken with Macnamara and might be considered a tacit admission that something was said. If so, what possible reason could there be for denying it?

Macnamara travelled to Paris to seek answers for himself. By Thursday, 4th September, the French police still hadn't contacted crucial witnesses such as Dodi's bodyguard, Kes Wingfield (who had been with Diana and Dodi on the day they died) or Paul Handley Greaves, head of Al Fayed's personal security, nor indeed John Macnamara himself. So, through the deputy head of the Ritz hotel, Claude Roulet, Macnamara contacted the Commissioner of the Brigade Criminale – Madame Comiele – and went to see her on that same day at around 4.00pm, taking 'Kes' Wingfield and Paul Handley Greaves with him. It was explained to Madame Comiele that they all had evidence to give which might assist her – especially Kes Wingfield, who had been with Dodi and Diana all day until they left the Ritz hotel.

Arrangements were made for statements to be taken and so, using an interpreter, the police started with Kes Wingfield while Handley Greaves and Macnamara waited for their turn. They waited for two hours but eventually left without giving a statement and, despite offering to attend a further meeting, little, if any, effort was made by the French police to recall either of them. Kes Wingfield was interviewed for five hours and described all the details from when he left Le Bourget Airport earlier in the day on 30th August to the departure from the Ritz Hotel just after midnight. However, the presiding judge Stephan's final file consisted of only one page of his testimony, so clearly much of his evidence was never included.

So now back to the inquest. John Macnamara was asked by counsel: 'at some stage did you become aware that there was at least the likelihood – *which in due course became obvious* [my italics] – was the need for a post-mortem examination to be held in England?' Just a few moments later, this point is twice more re-emphasised: *'Now you were aware, were you, that there would have to be inquests into these deaths, were you?'* And, *'Do you remember in your discussions with Mr Burgess that day, he explained there had to be inquests because these were violent or unnatural deaths?'* (My italics.)

Of course this only serves to emphasise how very *obvious* it was that a post mortem would be needed in England and, since this law had been in place since the early eighties, why was Diana embalmed in France against French and British law? This surely implies that there must be another reason, such as to disguise a pregnancy or the possibility of noxious substances. (It was crucial that the motive for murder that would present if Diana's pregnancy could be proven was removed.)

Diana's embalming was carried out by Professor Dominique Lecompte on instruction from Madame Coujard and took place around

2.00pm on 31st August, an hour before her body left the hospital to be transported home. Then, after the post mortem in England, she was re-embalmed. (Could this be to ensure that no traces of vital evidence remained?) This does beg the question as the purpose of the French embalming given that this only served for a matter of hours.

Macnamara was placed in a difficult position when asked for his views on the embalming because in order to answer the question freely, he would be required to dispute evidence already given by Sir Michael Jay, the then British Ambassador to France, who denied giving the order to embalm. There was insufficient evidence to support Macnamara's opinion that Jay did indeed give this instruction, but when we look at the source of this information we can see why Macnamara felt that he held his opinion on good authority.

Macnamara described having met with a freelance journalist, Peter Allen, who said he had interviewed the French Public Prosecutor, Madame Coujard. It was she who confirmed that instructions to embalm came from Sir Michael Jay (in fact, this was reported in the British *Daily Mail* newspaper on 27th June 2005). Madame Coujard told Jay that this was illegal under French law and asked on whose authority the request was made. Jay told her it came 'from the highest authority in Britain' – the then British Prime Minister, Tony Blair. Peter Allen did not attend court, but Macnamara firmly believes that Madame Coujard did indeed make this statement.

The subterfuge continued when Diana's body was returned home to England. Dr John Burton, coroner for the royal household, was present at Diana's post mortem where he publicly and volubly stated that there were no visible signs of pregnancy, saying, 'I looked inside her womb.' It's known, however, that in the early stages there are usually no detectable signs of pregnancy, even without embalming and Burton's comment certainly doesn't preclude this possibility.

Remember that the French radiologist, Dr Elizabeth Dion, had previously stated she observed clear signs of pregnancy in Diana's womb. However, Dr Dion didn't attend court to give evidence in common with many other dangerous witnesses and was not required to do so. Instead a written affidavit was accepted that didn't say where she was on that fateful night, or how she could have seen such a foetus in Diana's womb with clear signs of a developing pregnancy from the radiogram if she wasn't there. As a result of an affidavit being accepted from this key witness, the jury was denied her cross-examination that related to one of the main considerations for motive. (More later.)

Much was made in court of whether John Macnamara had identified Dodi's body at Fulham Mortuary when he attended there on 31st August 1997 at 5.50pm, the day of Diana and Dodi's murder. He had been awake since just before 1.00am and wasn't to obtain much sleep on the Sunday night either. Macnamara identified Dodi by checking and affirming from a passport photograph that this was indeed him and he signed a document confirming identification on the Monday when a policeman – Sergeant Wall – came to Harrods. But when asked at the hearing, years later, whether he had signed anything to confirm his identification, he couldn't remember doing so since the inspection of Dodi's body took place on the Sunday afternoon when there was much else going on.

As the authorities wouldn't allow Macnamara to view this document for him to ascertain whether or not it was his signature, he initially denied signing it. When finally permitted to see it, he accepted it as his signature, although he still didn't remember signing. One could argue that allocating several minutes of debate to this, in the general scheme of these inquests' theoretical purpose, was irrelevant but it did perhaps create an element of doubt for the jury as to John Macnamara's credibility. (Imagine if a similar line had been taken with MI6 witnesses, ostensibly because of their memories! At least Macnamara didn't obfuscate his answers.)

Macnamara said that a police officer – Detective Superintendent Jeffrey Rees, who had been seconded to liaison duties by Sir David Veness – was also present at the mortuary. As mentioned earlier, Macnamara had had previous dealings with him when Mohamed Al Fayed was investigated in 1998 following alleged claims that he had been responsible for gems going missing from a safe deposit box being retained at Harrods for Tiny Rowland – the man who Al Fayed had defeated in a fierce battle over the purchase of Harrods. The police finally dropped all proceedings in this matter. (Al Fayed was required to pay Rowland's widow compensation because the described loss was a Harrods liability.)

But why would David Veness, an assistant commissioner of police who works with the Security Services, specifically choose his man to go to the mortuary – sending a helicopter to fetch Rees from his holiday home in Lincolnshire – in these circumstances? Another officer, Geoffrey Hunt, was available and on duty for such matters as stated before. This is reminiscent of Judge Devidal being overlooked by the French President, who instead appointed Judge Stephan – a man he personally knew and in whom he had absolute confidence.

Macnamara spent two days at the Ritz Hotel supervising the security staff in a reconstruction of the CCTV that showed footage from 7pm on 30th August until the departure of Dodi and Diana at about 12.20pm on 31st August. He was questioned over his investigation into the claim that Henri Paul was 'drunk as a pig', as headlined in the British tabloid newspaper, the *Daily Mirror*, on the Monday following the attack. Macnamara had been assured by Kes Wingfield, Dodi's bodyguard, that Henri Paul had been drinking pineapple juice and had not taken alcohol during that evening, but when he arrived in Paris and questioned the Ritz barmen, Sébastien Trote and Philippe Doucin, he was shown a receipt indicating Paul had drunk two anisettes (such as Ricard) that are yellow when diluted with water – which could indicate why Wingfield thought they were pineapple juice.

Macnamara asked Frank Klein to ensure the receipt was kept secure for the French police since he presumed they would display an interest in such evidence and soon attend at the hotel. He had also accompanied a forensic pathologist from Scotland, Professor Peter Vanezis, to Paris in a futile attempt to ascertain the truth of these accusations against Paul; access to Paul's body was not allowed.

The court went to great lengths to insinuate that Macnamara had deliberately misled the public by telling both an American interviewer and the press that Henri Paul had drunk only pineapple juice that night. But Macnamara was interviewed before the French police had looked into the matter (the police were given the CCTV footage when they arrived at the Ritz, ten days after the crash) and so he was reluctant to pre-empt the findings of a French investigation when it could be discovered that the receipts were a forgery or mistakenly attributed to Henri Paul. It's common practice for police not to release evidence until they have fully scrutinised it and, remember, Macnamara had once been a senior Scotland Yard policeman.

There was no intention to keep this information from the police as suggested by some newspapers although it would possibly have been better had Macnamara not permitted the interview, especially at this juncture, because they are often embellished (equating with Henri Paul with being 'drunk as a pig'). The bar receipts were secured and awaited the arrival of the French police. But Macnamara wasn't to know that the police would not come to the Ritz until ten days after the crash, or that there would be neither French nor a British 'investigation'.

The court appeared to treat Macnamara as though he was responsible for the whole investigative charade instead of someone who was simply pursuing justice, albeit in a private capacity, for a bereaved father. Why did the court not question the need for him to be in Paris in the first place? His presence would have been unnecessary, had the British police bothered to investigate. Instead, he was admonished by the court for withholding this evidence being 'an important discovery in releasing the truth to the public'. Why then didn't the British police deign to immediately attend and seek these important truths to release to the public, such as the Mishcon note for example? It's not uncommon for the British police to assist with investigating British citizen's suspicious deaths on foreign soil. Why did they leave it to the French police when it was clear that not much, if anything, was happening?

Macnamara gave a reason for his cautious position with the media regarding the evidence of the bar receipts. Yet Scott Baker made the point that, 'If you tell lies on some occasions how can the jury tell if you are telling the truth on others?' Most interesting…

Readers will again recall MI6 testimony where it was proven they were repeatedly equivocal during the inquests and refused to answer many questions. They were also found to have perverted the course of justice in a former court of law. Why didn't the court ensure that these truths were released to the public? No comment was made nor sanction applied against MI6 despite everyone knowing they were behaving in this unacceptable manner. I submit, therefore, that we must presume the court was telling us to totally disregard MI6 evidence since, by the court's own standard test, they cannot be trusted.

Macnamara's position regarding the bodyguards remains immovable. (A full critique on the bodyguards appears later on in this book.) It is important to consider the logic of his reasoning and draw your own conclusions because, in common with all matters relating to the Security Services, it takes much scrutiny and great care to establish the truth since they have the entire state machinery on side.

The two principal bodyguards in this saga are Trevor Rees-Jones (now Trevor Jones) and Kes Wingfield, both of whom were employed by Mohamed Al Fayed but reported to John Macnamara. It was their role to look after Diana and Dodi's safety. There was another Al Fayed bodyguard, Ben Murrell, who was also in Paris and in charge of looking after the Villa Windsor – a large house in Paris once occupied by the Duke of Windsor and Mrs Simpson but leased by Mohamed Al Fayed from the City of Paris. Diana and Dodi visited the Villa during that last fateful weekend and, following later testimony from Klein, it's my view from the evidence that Diana and Dodi were considering taking this as one of their homes once married.

The bodyguards had specific guidelines such as always keeping the London control desk informed of their actions, particularly when – and if – any plans deviated from the norm or were considered inadvisable, as Trevor Rees-Jones admitted was the case here. This of course didn't happen. But several inconsistencies led to Macnamara's serious concerns as to their evidence.

Rees-Jones and Wingfield employed a ghost-writer to write a book, *The Bodyguard's Story* (2000), about that day in Paris. Most of its content flies in the face of what John Macnamara believes to be true. The book gives credence to the view that the deaths were the result of a terrible accident and some of the statements contained within its pages were revealed in court. However, interestingly, Kes

Wingfield confessed to not knowing whether some points raised in the book were true and, post disclosure during the inquests, even tried to disown any part in the book's authorship.

One of the main points discussed in the book was whose idea it was to leave the Ritz using a decoy vehicle. Both bodyguards vehemently maintained in their book that the order came from Dodi. During the inquests, the lawyer showed that this order couldn't possibly have come from Dodi and so this, and several other contradictory statements that both bodyguards gave to police over several years, were now proven false (see later evidence). For example, on page 19 of the book, Rees-Jones says: 'If Dodi did something that was contravening what his father wanted, I had to report to his father, not to him.'

Then, on page 81 he says with regard to Dodi, 'Well, I couldn't give a toss because we work for Mr Fayed and nobody else.' All this indicates that they wouldn't have taken the order from Dodi, even if he had given it. So why did they follow this course of action since both knew that they should have contacted London and also that it was a crazy plan, so described by Rees-Jones? Does this imply they were either grossly negligent that evening or had some other agenda to fulfil?

As already stated, many of the comments in Rees-Jones's book contradict Macnamara's views. Another example is that on returning to London, Rees-Jones told McNamara he had accompanied Dodi to the Albert Repossi jewellery store in Place Vendôme to buy a ring early on the Saturday and that he believed it was an engagement ring. His book commented that, 'Although Trevor has a vague recollection of Dodi leaving the boutique carrying one of those small elegant shopping bags with strings, it has been continually reported that the ring was picked up and taken back to the Ritz by Roulet [the Ritz assistant manager] and given to Dodi later.'

Another remark described the effect of how airbags work in motorcars when the airbag system is inflated, which Rees-Jones used as the explanation for the amount of carbon monoxide in Henri Paul's blood. He then continued to describe in precise medical detail what would happen to a body in such a situation: 'The impact and extreme deceleration leave Diana's heart displaced from the left to the right side of its cavity and with injuries so serious – the severing of the vital pulmonary vein and rupturing of the pericardium, the heart's protective sac – that there is no example in international medical history where a person suffering from such an injury survived, the judge's medical experts would ultimately report.' (In any event, Mercedes confirmed that they do not use carbon monoxide in their car's air bags and the firemen at the death scene said they checked for the presence of gases and there were none, so this couldn't possibly be true.)

Macnamara believed that there is no way such information came from Trevor Rees-Jones. Instead he was clearly trying to put forward a specific point of view on matters about which he had no knowledge and one must wonder why and from whence this information came. One wonders whether, in such situations, the Security Services would seek to influence some people in exchange for cash, a longer, healthy life and then their silence.

Another interesting insight is the comments of Karen Mackenzie, Al Fayed's Park Lane housekeeper. She recalled that, as she entered a lift together with Trevor Jones at these offices, he said to her: 'If I remember, they will kill me.' (More later.) The central theme of John Macnamara's discontent stems from his knowledge of the various lies that were being proffered and accepted as truth.

But before we end this section on Macnamara, let's look at what he discovered regarding American Secret Service surveillance of Diana before she died. At the Inquiry, evidence emerged from Mr Gerald Postner, an American investigative journalist and lawyer that he had personally listened to recorded conversations between Diana and Lucia Flecha de Lima, wife of the Brazilian Ambassador to Washington. These had been intercepted and recorded by the CIA in Washington, DC. In addition, the US Government admitted possessing around 1,056 pages relating to matters concerning Diana, confirmed in a letter dated 5th November 1998 from Joann Grubb, director of policy for the US National Security Agency (NSA), and delivered in response to requests from Mr Al Fayed's Washington lawyers, William & Connolly.

One of these surreptitious recordings was confirmation that Henri Paul met with the Security Services on the Saturday afternoon before the attack. An application was made to the court in Washington, DC for the release of these documents held by the NSA and was heard by District Judge Kennedy, who granted a subpoena. Judge Kennedy also directed that the US Defense Intelligence Agency appear for deposition and produce these documents. In addition, subpoenas were issued on the United States Department of Justice, The Central Intelligence Agency and the Defense Intelligence Agency.

On 29th March 2000, however, Judge Kennedy retracted his earlier direction and we are sure readers won't be surprised to hear that these subpoenas were then rescinded. The Defense Intelligence Agency was released from its obligation and the CIA refused to produce any information, which you may find surprising if there was nothing that was relevant. A further application had also been made through the District Court of Maryland on 4th February 1999, but was denied by District Judge Frederic N Smalkin.

John Macnamara visited Washington on several further occasions and sought subpoenas through the courts in Washington and Virginia for these records to be produced. He was assisted in this mission by Senator George Mitchell, who had served as United States Attorney for Maine, as United States District Judge for Maine, majority leader of the United States Senate and was also entrusted with the sensitivities of Northern Ireland politics, where he successfully assisted with a negotiated settlement. On 18th August 1999, Macnamara went with Senator Mitchell and a legal team to the Pentagon, where they saw Robert Tyrer, chief of staff for the Under Secretary of Defense. Permission was sought for Senator Mitchell to review these records and determine whether there was anything of relevance to Diana's murder, but it was denied.

It was arranged instead for Mr Tyrer to examine all the records relating to Diana and determine himself whether there was anything of relevance to the attack in Paris. A second Pentagon meeting with Robert Tyrer was held in September 1999, when he announced that he had reviewed the documents and was satisfied there was nothing in any way related to the deaths of Diana and Dodi. There was no guarantee of course that all documents had been handed over to Robert Tyrer by the CIA or NSA, and John Macnamara expressed this concern. Senator Mitchell wrote to Robert Tyrer that he was 'particularly concerned that the set of potentially relevant documents provided to you may have been incomplete'. Tyrer wrote back, dismissing this point.

Isn't it strange that Senator George Mitchell was entrusted with positions of very high office by the US and British governments but wasn't permitted to view documents that he could read within the confines of the Pentagon walls, vetoed on the grounds that National Security would be threatened? Is anyone able to conceive how Senator Mitchell would threaten US National Security, especially concerning information that we are told didn't contain any untoward detail?

Perhaps the reason was simply that, being a man of integrity, these governments couldn't entrust him with the truth. But we wonder why the US Government wouldn't assist justice. This must have come as a request from the British Government to the US Government.

Frank J Klein

When the Alma crash took place, Frank Klein – president of Al Fayed's Paris Ritz Hotel – was on holiday in Antibes but he was nevertheless able to clarify some of the evidential dissent that occurred afterwards. Klein's role was to oversee activities at the Ritz but he had managers for each department and so wasn't aware of day-to-day matters.

He regarded Henri Paul as a business acquaintance and had worked with him for twelve years so knew his proclivities. When questioned on Paul's drinking habits, Klein confirmed all his staff had regular medicals and that the Ritz has its own doctor; there was no sign of Paul having a drink problem and nobody ever mentioned it before that sad day in Paris. Klein also added that he would never contemplate engaging someone with a drink problem and insisted that Paul 'took alcohol like myself or somebody else, on a normal basis'. He believed that Paul couldn't have known he would be driving his boss that night or he wouldn't have taken any alcohol at all.

The court acknowledged Paul was there to help Dodi and, despite not being on duty, the police later attested to Paul still only having had two Ricards, which hardly accords with a propensity towards alcoholism. It was suggested that the measures of Ricard were rather generous but Klein said that they either came from a bottle measure or a glass of a specific size, adding: 'We have to make a profit.' He added that Henri Paul had been recommended by members of the judicial police and was very discreet, so he was obviously considered dependable.

A rumour had been initiated from some source that Henri Paul wasn't licensed to drive the large Mercedes car but here Klein confirmed that a licence is required only if a driver wishes to drive for hire or reward – but that was not the situation here.

Klein said that although Paul wasn't permitted to drive the Mercedes, this only related to internal authorisation from Etoile limousine cars; there was nothing that forbad him from driving large Mercedes cars under French law and he did occasionally drive during the course of his duties. For example, he collected Diana and Dodi's baggage from Le Bourget Airport and took it to Dodi's apartment on the rue Arsène Houssaye earlier on the Saturday afternoon. Paul had also been on special driving courses in Stuttgart after a previous head of Ritz security, Josef Goedde, had attended. So it is clear that, contrary to reports, Paul was used to driving large Mercedes cars.

Paul's dealings with the Security Services of several countries, including the British, is not in doubt, so it does make one wonder why the court and the Security Services tried so hard to deny it. Klein confirmed that many of the larger hotels have established contacts with the Security Services of various countries, re-affirmed by Richard Tomlinson. This is because they need to cooperate with dignitaries' own security people when presidents, prime ministers, kings and queens visit their hotels; it was part of Paul's job.

However, the money, totalling around £20,000, that was established had entered Paul's bank accounts between 19th June and the first week of August (c. $2,000 was also found on Paul after his death) confounded Klein just as much as anyone else. He said that he had no idea where the money came from; Paul's duties wouldn't enable him to generate these sums in tips since he wasn't a concierge and didn't run errands. Even a man who had worked with Paul for twelve years couldn't explain the source of this money.

Another issue that confounded Klein is why Paul drove to Dodi's apartment at the rue Arsène Houssaye via the Alma tunnel. The direct route is via Place de la Concorde and then the Champs-Elysées. Klein said that no one would ever go via the Alma tunnel since it's a circuitous route and one would probably need to drive on to the Trocadero, which is even busier than the Champs-Elysées. He was asked: 'If you live and work and drive in Paris, you would not go via Trocadero?' To which he replied: 'Never ever – nobody would.'

One of the bar staff at the Ritz, a Monsieur Willaumez (who was on duty on the night of the attack and whom it was stated in court had a problem with Henri Paul because Paul had previously needed to admonish him) said that Paul drank far more than the two Pastis previously mentioned, but he did not explain why the bar receipts didn't reflect this. Willaumez even said that Paul had staggered into the head barman, Vincent l'Otelier, but l'Otelier did not confirm this and CCTV footage of Paul's movements around the hotel didn't substantiate it either. The authorities had relied on a bar receipt to show Paul had drunk two Ricards that evening, but despite having no further receipts or any other evidence to support Willaumez' claim, the court still allowed this point to stand.

Willaumez also claimed that Klein had tried to prevent him from speaking with police about the drinks Paul had taken that evening. He accused him of saying, 'We must stick to that version for the good of the Royal Family' with regard to Kes Wingfield's stated opinion of 1st September that Paul had only taken pineapple juice. Klein emphatically and convincingly rebutted this allegation. He said that, having received a call from John Macnamara about British press reports that Paul was 'drunk as a pig', he immediately checked the bar receipts and found that he had consumed two Ricards. However, because of the inevitable media frenzy surrounding this affair, he didn't want the press to receive information ahead of the police. He told staff: 'You don't speak to anybody in the interests of the Royal Family and the family Al Fayed.'

Klein was furious that Willaumez had suggested he should lie to the police, responding, 'How should I say you cannot speak to the police? I am old enough, I am living in France for thirty years and it would be…it is ridiculous.' But Klein wasn't to know that the police wouldn't turn up at the Ritz until ten days later. So, why did Willaumez make this claim?

Klein was also able to shed light on Dodi Fayed's intentions regarding marriage before he died. He received a call on 14th August from Dodi and remembered the date because it was the day before the French National holiday began on 15th August, when he was due to return to Antibes. Klein knew Dodi was in Monte Carlo because Dodi had said, 'Frank, I passed by a jewellers' shop,' mentioning it was Van Cleef & Arpels and then said, 'I want to – I need to buy some jewellery. I am getting engaged.'

Klein then phoned Madame Ray, directrice of the Van Cleef & Arpels store, to arrange a private viewing of some engagement rings and described what Dodi had told Klein he wanted to see, saying, 'There must be something in your shop or in your window, something with red or blue.' (Diana's blue sapphire engagement was bought there. It is the ring that Prince William recently gave to Kate Middleton.)

She replied, 'Yes, we have this in our window,' confirming the items that Dodi had described. Klein called Dodi back and told him, 'There is Madame Ray, who is waiting for you but I think they are going to close at 6.00pm.' (Klein knew Madame Ray because she had previously worked at the Van Cleef & Arpels store at Place Vendôme near the Paris Ritz.) Unfortunately, Klein spoke to Dodi from a Ritz landline and so the call could easily have been infiltrated.

Another conversation then took place between Klein and Dodi over 18th–19th August, while Klein was in Antibes, in which Dodi mentioned he would probably come to Paris with his 'friend' by the end of the month. Klein told Dodi there was no room available at the Ritz. (Rooms did later become available due to cancellations by the time Diana and Dodi arrived, but in any event, Klein said that Dodi often stayed at his apartment if no rooms were free.) He further added that Dodi had called him on Friday, 29th August from his boat saying that, 'I come to Paris, I am coming with my friend…friend/girlfriend and I am going to get married, and I am staying there and I am going to live there [the Villa Windsor].' Klein checked on when the refurbishment of the Villa would be complete and found it would be several more weeks so Dodi asked him to prepare a portfolio of other properties. Clearly, he wasn't prepared to wait.

For those who dispute Klein's description of events we must wonder why he would make all these provable claims if they hadn't occurred, since it's known he intended pursuing other properties with Mohamed Al Fayed on the Monday after the crash. It's certain Diana and Dodi were not delaying their new beginning but were making plans for moving in together known and it's clear from the evidence of these phone calls that the Security Services would have had at least twelve days of knowing the seriousness of the couple's relationship before the 'accident' took place.

The Villa Windsor in Paris is of special relevance in this story because, being a large house in the Bois de Boulogne and under the auspices of Mohamed Al Fayed, it was a natural location for Diana and Dodi to consider as one of their forthcoming homes when married. It is significant that they visited the Villa on their last visit to Paris – why else would a couple, who had recently viewed engagement rings and been inseparable for several weeks, concern themselves with visiting an empty house, despite having only limited time on their short Paris visit, since it's known they were intending to return to the UK on the Monday after they were murdered?

The main argument against the theory that this visit was carried out in order to consider a future home was that Diana allegedly stated she thought it looked like a mausoleum. Even if true, this doesn't alter our logic since the purpose of the visit was to enable the couple to decide whether the Villa was an option, not necessarily their first abode. It was known that the Villa wouldn't be ready for several weeks and that Dodi had already asked Klein to prepare a portfolio of other properties (remember, wealthy people often have several homes).

If the Villa wasn't suitable, Diana would have discarded it but the central issue is that they were clearly looking for a home together.

Klein was further questioned regarding a visit to the Villa Windsor on one occasion in which two American journalists were present. Ben Murrell, an Al Fayed bodyguard who was in charge of the Villa Windsor, offered an incredible account of events surrounding this visit. Murrell claimed that Klein was at the Villa with Michael Cole (Al Fayed's publicity man) when Murrell told them both that David Pinch, another Al Fayed bodyguard, had instructed him to tell the journalists a lie.

Pinch allegedly wished to accentuate the seriousness of Diana and Dodi's relationship so he asked Murrell to claim that the couple met with a famous Italian designer, Ardo Grossi, while at the Villa, with the obvious suggestion that they were intending to live there. Murrell said both Klein and Cole were happy to accept this falsehood.

Klein said that he visited the Villa occasionly and hosted journalists but he didn't remember this visit or these particular American journalists; not unreasonably pointing out that Murrell, who was making these claims, should be the one with the names. Michael Cole didn't even recall meeting with Murrell. That Diana and Dodi visited the Villa is testimony to their intent but why did Pinch suggest a third party was present when this could easily be disproved? Murrell also said that Klein had asked what he was going to say at the inquests, though Klein denied this, saying it was 'a false and very wrong allegation against me'.

It was important for the disinformation experts to dismiss Klein's testimony and the police lawyer was in full swing, accusing him of perverting the course of justice by giving false evidence – it's amazing that he had the impudence. However, the lawyer then stumbled.

Klein thought he could offer evidence of Willaumez having been given a warning by Paul and that this would be written in his staff file, but when the evidence was sought there was none. Klein had forgotten that after a specific period of time, under French law, these written warnings must be expunged. Indeed, the penalties for failing to comply can be very high. The lawyer for the police, continuing his insinuations, claimed that Klein had kept this file secluded from the investigative authorities.

The court, however, then established that these files were not available to Klein and the coroner had himself needed to obtain an order from the French court for them to be released, after which they were transferred from the French authorities to the French police. They had never been in Klein's possession.

Another lawyer then intervened and asked whether the lawyer for the police was asking questions or making speeches since he hadn't given Klein any chance to respond. It was suggested that he was throwing mud in the hope that the jury would take a dim view of Klein's evidence, which seemed the sole purpose of his attack. It's disturbing that the court didn't see fit to intervene since it was the coroner who had clarified how and when this file became available; surely he knew this was a misleading line of questioning. Klein didn't, of course, receive an apology for these incorrect insinuations in court.

Diana's pregnancy was another issue that needed to be refuted since this was one of the main planks of any conspiracy. Klein referred to witness evidence that he gave to police, one or two months after the crash. He had received a phone call at the Ritz from a woman who was the aunt of a male nurse at the Pitié-Salpêtrière Hospital in Paris, where Diana was taken after the crash. This woman had some inside information for him: she gave the name of another nurse at the hospital, who had made a statement confirming Diana's pregnancy and gave it to the police. The name of this nurse is Jocelyn Magellan and her address was 24 rue Schwartzberg, 77144, Montevrain. She was going to meet with Klein but didn't turn up – perhaps too frightened to come forward. Klein said he believed she was from the French West Indies, either Martinique or Guadeloupe, but he didn't know what the French police did with this address or whether they pursued this witness. Jocelyn Magellan has not been heard from again.

Klein also said he met Elizabeth, the wife of James Andanson – the paparazzo who owned a white Fiat Uno and was believed to have been in the Alma tunnel that night in Paris. They met at Klein's offices two or three weeks after her husband James's body had been found at the Plateau d'Albion in the South of France in May 2000. Mrs Andanson told Klein: 'There may be a way we can work together in the investigation.' Asked what she meant, Klein said Elizabeth Andanson had replied that she didn't believe her husband had committed suicide and she linked his death to Diana and Dodi's case.

Andanson had been involved in the harassment of Al Fayed's property at St Tropez, South of France between 14th–20th July 1997, when Diana and Dodi were staying at his 'Fisherman's Cottage'. The paparazzi used helicopters to take photographs and Klein had needed to contact the Mayor of St Tropez to complain of the noise and risk to security. Andanson had also been chasing Al Fayed's yacht, the *Jonical*.

This is a totally different view from Mrs Andanson's later avowed belief, displayed at the inquests, that her husband had killed himself – what, or who, changed her mind? As we will see later, this was not the only contradiction to come out of Elizabeth Andanson's evidence: she also said her husband wasn't interested in Diana and Dodi despite having just joined the hottest paparazzi agency in France and with copious evidence that he spent the whole summer in their pursuit.

Klein described the moment he heard from John Macnamara, who told him that he had just received a call from the then coroner, Mr Burgess. Burgess had in turn received a call from Scotland Yard to say that the deaths were suspicious and repatriation may not be immediately possible. Klein was already in the courtyard of the morgue with Claude Roulet, the Ritz manager, when he received this call so went immediately with Roulet to try and see Professor Lecompte, the forensic pathologist who later carried out the embalming. After a while, Lecompte came down into the courtyard. 'Wait,' she told them.

At this time Dodi's coffin was already in the car for transportation and Lecompte went to her office, taking twenty minutes, which made Klein nervous because he knew that Dodi had to be buried before sunset under Islamic law. He went to look for her office and, after finding her, Lecompte confirmed that she was in touch with the authorities (Klein thought Chevènement, Minister of the Interior). After a further hour, she cleared Dodi's body for repatriation to the

UK but also said the Chief of the Judicial Police – Patrick Riou – wanted to see both Klein and Roulet. They went to him and he asked, 'Who called you?' Riou told them that the French police hadn't seen, or been informed of, anything suspicious. It would appear that he wanted to know whether there was any information that he didn't possess.

The assault on Klein's evidence was unrelenting throughout the inquests, in common with all those who knew too much. It's worth noting his final response:

'I am a free man and I say what I know and I speak the truth. I am very shocked and I am a president of a company and I am very shocked that the Professor Lecompte and the French judicial experts, you know, are not coming here to give evidence and the reason is they give a code. The French law code is 694.4. There is a code, which is under the secret act and *ordre public* [Public Order Act]. For that reason the French judicial experts are not giving evidence and those experts are in this investigation since 1997. I am shocked myself; I am shocked. OK, I do not criticise the questions you put to me but I am very, very shocked that we are speaking here about…I have come back and I come back with pleasure to help [Klein had been recalled for further evidence]. What of Mr Murrell, who is sending false… who has sold false stories to the newspaper and he got paid for it? I think that was a disgrace.'

We must consider now why it was thought necessary to invoke the Public Order Act to deal with a mere road traffic accident. What imperative truth demanded that the people be deceived?

Key Participants

Henri Paul/the Medical Profession

The fundamental issues concerning Henri Paul's role that night are:
  (1) Was he drunk at the wheel?
  (2) Did he work for the British Security Services?

We must also consider whether anyone would have survived this attack, whether drunk or sober because, if not, then the issue of drink becomes irrelevant. Of course if people could be persuaded Paul was drunk, it would be easier to accept a verdict that the deaths were due to an unfortunate accident as a result of his incapacity. But to blame him, the court agreed that the evidence must be uncontaminated and unambiguous to prove his culpability. You decide if it was.

On the second issue, preceded by the inevitable denials, MI6 were forced into admitting that they recruit hotel security staff as a matter of course, with former MI6 agent Richard Tomlinson even confirming they are considered an indispensable recruitment target. In addition, there is much to suggest Henri Paul's involvement with the Secret Services of many countries; Frank Klein confirmed this same point. Tomlinson also stated to the court that he saw a file while serving in MI6 that contained information on a security man at the Ritz who was a pilot. Since Paul was the only pilot among them, dare we presume MI6 were again being economical with the truth when they denied their connection with him? Once again, you decide why they denied it.

But first, let's go back to the issue of whether Paul was drunk. This should have been a simple matter to clear up, but as usual there were too many irregularities. Some written medical witness statements were read out at the inquests, but only direct questioning of the doctors involved could have answered the pertinent questions. But they were almost certainly prevented from attending by the authorities in like manner to the paparazzi that were proven in court to have been prevented, *through political intervention*. We are left with the fiasco of not knowing where blood samples came from, Henri Paul's carbon monoxide levels showing at twenty per cent (enough to have made him visibly disoriented or comatose) and blood taken for DNA tests that were not carried out.

The French police's procedures that night were criticised by Lord Justice Scott Baker, who accepted there could have been *another agenda fomenting*. In fact, the police didn't even record Henri Paul's body correctly in the mortuary, despite the level of international interest in his death. Major Mules of the French police showed Paul's body as being No. 2146 when it was 2147; Scott Baker commented that this displayed a 'lack of care, at the very least' (the corpse next to Paul was a car exhaust suicide – carbon monoxide).

Similarly, police recorded the date of Judge Stephan's visit to the morgue to oversee tests on Henri Paul as 5th September and not 4th September, as shown on the 'Official Report of Visit' document exhibited in court. Scott Baker said the jury might consider this another example of the 'carelessness that we have seen so many times before'. Whether the following irregularities were careless or deliberate is for you to judge.

The official result of the investigation into the deaths was that the blame lay at the feet of Paul but the evidence was extremely flawed and indicated that he was set up.

Lord Stevens, the former head of Scotland Yard who ran the Paget inquiry (the special investigative team or fiasco, depending on your view, that was set up about seven years after Diana's murder) tried to downplay the comments of his Paget officer, Detective Inspector Scotchbrook, who had written a note saying that Henri Paul had only had two drinks and no more. That, according to Stevens, isn't what Scotchbrook had meant to say; he didn't clarify what she did mean to say. But why did Stevens even attempt to downplay Scotchbrook's evidence?

Scott Baker also made reference to Lord Stevens' Paget report, stating 'too much emphasis is placed on assumptions that the blood being tested was from Henri Paul', which Scott Baker says, 'is very much in issue'. He added, 'The jury will have to consider whether wrong samples got into bottles or whether there was a deliberate mix -up.' This, together with the judge's criticism of the carelessness seen in police behaviour, puts the whole Paget report in doubt. Indeed it was suggested in court that Lord Stevens had been 'got at'.

Questions also rose about police activity with regard to the drugs that Henri Paul was taking. An empty packet of Ayotal tablets (a drug used to help people stay off alcohol) was apparently discovered in Paul's trash bin since traces of it were found in some samples supposedly taken from Paul. Scott Baker questioned whether police relied on this empty packet to confirm the blood was from Paul but accepted that it's unlikely these tablets were taken by him since he had been drinking and the combination would have made him ill (clearly considering French police corruption).

This raised further doubts as to police integrity and Scott Baker even appeared to suggest that someone planted this 'evidence'. So, together with the probability of planted evidence and 'the blood source being very much in doubt', plus the jury being told to consider whether 'there was a deliberate mix-up', it defies belief that this evidence was permitted to stand.

The report from Professor Lecompte shows various discrepancies between Paul's height and weight, in addition to the serious questions raised over blood testing. Different doctors gave a variety of findings in their blood analyses but the overall results were bizarre and the absence of DNA testing, which one presumes should have been of the utmost importance, was also unexplained.

Why a doctor would take samples from a corpse in such a high-profile situation and then not bother to carry out the DNA test procedure for which they were taken, despite retaining them for three years, is something of a conundrum. These samples then mysteriously disappeared when people started asking questions about where they were. In fact, as Scott Baker stated, there is serious doubt that any of them came from Henri Paul.

The obvious thought that springs to mind is that either these blood tests were not from Henri Paul and were more probably from the corpse that lay next to Paul in the morgue. Or, perhaps, that they were and the blood alcohol levels were very low when certain other people then ensured this evidence never reached court. All we have is a weak assertion from Scott Baker that a DNA test 'must have been done on Paul's blood' and we are expected to presume the results then went missing, with no one having a recollection of what these results showed. There wasn't even anybody to confirm that the tests were done. Does anyone believe this?

You will recall that the police quickly produced 'results' for Paul's blood alcohol level within hours of the crash because the political machinery needed to blame him for the deaths to remove suspicion from the Security Services. No one believed this fabrication then and no one believes it now, but the difference is that here we have a senior judge concurring with accepted, dubious evidence despite his own criticism of both the blood tests and police behaviour. Why did the police feel it necessary to manufacture these results within a few hours of the attack because it's proven they were not available between the crash and the police announcement that Paul was drunk? So this statement was clearly a fabrication?

Blood samples were taken from Henri Paul's neck, an anatomical area known to give unreliable results for analysis. This was confirmed and carried out by the medical Professor Shepherd, who saw photographs of the autopsy room and noted blood in sample bottles from a procedure carried out before they opened Henri Paul's chest cavity. Professor Shepherd could see an incision in the side of Paul's neck. However, forensic pathologist Professor Lecompte wrote on 9th September 1997 that the blood had come from the left hemi thorax area but soon after this examination, and on the same day, she said it had come from the chest cavity because there was insufficient blood to conduct proper tests. Much later, on 9th March 2005, she told British police that the blood had come from the heart using a clean scoop, so we see how much confidence can be attributed to medical testimony.

Chest cavity blood is known to have the risk of being contaminated, so even if a proper test was done, it's improbable that the results would be reliable. Professor Lecompte made no comment at the time, but she should have been available to answer this and many other questions. Given all the problems with the medical evidence, is it any wonder all the medics preferred to stay away from court? But you must decide how all these senior medics could get it so wrong.

French toxicologist Dr Gilbert Pepin did another test without making it clear that it was not from another sample 'as he should have done', according to Scott Baker. 'Why did Pepin adjust these results without telling anybody?' he admonished. However, he added, 'There isn't anything necessarily sinister about it,' clearly having considered there could be something sinister.

The forensic pathologist Professor Peter Vanezis said that for Henri Paul to have that level of alcohol in his bloodstream and still be able to drive a car he would have to be a regular drinker, but he had nagging doubts over whether Paul was twice over the limit because 'of the way his samples had been handled'. He added that the vitreous humour samples were likely to have come from Paul and these were 'apparently' taken from him in the presence of Judge Stephan.

Scott Baker continually questioned the veracity of the results throughout proceedings, which is understandable because none of the experts were certain and most gave ambiguous testimony. Yet still he permitted the jury to find Henri Paul guilty of manslaughter despite this verdict being dependent on Paul's blood results and having already stated that the samples taken on 31st August are 'probably in doubt'.

Professor Johnston is a professor of clinical pharmacology who dealt with the CDT test. He said, quite unambiguously, that more than one measurement was needed for a test to be of any value and that there could be an overlap between those who drink a lot and moderate drinkers. He was, however, disturbed by the closeness of results for the alcohol tests and he also thought that the most likely explanation for the twenty per cent carbon monoxide readings was that the blood was not from Henri Paul.

Dr Veronique Dumestre-Toulet, a toxicology expert with the Court of Appeal in Bordeaux, then introduced further bizarre uncertainty over samples with incorrect dating; this time by around a week. She said a sample sent by Dr Pepin on 15th September arrived on the 16th and she did the analysis on the same day. However, the record on the analysis sheet shows the 10th. Does anyone believe there could be quite so much error in so many professional reports or does this once more lead us into believing there is more at work here than simply widespread professional incompetence? During the entire inquests, no one was able to say unequivocally that any of these samples were from Paul.

The British forensic pathologist and expert witness Professor Robert Forrest said that if one took alcohol on a regular basis then one would acquire a degree of tolerance and resilience so the effects of a small extra amount would be manageable to such a person. So how could he subsequently conclude that Paul's judgment was impaired, especially since this evidence concurs with that of the crash expert Dr John Searle? Forrest was 'comfortably satisfied' that the results came from Henri Paul, which surely meant that he couldn't be at all certain. One is either satisfied or not, and any qualification is an expression of doubt.

Another drug found in an analysed blood sample also raised questions of whether the sample was from Henri Paul. Albendazole is used for treating worms yet no one close to Paul had any recollection of him ever having needed to take it and the condition was not mentioned in his medical records.

It would be interesting to know what happened to the corpse in the same morgue as Henri Paul that night, who committed suicide by inhaling the exhaust fumes from his car (which would create high levels of carbon monoxide in the blood). Is it too outlandish to think that perhaps the suicide's body was placed next to Paul in the morgue and given the number 2146 to establish an excuse for the 'error' of the blood samples being switched, should it be discovered?

With regard to the carbon monoxide, Scott Baker summed up: 'None of the experts could provide an explanation for that sort of level, *assuming that the blood came from Henri Paul* [my italics]. It's a mystery, and a mystery that you must take into account.' He again questioned whether the blood came from Paul and directed the jury to consider this but surely they would also need to consider why the medics and police had deceived the investigation since this had to be deliberate?

Scott Baker then told the jury that they would have to consider whether the wrong samples got into bottles or there was a 'deliberate mix-up' but failed to tell them there was so much flawed evidence that it should be disregarded for evidential purposes. He then told them to ignore the presence of twenty per cent carbon monoxide in the blood sample supposedly taken from Paul because expert evidence had destroyed its credibility, but again didn't question what the motive might have been for falsifying those results in the first place or question who could be responsible and where those blood samples came from.

Scott Baker continued that levels of Prozac and Tiapride also found in Paul's blood were very similar and suggested the jury may want to think carefully about this too. He questioned, 'Is this Paul's blood?' adding, 'There are question marks, therefore, about the conclusions to be drawn from the analysis of the blood samples said to have come from Henri Paul.'

Perhaps the most baffling statement from Scott Baker is the following – baffling because after this, it's hard to see any plausible and honest justification for permitting this blood evidence to stand. He said:

> 'Even if you were satisfied that the 31st August sample had come from Henri Paul, you would want to consider whether this inexplicable reading causes you to have doubts about the whole process of analysis. If the carbon monoxide readings must be wrong, what about the alcohol readings, the Prozac readings, the Tiapride readings?'

Yet this senior judge didn't tell the jury to ignore the blood sample evidence; why not? Could it be that in order to avoid the world realising Diana had been murdered, this 'accident' must be pinned on some poor soul who couldn't counter the accusations, so it was necessary to allow the blood 'evidence' to stand for the court to have its satisfactory finale and preserve the monarchy.

In his summation, when describing permissible verdicts, Scott Baker told the jury they might find unlawful killing through the gross negligence of Henri Paul because of 'the speed and manner of his driving and any alcohol he *may* [my italics] have consumed'. But from the evidence we know that Paul was driving fast because assassins were in hot pursuit, so if one remembers that Paul was working with MI6, everything becomes clear. But the jury were also told that for a manslaughter verdict, they must *be sure* (my italics) that Paul knew he ran the risk of death but ran it nonetheless. If you agree with this book's view that Paul cannot have known who these 'aggressive' and 'loitering' and 'blocking' vehicles were as described above then the condition required by the court cannot have been met.

But it is worth reiterating here that Scott Baker also said during his summation that the jury were not permitted to find for unlawful killing by persons unknown because there was insufficient evidence for them *to be sure* that this was an 'Unlawful Killing by a Staged Accident'.

So it's all right to consent to a verdict because someone *may* have consumed alcohol (despite seriously questioning the value of all Paul's blood evidence) and to find a deceased person guilty of manslaughter despite the jury having been told they must *be sure* (my italics) Paul saw that he ran the risk of death but continued nonetheless when it's clear he cannot have known what these aggressive vehicles were. But not acceptable to permit an 'unlawful killing by persons unknown' verdict because Scott Baker 'can't be sure' that it was *a staged accident* having already conceded that there is evidence of a staged accident. Consequently, the monarchy is safe.

Paul was briefed by MI6 and unwittingly assisted in his own murder; all these 'errors' didn't occur through professional incompetence but through the connivance of MI6.

Scott Baker changed his mind with regard to the relevance of the money that Paul had in his bank accounts. But if one is to question whether Henri Paul was in the pay of MI6, central to this whole affair, then examination of these illicit funds might well explain why he drove the Mercedes on a detour through the Alma tunnel. Scott Baker said the jury may have 'speculative ideas' about the money that had been regularly going into Paul's bank account but asked whether, 'In any event, are these mysteries relevant to any verdict?'

It is interesting to recall one of Scott Baker's initial eight building blocks for the 'conspiracy to murder' theory that he undertook to unravel at the commencement of proceedings. One was to establish 'the explanation for the substantial amounts of money in his [Paul's] possession and in his bank account'. So why did he then question whether this was now relevant? We can only wonder at how the jury coped with all the perverse reasoning that abounded in court.

Is it acceptable that Paul should be vilified for all time, especially when as Scott Baker said, 'There are doubts about the whole process of analyses.' This 'evidence' was an MI6 defence pose that needed to be sustained whatever the cost, but by Scott Baker's own admission, it is seriously flawed.

It is my contention that allowing this blood evidence to stand and not permit the jury a verdict option of 'unlawful killing by persons unknown', is an abuse of justice, pure and simple.

The Paparazzi

The paparazzi are discussed where considered appropriate during the course of this narrative but, essentially, only to put their role into perspective and remove them from the firing line. Their prime but unwitting purpose was to serve as adjuncts to murder. Without the presence of the paparazzi imagine how a group of assassins could claim that other people accidentally struck Diana's car that evening considering the evidence you are reviewing here. It would be very difficult to mask an attack.

It's why Henri Paul was volubly goading the paparazzi outside the Ritz that evening; to ensure they would be available later for their essential, but unwitting, scapegoat duties. It was also essential they arrived soon after the attack in the tunnel but not soon enough to witness the attack; here the timing was crucial. Sooner and they could have given specific evidence against the assassins but too late and people could more easily prove that the paparazzi had nothing to do with the attack.

(This evidence was crucial and could have brought the curtain down on this whole nefarious affair, so the paparazzi were prevented from attending court *through political intervention*. You will soon read Scott Baker's confirmation of this in response to the lawyers questioning.)

James Andanson

One of the biggest mysteries in this affair is the role of James Andanson, who owned a white Fiat Uno and who confided in his friends, including Frédéric Dard, that he was at the Alma tunnel during the attack. The court declared that Andanson was 'not appropriate to these proceedings', despite his bizarre death in May 2000. But Scott Baker still permitted the court to spend significant time cross-examining witnesses such as Andanson's boss, Hubert Henrotte, and family friends, François and Josephine Dard, plus Andanson's wife and son, who were all questioned in detail. Why, if Andanson wasn't relevant to these proceedings? His family were not in the tunnel. But if one is to interrogate his family then why wasn't Christophe Pelât invited to attend court and given an opportunity to describe the two holes that he saw in Andanson's skull?

One also wonders why it's appropriate to consider Andanson's whereabouts and proclivities at length but not the manner of his very strange demise, especially considering the significant evidence that emerged from this questioning. The French police were also surreptitiously dismissive. Surely it is obvious that James Andanson was central to this whole inquiry.

Yet if James Andanson wasn't involved, don't you think it an amazing coincidence that, considering his prominence in this saga, some thirty-three months after Diana's murder he 'committed suicide' by driving 600 miles from his home onto a remote army range, where he burnt himself to ash, having first shot himself *twice* in the head? This is especially interesting because he was known to have been bragging to friends about being in the tunnel that night. Looking at the evidence, it's clear Andanson wasn't the suicidal type; certainly his wife and son initially believed MI6 were responsible for James Andanson's death, as Elizabeth Andanson informed Frank Klein.

One of the firemen who attended at Andanson's 'suicide', Christophe Pelât, saw two small holes in Andanson's skull. Everyone waited for Pelât's testimony in vain since he wasn't even called to court, despite offering to attend. It would be interesting to know how Andanson managed to shoot himself twice in the head, set fire to his car with sufficient fuel to ensure his total cremation and then propel his BMW car keys to a safe haven (seeing as the keys were never found).

Andanson's story is one of the main issues concerning Diana's murder but, as Scott Baker says: 'If he wasn't in Paris, then he couldn't have done the deed.' But the evidence Scott Baker relied on in his summation for accepting that Andanson wasn't in Paris that night was from a photographer, Pierre Suu, who also didn't volunteer to attend court nor did the court require his presence. Suu said if Andanson had been in Paris, then he would have been noticed. Yet interestingly, he stated in a subsequent interview that 'he had nothing to do with that' (reference chasing Diana through Paris). But if he wasn't there, how could he know where Andanson was? As a result of this rather weak and distant assertion, the court ignored other evidence that Andanson was indeed in Paris.

In fact, Andanson produced an alibi for the night of Diana's death, but this is shown to be very flaky. If involved in the Princess's murder, it's obvious he would try to establish one and naturally MI6 would have assisted, and insisted it was in place. So the issue is not so much whether he had an alibi, but whether it survives scrutiny.

Hubert Henrotte was James Andanson's boss at the Paris-based Sygma agency in 1997 and he gave evidence on his employee's state of mind, together with relevant detail pertaining to the summer of

1997. He confirmed that Andanson was one of his photographers but said there was a disagreement between them during that summer because Andanson was keen to pursue a better-paid paparazzi-type role rather than the more decorous work predominantly produced by the agency (described as eighty per cent normal photography and twenty per cent paparazzi). Henrotte didn't want his agency to become too focused on paparazzi shots. Andanson, on the other hand, had been complaining to Henrotte that Sygma wasn't properly organised; specifically, other agencies were getting better images of Diana in the South of France.

On 28th or 29th August, Henrotte thought that Andanson was planning to join the paparazzi pack once again. He had become good friends with the most famous one of all – Daniel Angeli – whom Henrotte described as 'king of the genre'. Andanson was visibly planning a more aggressive pursuit of his career to improve, and take control of, his finances. He knew something was imminent with Diana because eight or ten days before arriving in Paris, she had said 'great news was coming'. Andanson's interest in Diana led him to introduce her official photographer, Tim Graham, to the Sygma agency and he knew by the previous Thursday, at least, that Diana and Dodi were flying from Sardinia on the Saturday. He informed Henrotte, who knew Andanson had contacts with airport police.

That Andanson was keen to follow Diana is not in doubt. During the summer he had even hired a boat to get closer to her, which was confirmed in his diary. When he returned home from the South of France on Thursday, 28th August, his diary entries showed that, on Saturday, 30th August, he entered a *'rapport sur le voyage de Lady Di'* (a report on Diana's trip). However, despite knowing that Diana would be in Paris on the Saturday, Andanson claimed to have been going on a photo shoot assignment of Gilbert Becaud for Henrotte in Corsica that day. But do we believe he went?

Henrotte was grilled over the airline ticket to Corsica that he says was booked for Andanson but which he paid for himself; a fax sent to Andanson's home was found by police, confirming that the Corsica flights had been prepaid by Henrotte's Sygma agency. There was clearly no need for Andanson to purchase another ticket, certainly not for transportation purposes. All it did was to enable him to show that a ticket was bought at the airport but without associated proof that he actually took the flight.

Elizabeth Andanson took the stand and confirmed her husband had been 'in turmoil for weeks'; he was planning to leave the Sygma agency before the 31st August and wrote 'la lettre', his letter of resignation to the Sygma agency, on the Saturday morning before Diana was murdered. Eventually he faxed his resignation on 5th or 6th September 1997. Mrs Andanson remembered he had decided to sell his photographs from the Becaud assignment of the 31st August in Corsica to the Sipa agency. They didn't materialise.

It was questioned in court whether Mrs Andanson knew of her husband's intentions to resign before driving the 360 miles round day trip to Paris on the afternoon of Saturday, 30th August 1997 (the same day her husband had written his letter of resignation and the day before Diana's murder) to seek a loan from her husband's boss, Hubert Henrotte, of around $5,000 for her son James Jnr's education in England. Under oath, Elizabeth Andanson denied doing so in court. She also said her husband was at home that day. So he must have left home in the early hours without her knowledge because it seems that James Andanson or someone using his credit card travelled to Vierzon, a town in the centre of France, very early that Saturday and apparently arrived back later that morning.

If this is so, Elizabeth Andanson would have then left to go to Paris within moments of her husband's return and, according to her, when she arrived back home later that day James Andanson would have again left for Paris to catch the plane to Corsica but without her knowledge. We know that Andanson knew of Diana's death because Mrs Andanson gave evidence that he telephoned her at around 5am on the Sunday morning to ask that she contact his boss about it.

Elizabeth Andanson was questioned over road toll tickets provided by the toll company, Cofiroute, which show that somebody using James Andanson's credit card, the one he regularly used and ending in 1300, took the journey to Vierzon in the early hours of Saturday morning. The card was used to pay for the exit at Vierzon East at 4.55am. Somebody made an almost immediate turn-around, with a further ticket being purchased back at Bourges at 5.08am, just thirteen minutes later, with the same card. The costs for this trip were included in Andanson's expenses claim, which indicates it was either James Andanson or his wife, though she denied all knowledge of the trip.

The journey to Vierzon from Andanson's home in Lignières is around 100km in the direction of Bourges and Paris, mostly on the toll road. Vierzon also has a main railway station that connects to Paris, with a vehicle-transport train service and so, allowing for a few minutes' return travelling time between the Vierzon East exit and the return point at Bourges, the driver spent no more than seven minutes in Vierzon. What could have induced Andanson to get up early on the Saturday morning and drive a 200km round trip to spend just minutes in Vierzon on the day before Diana's murder and, according to Elizabeth Andanson, keep this knowledge from her? Could he have been positioning vehicles for other duties?

Either someone took James Andanson to Vierzon on the Saturday to catch the Paris train and has not come forward, or more likely, he was given a lift to Vierzon then went on to Paris when his driver incurred the return charge on the toll road. Andanson routinely used both his Fiat and a motorcycle for separate activities during the course of his paparazzi work.

He had left the motorcycle in the South of France but had it returned by train to Vierzon so it wasn't unusual for him to have both vehicles concomitantly in action; he must also have had assistance in positioning the vehicles because he could hardly have driven both his car and motorcycle home. Asked about her husband's motorcycle being collected from the train, Elizabeth Andanson replied, 'I cannot remember.'

A possibility is that the Fiat was driven to Vierzon and put on the train with the motorcycle being ridden on to Paris, or vice versa. The second driver would have needed a lift to return home and incur the toll charge, but the toll receipts proved this journey took place on the Saturday morning and Mrs Andanson confirmed they didn't have any friends in Vierzon. She couldn't offer any explanation and said that she knew nothing of this journey.

To sum up, we know that Andanson was close to Paris, knowing

Diana would soon be arriving and that all other paparazzi would be descending – and we are expected to believe he just returned home and then headed off to Corsica. Even discounting his level of interest in Diana, it is hard to credit that any aspiring paparazzi would miss out on this news event especially since he had just joined the hottest paparazzi agency in France. After all, the climax of a story he has pursued all summer was developing and he was virtually on site, yet he apparently went on an unproductive jaunt elsewhere. Interestingly, no photographs were ever received by the Sipa or Sygma agency from this supposed Corsica assignment; you might consider this a bizarre outcome for a very determined and aspiring paparazzo.

Andanson's son, James Andanson Jnr, provided a written statement saying that his father telephoned home in the early hours of Sunday, 31st August to say that Diana had been involved in an accident and asked if they would contact the Sygma agency's chief editor. Elizabeth Andanson was asked what time her husband had called and to confirm her son's statement, in which he said, 'I think I remember that he telephoned us at about 4.30 or 5.00am on the Sunday morning on 31st August 1997 and asked us to notify Mr Cardinale that Diana had had an accident.' Again, she said she didn't remember the details. When questioned, his son said he didn't now remember the conversation either, despite his previous written statement that confirmed he did.

One wonders why Andanson didn't phone the Sygma agency himself rather than ask his wife or son. Perhaps he was under pressure over a different issue in the early hours after Diana's murder and didn't wish to risk Henrotte ordering him back to cover the Alma story and so destroy his shaky Corsican alibi?

Elizabeth Andanson said her husband telephoned from somewhere close by (it wasn't established how she could have known where Andanson was). The toll tickets that he relied on showed an exit at 5.48am. The plane ticket to Corsica was purchased at 6.23am from Paris Orly Airport, exactly six hours after the crash and just over two hours after Diana was pronounced dead. All this information was confirmed by Mrs Andanson's bank statements.

Her credit card, numbered 1014, was used to buy this ticket and she confirmed in a written statement to police that, 'I sometimes borrow my husband's credit cards but he never borrows mine,' presumably indicating it was she who made the purchase. But if so, then why and where was Andanson? He had ample time to catch the plane to Figari in Corsica and could have laid his own trail of toll tickets before flying, although it's probable someone else would have prepared the 'evidence' for him.

The Fiat has always been central to this affair and Elizabeth Andanson acknowledged that a journalist had telephoned her one evening in February 1998, saying the 'Fiat Uno had been found in a dump and everybody was going to think it was her husband who was driving it' on that night. She said her husband had immediately told her that he had toll road tickets to show where he was at the time, but as we have seen, this isn't authoritative. But how remarkable that Andanson knew immediately he had tickets available when told that the police would want to speak with him? Perhaps he knew he might need an alibi and prepared accordingly.

The alibi isn't satisfactory, however, for the simple reason that if James Andanson did catch a plane, all it confirms is that he had about five hours to be involved in murder and then drive about twelve miles from central Paris to Orly Airport after his debriefing; the timing fits very well with a convenient escape from the murder scene. He was trying to use the toll road tickets to put him elsewhere when the Alma attack took place, but as we have seen, there was still ample time for him to have been party to a murderous attack on Diana's Mercedes.

An interesting thought now occurs. Since Mrs Andanson and her son initially thought her husband James was murdered by MI6, what made them change their minds? But it is more important to consider what first made her think that the British Security Services had any reason for killing her husband. (Why would they wish to kill a photographer?). Surely this indicates, at least, that she thought she had some reason to suspect her husband's involvement in Diana's murder?

Many stories abound concerning the state of the Andanson's Fiat Uno and Elizabeth Andanson seemed keen to stress that it had not been roadworthy for some time. However, under examination, she didn't offer any specific reason why she felt unsafe driving it. These stories include the Fiat being used as a chicken hutch; another for using the trunk to put out the garbage and then to Elizabeth's mother having use of it for some months prior to it being disposed of (which was, remarkably, eight weeks after Diana's murder when it had been damaged in the exact place where the 'unknown' Fiat had been damaged in the tunnel – this is known because of debris that was collected from the tunnel that matched a Fiat Uno).

Access to the car was then denied to everyone – even Mohamed Al Fayed, who tried to buy it in February 1998, but he was told he couldn't have it for reasons of 'safety'. (*Whose* safety?) Andanson told police he was in St Tropez that weekend and had sold the Fiat in June of that year, though of course both facts were quickly proven to be lies. Having laid the trail for Corsica, why did he feel the need to lie about being somewhere else – perhaps he felt the Corsica alibi too feeble to rely on? But why did he need an alibi at all and why lie about having sold his Fiat in June 1997?

Elizabeth Andanson also added that the Fiat didn't have a tax disc or insurance and hadn't received any technical inspection – just the things that would concern an assassin for a single hit. Even if true, however, would she know whether her husband had spent time working on the car for a very specific purpose?

She was asked whether her husband had displayed any interest in Diana and Dodi's deaths. Somewhat incredibly, she said: 'He had no interest whatsoever and was more preoccupied with his new job.' He was now a full-time *paparazzo* with the largest agency in France – this was his new job! Andanson must have been the only person on the planet who wasn't interested in Diana and Dodi having been the most interested only days before and having made his living from pursuing Diana, so he should have been even more interested than anyone else, from a professional point of view. This is totally implausible but it appears certain James Andanson needed more cash than he made.

A statement was read out that Mrs Andanson gave to the British police (dated 26th April 2006) with regard to James Andanson's death: 'Frankly and honestly, I think he did it [committed suicide] for professional and financial reasons. There were the far-reaching changes in the press which worried him a lot and about which he was right to be worried. Our son had become champion of France a year after starting out in motorsport and that involved expenditure. Furthermore, my husband was having trouble adapting to changes in the press, where the use of digital technology was one of his concerns; my husband had started to age and he was tired. Even though he expressed his concerns to me fairly often, he never followed my advice.'

Just a little earlier she was adamant that he was not concerned when asked about his financial position concerning his son's rather expensive career. Yet it was obvious that Andanson was experiencing financial difficulties. Andanson Jnr was an aspiring racing driver, a sport in which the costs and expenses are high (a figure of $300,000 per year was mentioned). This clearly indicates that his father was in need of funds way in excess of his earnings, which certainly illustrates motive.

James Andanson was a worried man, who couldn't cover his financial commitments. Elizabeth Andanson admitted that, on the day her husband died, she went to the bank to ask for a loan to repair her son's racing car. (She hadn't told her husband because she didn't want him to have 'additional worry.') Her son then added weight to this by saying of his father, 'He seemed unduly worried on the Thursday before his death and perspired a lot,' which all accords with Andanson's bizarre death a few days later and explains why the Andansons originally expressed their opinion that MI6 was responsible for James Andanson's death.

It was put to Mrs Andanson that her son, James Andanson Jnr, had said: 'I do not remember where my father was, but one thing is certain, he was not at home that night.' Elizabeth replied, 'Well, he was wrong.' She was then forced into admitting they had a family dog that sometimes wore a red bandana. This was mentioned because of witness evidence (from a French couple, George and Sabine Douzonne) stating that they saw a man exit the tunnel after the crash, driving a white Fiat Uno with a dog on the rear seat wearing a red bandana.

Elizabeth Andanson was also challenged regarding evidence from family friend, Mrs Josephine Dard, who had said that James Andanson had told them he was in Paris that evening and had been in the tunnel. Elizabeth replied that it was, 'Her word against mine.' Then there was the mysterious call from a man named Philippe Poincloux, who had telephoned James Andanson the day he died. Elizabeth seemed perturbed on being questioned about him. She said this call was for her son, not her husband. When asked, her son said he didn't know Poincloux – he had never spoken with him.

We know a man telephoned Andanson on the afternoon of his death and told him they must meet. Perhaps this was to discuss certain indiscretions regarding Andanson bragging of his presence at Diana's assassination? Why has Philippe Poincloux never been traced or even, to my knowledge, sought?

James Andanson Jnr then took the stand and said that on the night of 30th August, he had gone out to visit a friend near his family home at Lignières, returning at between 12.30 and 1.00am. He was reminded of his previous statement to the police in which he said that he had borrowed his mother's car, but then launched into a barrage of excuses as to why this was wrong (and it was his father's car, after all) supporting his mother's evidence that his father was at home that night. James added that his parents each owned a BMW and one of them had a CD player (his father's car), the other did not.

James was reminded that he had said his father was away at the grape harvest in Bordeaux that weekend but it was shown from James Snr's diary that this was the following weekend (6th and 7th September). In any case, how could Andanson's son have thought that he had borrowed his father's car, if he also thought James Snr was in Bordeaux?

The reason Andanson Jnr gave for knowing his father was definitely not at home that evening was because his car wasn't in the garage when he returned home. Remember, he had said – and this is worth repeating – 'I do not remember where my father was this weekend but one thing is certain, he was not at home.' He then contradicted his mother by saying that his father must have been in

Paris because he would have wanted to cover Diana's visit – going against Elizabeth's evidence that Andanson wasn't at all interested.

Also, why would James Andanson go to Vierzon early on the Saturday morning and hide the fact from his wife without good reason? But, if he didn't hide it, then why did Elizabeth Andanson state that she knew nothing about it in court? If he were visiting Paris on the Saturday just to handle a routine assignment, surely there would be no need to be coy about it.

But this is, perhaps, the most crucial thought on this matter. Andanson Jnr stated that when he got back home that evening, there was no car in the garage. So the fact remains that, despite changing his story to borrowing his father's car and not his mother's, there was still no vehicle in the garage when he returned. Either way, he had just returned in one car and the other wasn't in the garage; both he and his mother confirmed to the court that she was at home – so where was the other car and where was his father?

This was not the only curious fact to emerge. Françoise Dard and her husband Frédéric were family friends who had known Andanson for about thirty years. At the inquests, she and her daughter, Josephine, gave evidence that Andanson had boasted he was in the Alma tunnel when the crash took place. He said he had photographs of the Mercedes that would be *'un Baum'* – in other words, they would rock the world. Josephine Dard added that Andanson had described chasing Diana's Mercedes through Paris on his motorbike.

It is my belief that Andanson was murdered because he was too loose with his tongue and had been giving details of the attack to various people, including Monsieur Frédéric Dard, Françoise's husband, who happened to be a famous French crime writer. Five weeks after Andanson's 'suicide' on 3rd May 2000, Frédéric Dard died of *a heart attack* on 6th June – it would be interesting to know what he was working on at the time.

Josephine Dard reluctantly confirmed that her father had discussed the idea of writing a joint book about Diana's murder a few months before Andanson's 'suicide'. It's obvious why they believed they were special as a team: Andanson's knowledge of events and Dard's writing skills. One wonders whether Andanson made further compelling and incriminating observations to Dard that leaked beyond the confines of their private discussions.

Throughout this hearing, the court repeatedly suggested that Andanson was given to exaggerated statements. We are told of conversations between the Dards and Andanson that were used to prove he was not credible, such as his assertion that he was Irish or the court's suggestion that he claimed to have taken photos actually taken by another. Of course, following these suggestions, the jury might well have dismissed Andanson as a fantasist.

However, Andanson was clearly one of the most successful photographers around, reaffirmed by examples of when he had informed the Dards on some matters before they became public knowledge. Character assassination would assist in having the jury dismiss his reputed comments as spurious, of course, if that was what they wished to do. But remember, the court declared him 'inappropriate to these proceedings', so why spend so much time considering his family? (It is my view that the court hoped to dismiss public concerns surrounding Andanson but without needing to consider him in relation to Diana's murder because that would have been extremely dangerous. There would then have been no excuse for not hearing Christophe Pelât's testimony of having discovered Andanson's body and seeing two bullet holes in his skull.)

It is also remarkable how, despite the court instructing that no one should believe a word Andanson said, they then relied on him having told the Dards that he used his motorbike in Paris, with the implication that he couldn't, therefore, have been driving his Fiat. But if they couldn't believe a word he said, what is the value of this information? You can't have it both ways. (Perhaps this is reminiscent of Richard Tomlinson's, and much other, evidence.)

Andanson couldn't use an old Fiat for chasing after Diana's Mercedes during what he knew would be a hot pursuit through the streets of Paris, attracting great attention especially if there were later more clandestine intentions. But it explains why his motorbike and Fiat would be in Paris for very different duties and why he required a train for transportation. When challenged on this point, Elizabeth Andanson did not refute the idea of the train journey for her husband but merely said that this couldn't be so 'because there was no expenses claim for a train journey'. But perhaps we should again remember Lord Scott Baker's comment that criminals don't write down details that could later be used as evidence against them.

The court also questioned why Andanson didn't sell his photographs of the crash scene with the implication being there must be doubt that he took them, so he must therefore be lying about being in the tunnel. This is typically disingenuous since publishing these photographs would have ensured his arrest, put MI6 right on the spot and brought the curtain down on the whole nasty affair. It would be confirmation that he was there in the tunnel and had been lying about more than his already-proven lies to the police regarding being in St Tropez and having sold the Fiat in June 1997.

Whichever way you look at it, there are numerous unresolved and questionable issues regarding James Andanson's involvement in Diana's death. Now he has gone to his grave but have his secrets gone with him?

Other Participants

The Bodyguards

Diana and Dodi's two bodyguards, Trevor Rees Jones (now Trevor Jones) and Kieran Alexander Wingfield (Kes), are two of the people most closely involved with the couple during their last moments. However, in common with MI6 witnesses, both claimed incomplete or absent memories for the most important questions, especially concerning the five-hour period from 7.00pm through to the fateful journey. So, bearing in mind the issue of whether Henri Paul worked for the British Security Services and thus controlled the evening's activities, let us decide whether their testimony either adds credence to MI6 culpability or assists in refuting it.

On giving evidence at the inquests, Rees Jones had recollection of some points from this five-hour period but none that might assist proof of murder; he further claimed he had no memory of the conversation that he and Kes Wingfield had had with Diana and Dodi when they emerged from the Imperial Suite, nor what Henri Paul had said when he joined them downstairs. He even stated: 'It looks like there is a possibility that Dodi would have put his head out of the door, as I said, and said something, but specific recollections I do not have.' This is strange given that he had spent eleven years stressing Dodi directly issued these instructions.

Testimony was heard that Rees Jones' friends have said that he had recollections of a white three-door hatchback car and two or three motorbikes and of being pursued into the Alma tunnel, though nothing of the Alma crash itself. (Rees Jones denied making this crucial comment.) But this would be further proof that the paparazzi were not first to the tunnel and should never have been incarcerated; witnesses proved that these vehicles vacated the scene almost immediately after the crash; they didn't hang around as it's known the paparazzi did.

If it could be proven that it was Henri Paul who issued the instructions for the rear entrance departure that evening and not Dodi, then Rees Jones's main defence of not challenging this because it would have meant calling the boss a liar would be destroyed. So Rees Jones's insistence that it was Dodi who issued the command during Rees Jones's statements to police over the previous eleven years, and now at these inquests, had to be questioned.

Rees Jones was reminded of these previous statements and some were read out in court. In one, he claimed that he spoke to Dodi as he popped his head out of the Imperial Suite and they had a long conversation that would have taken several minutes to complete. However, CCTV footage showed Dodi had only done this once, for a mere twenty-eight seconds. It was impossible for this information to have passed between two people in such a short time. Rees Jones finally admitted it must have been Henri Paul who gave the order to leave from the rear of the hotel, much earlier in the evening.

The bodyguards could, and should, have questioned the decision for Diana and Dodi to leave by the back door with London, but hadn't done so. Rees Jones then said that Henri Paul had said, 'I have got it from Dodi,' adding, 'I think we expressed our concern.' It was a far cry from his former position of maintaining that Dodi gave the order. One might question why he now remembered this point and at this particular juncture. Of course, Rees Jones had been permitted to view the CCTV evidence on the previous night and that didn't support his previously held position. The evidence that Henri Paul controlled the events that took him to his death, via MI6, was inexorably growing.

Rees Jones made a mysterious telephone call from the Ritz on his mobile/cell phone between 22.00 and 22.30pm that lasted ten minutes. This was after Diana and Dodi had returned to the hotel but he cannot remember who he was phoning, despite the call being of considerable length. He claimed the call was either to Ben Murrell, the bodyguard at the Villa Windsor, or to his central operations room in London. Yet at this point, having just returned to the hotel, Rees Jones didn't know what the evening's plans were, so he wouldn't have had anything to communicate to either Ben Murrell or London. He finally admitted this, but it's impossible to identify the recipient because Rees Jones's telephone records have gone missing.

Mrs Karen Mackenzie, an office worker at Al Fayed's security offices in Park Lane, London, gave a written witness statement on 11th March 2004 saying that she had worked at 60 Park Lane for eleven years where Dodi Fayed had an apartment and she was aware of the various visits of Diana, Princess of Wales just prior to the Paris incident. She knew Trevor Rees Jones because he was the bodyguard for Dodi and used to be in the upper floors of the building; she spoke with Trevor regularly.

Trevor visited about six weeks after the crash and stayed at the adjoining building at 55 Park Lane that has three adjoining floors with number 60. She saw him outside the laundry room but was shocked when she saw that he looked in such a poor state and had lost a lot of weight.

The next time she saw him was a few weeks later towards the end of his stay at number 55 Park Lane. Karen then said, in her own words. 'We passed the time of day for a few moments before the lift arrived. As we parted and Trevor got into the lift, he said to me, "If I remember, they will kill me."'

An incident was then cited which occurred when Rees Jones did a stint at a sports shop in his hometown of Oswestry during his period of crash rehabilitation. While there, he received two or three letters and a number of telephone calls on one day that were 'threatening in nature'. The caller said that they knew who he was, where he worked and where he lived, and told him to keep quiet, adding, 'You know who we are.'

An interesting story about Rees Jones is worth mentioning here. When he had recovered sufficiently to be interviewed, he was driven in a car from the Ritz Hotel to meet with Judge Stephan. The car was stopped by French police and Rees Jones was ordered to transfer to a British Embassy vehicle; Al Fayed's security personnel objected to this transfer but were told that if they obstructed the police, they would be arrested.

After Rees Jones had given evidence to Judge Stephan, he was again driven away in an embassy car. This is reminiscent of John Macnamara's team being told that if they assisted the French police and found any more embarrassing evidence such as James Andanson's Fiat Uno, they too would be arrested. One must question why the police would insist on keeping control over those who were merely seeking justice or giving evidence.

The other bodyguard, Kes Wingfield, was grilled at some length, but despite not having had an accident, his memory was also found to be shaky on most of the important questions. It was also contradictory concerning various statements given over the past eleven years. For example, it had been widely reported that Dodi had said, 'It's been okayed by MF [Mohamed Al Fayed], it's been okayed by my father,' regarding the departure from the rear of the hotel that night – an important ruse to obtain a clear head start before the paparazzi realised they had left the hotel so that Diana and Dodi could avoid being hounded. This had been included in three separate sworn statements to police from Wingfield and espoused by him for eleven years. This was now disproved in court.

In the early evening at around 7.00pm, when the bodyguards travelled with the couple from the Ritz to Dodi's rue Arsène Houssaye apartment, Wingfield confirmed that paparazzi were waiting when they arrived and, on leaving the apartment for the Chez Benoît restaurant prior to returning to the Ritz, paparazzi were waiting there too in addition to Ritz staff members.

Wingfield denied knowing there would be people waiting at Chez Benoît but, having experienced a similar event outside Dodi's apartment, they still allowed Diana and Dodi to travel to the restaurant without an in-car bodyguard, while both he and Rees Jones followed behind in another vehicle. It also appears that MI6 didn't need covert spying techniques to determine where the couple were going – all they had to do was ask the paparazzi.

It was shown that no authority to break with normal rules for close protection work had been given – or sought – from London before proceeding with the rear exit option. Wingfield says it wasn't London's call, yet still stressed that either he or Rees Jones would have contacted the operations room, had they considered it necessary. When challenged that his records didn't show any phone call to London that evening, in response he sardonically suggested that the lawyers should check Rees Jones's records, since he knew these had inexplicably disappeared.

Wingfield was asked how, in general terms, he came to learn of the plan to leave from the rear of the hotel. He immediately responded that, having watched CCTV the previous evening, he remembered Henri Paul coming up to see them in the foyer, saying, 'Dodi has changed the tasking,' during which time Paul, apparently, described a plan for the rear exit. Wingfield here changed his story because he had previously said the first he knew of the plan was fifteen minutes before departure but CCTV footage once more proved that he knew from at least 11.15pm, so had plenty of time to question this decision and obtain countermanding authority from London.

It was also proven that it wasn't Dodi who gave him the order but Henri Paul, who in turn had claimed that it came from Dodi. So Wingfield had permitted Paul to make this decision and could have easily explained his intervention to Dodi, had he decided to telephone London. He didn't bother to check despite Trevor Rees Jones having described it as a 'terrible plan' – like Rees Jones, Wingfield cannot remember the content of the conversation with Henri Paul, including when he was downstairs with Rees Jones and Paul. He did, however, remember that Paul was definitely not drunk but behaving in a normal manner; posing problems for those who wished to claim that Henri Paul was responsible for the crash.

Wingfield was asked why Diana didn't wear a seatbelt and he responded: 'I know Trevor, I have known him of old, and he is a very professional guy and what he will have done is ensured that he mentioned the seatbelts to Dodi and the Princess. Without a shadow of a doubt, Trevor will have mentioned that, but he can't physically grab the Princess of Wales and put a seatbelt on her.'

This point is repeated later that day at the inquests. During the previous morning session, however, when asked by a different lawyer whether he had worked with Trevor prior to this engagement in the summer of 1997, Wingfield replied, 'I knew Trevor from the organisation, but I had never worked with him for any long period of time – only in passing,' which hardly accords with the afternoon's statement that he 'know[s] him of old'. It seemed he was caught in another contradiction.

Asked about his statements to police over the previous ten years, including his participation in Rees-Jones's book (the contents of which he now appeared to disown) he admitted that he had 'fleshed out a few assumptions'. He was then challenged over the three differing versions of events previously given to police and said this was due to 'memory lapses', in common with so much 'evidence' in this whole affair. He then couldn't remember whenever there was a contradiction that couldn't be circumvented, or blamed it on those memory lapses.

So whereas at first he couldn't remember his conversation with Henri Paul, he now had a recollection 'because of the assistance of the DVD'. He was challenged by one of the lawyers that the CCTV didn't tell him what was said and he responded: 'No, but it jogs the memory to what happened on certain occasions.' Finally, he acknowledged the story that he had maintained for ten years, concerning the plan to leave by the hotel's rear being Dodi's, had all been incorrect.

Ben Murrell was another Al Fayed bodyguard. He resigned in August 1998 (two months after Wingfield also resigned) and then sold a story to the *Sun* newspaper, in which he propounded the view that Henri Paul had been drinking and had had a good lunch on the Saturday before driving later that evening. The story says, 'Chatting with Henri Paul, Murrell noticed that he smelled as if he'd had a very good lunch. If he did smell of wine and garlic from a good lunch it was disguised for Kes (Wingfield), a non-smoker, by the offensive smell of Henri Paul's cigars.'

Now both Trevor Rees-Jones and Kes Wingfield had been with Henri Paul during the Saturday, so this does seem strange but it also begs the question as to why these people would issue such misleading statements. Remember, it was Murrell who sold his story to the newspapers accusing Ritz Hotel president Frank Klein and Michael Cole, Al Fayed's publicity chief, of being prepared to deceive the public about Diana and Dodi's intentions regarding the

Villa Windsor, which was robustly denied by both Klein and Cole.

There is no attempt being made here to implicate any bodyguard in the assassination plan since there is no evidence for that. However, I do believe there is some question over whether, had they stuck to procedure, this could have prevented a successful attack. I must leave it to the reader to consider the reasons for their curious memory lapses.

Even accepting that Rees-Jones sustained horrific injuries during the attack, does this account for him remembering irrelevant detail within this crucial five-hour period although none relevant to the question of murder? It's all somewhat reminiscent of MI6 testimony in which the big questions remained unanswered but we instead became bogged down with the minutiae. It makes one wonder whether human brain cells are naturally selective to the benefit of the British Security Services.

Paul Burrell

Before becoming footman to Charles, Prince of Wales, Paul Burrell did this same job for Queen Elizabeth and subsequently performed butler duties for Diana, Princess of Wales, from the spring of 1992. This was the time that Diana embarked on her quest for freedom, determined to begin a new life with people whom she could trust. It is small wonder that the person who was with her most of the time would become a permanent ear for Diana and one of the few people in whom she could confide. With the world against us, people often turn to someone willing to listen for solace.

Burrell undoubtedly supported Diana and had shown his disapproval of Charles, Prince of Wales. However, there is one strong tie that must never be forgotten: he had also worked directly for Queen Elizabeth II and he remained loyal to her. As a result of the Queen's dignified behaviour, in which she managed to stand aloof from the less savoury aspects of Palace conduct, she has retained the affection of most people throughout the realm and this was a position supported by both Diana and Paul Burrell.

One could, perhaps, understand the view that since Diana was dead, defence of the Queen was now paramount and might this not include preventing the truth of what happened on that fateful night of 31st August from ever becoming known? With this in mind, it's easier to take a kinder view of Burrell's position following what happened at the inquests, although I do not endorse it.

Let us start by considering the story of bodyguard-turned-agent Michael Faux, who was employed by Burrell. Faux said that previously, he hadn't been able to come forward because of a confidentiality agreement, but now felt compelled to tell the truth. Burrell apparently received a Bulgari ring from Tebbutt, a royal chauffeur, when he was in Paris, which had been removed from Diana's finger after the crash and this was still encrusted with her blood. DNA testing could prove it was hers and Burrell had told Faux it was an engagement ring (making nonsense of his previous testimony about which finger Diana intended placing it on and of her hopes of returning to Hasnat Khan, the Pakistani heart surgeon she once dated). This ring was in Burrell's possession and went missing, never to be found, which makes the number of curious mishaps associated with him very interesting.

Faux said Burrell asked him to dispose of this ring, along with other jewellery and papers that Burrell had hidden in the house next door to his own in Farndon, where a woman called Maddy lived. Faux described how Burrell was engaged to make an after-dinner speech on a Cunard cruise liner, the *Saga Rose*; Faux alleged he was asked to go with him when, at a convenient moment, he would take the ring, together with some papers and boxes of old books then tip them overboard. Unsurprisingly, Faux didn't like the idea, given that it would have been the criminal offence of disposing of evidence and so he backed off.

Faux went on to say he had also witnessed Burrell burning some letters on Palace-headed notepaper with writing in an old-fashioned typeface that would have come from the sort of typewriter used by the Palace. Other letters that Burrell destroyed were allegedly 'nasty' ones that Prince Philip had sent Diana. If true, why did the butler feel he had to destroy this important evidence? Was he still protecting the Crown?

Despite hearing this evidence, Scott Baker declared whoever was responsible for the disappearance of the Bulgari ring was an 'open question'. In a similar vein, no one knows what happened to Diana's landmine dossier, which had also gone astray (more on that later).

Burrell was keen to try and establish that Dr Hasnat Khan was Diana's true love and that she wanted to rekindle that relationship. Yet surely it's ridiculous to suggest that Diana would end her relationship with Dodi, who was so eminently suited to her, and then recommence a relationship with Khan who, by his own admission, had cooled things because he couldn't deal with Diana's celebrity. Scott Baker did concede this was pure speculation on Burrell's part.

So what was Burrell's motive in all this? Did he simply want to protect the monarchy as a loyal public servant, or was he 'advised' to follow this course by MI6? Thanks to his misguided loyalty, we need to rationalise the truth for ourselves.

Certainly, Scott Baker wasn't very impressed with Paul Burrell's actions, which can be seen from this summation: 'How you should approach his evidence, you may ask? You heard him in the witness box and even without what he said subsequently in the hotel room in New York, it was blindingly obvious, wasn't it, that the evidence that he gave in this courtroom was not the truth, the whole truth and nothing but the truth?' (The mention of 'New York' refers to the occasion when the *Sun*, a British newspaper, videoed and recorded Burrell in a New York hotel room, where he admitted not telling the whole truth to the court.)

Scott Baker went on to make reference to Burrell's claim of having been Diana's 'rock', pointing out that Mr Keen, one of the inquests' lawyers, had described him as 'a rather porous one'. Burrell was accused of trying to ensure that whatever he said wouldn't affect his future enterprises. Scott Baker went on to say:

'It may be that, having heard him give evidence in this court, you are left with a concern about whether what, if anything, he told you can be believed. I advise you to proceed with caution, especially when – and if – you are left with the impression that he only told you what he wanted you to hear.' When considering his evidence on the various notes that Burrell had mentioned, Scott Baker said, 'You may remember he gave inconsistent answers and, in the end, despite promises, produced nothing, including the last letter relating to what has been called the "secret".' In summary, Scott Baker described Burrell's behaviour as 'pretty shabby'.

Lionel Cherruault

The day after Diana's murder, London-based agency photographer Lionel Cherruault had his home raided by thugs in the middle of the night. In evidence, he confirmed that the police attending his home that same night had said he hadn't been burgled but instead intimated that it was the Security Services who had raided his home. Let's look at this disturbing story in more detail.

Early on the Sunday morning after the crash Cherruault had been telephoned by a colleague named Mark Saunders, at this time in the USA, who told him that Diana had been involved in an accident. Saunders said he had a contact able to obtain photographs of Diana taken at the crash scene and asked whether he wanted them, to which Cherruault replied, yes. Clearly anyone who heard this conversation would expect to find some potentially explosive photographs at Cherruault's house.

Cherruault had good reason to believe his conversations were being listened to. On one occasion, he placed his telephone receiver down and picked it up again almost immediately to hear his last conversation being played back. As a result of this and other incidents, he believed his phone lines were being tapped because of his work involving the royals; especially Diana.

At about 3.15am on the Monday morning, just twenty-seven hours after Diana's murder, Cherruault's house was burgled and certain computer equipment taken. The 'burglars' not only took carefully selected items, which would have contained any photographs of Diana and the crashed Mercedes – had there been any – but also searched his car, having taken the car keys from his house. They then left with his wife's car, presumably because they were disturbed by Cherruault who had heard a noise and gone downstairs so the criminals didn't have time to search it. No fingerprints were found in either this car or the house.

The police report, written at the time by investigating officer Sergeant Freeman (now detective chief superintendent) was read out in court and went as follows: 'It appears too much of a coincidence that the burglary took place when it did to not be connected with her death. The property stolen indicates the *thief* (my italics) would have prior knowledge of the house or the victim's business in that an older Apple computer was left at the scene, whereas the standard computer burglar tends to take all computers which are present.'

It clearly shows that this highly experienced police officer believed it wasn't a burglar. Following this, Cherruault accepted an offer from the police for an officer to visit and advise on security, which took place on 4th September 1997. This officer, William Kemp, had studied Cherruault's case before attending at his house and said on arrival: 'First, are you recording our conversation?' 'No, of course not,' he replied, thinking this very odd. Kemp then continued: 'I have to tell you that I have reviewed the report of your burglary and I have to tell you that this is not a burglary, but you were targeted,' to which Cherruault replied: 'What do you mean, "targeted"? Do you mean grey men, MI5, MI6, whatever?' 'You would be surprised what kind of people they use, but I have to reassure you that at no point were your lives in danger,' said Kemp.

In court Kemp tried to refute saying this, of course, but he was skilfully put on the spot and finally forced to admit that he did consider this to be a targeted burglary because it certainly didn't match the usual patterns. (But then, in common with several other witnesses, including Richard Tomlinson, much of their previous and spontaneous comments were changed at the inquest. In my view these witnesses were persuaded to 'play the game' and assist a suitable verdict. I do, however, have sympathy with Richard Tomlinson who had to endure an horrendous time at the hands of his former colleagues. I am sure he just needed to begin a normal life and not be in constant fear of losing it.)

We know that just after the murder, MI6 were urgently trying to keep the lid on all crucial details of the attack and anything associated with it that could possibly cause a problem, especially any evidence of a white Fiat Uno being in the vicinity of the tunnel that night.

The police even denied the Fiat's existence for two weeks after the attack and seized photographs from the paparazzi and anyone else that might endanger their subterfuge. This 'burglary' at Cherruault's home fitted in perfectly with that logic.

In the inquests' summation, comments on Cherruault are reduced to a few lines, in which his conversation with the police officer was described as 'some misunderstanding between them'. An amazing further coincidence is that there are no photographs available of the period between Diana leaving the Ritz and the crash scene. Considering all the paparazzi activity at that time of which we have heard so much, doesn't that seem strange or perhaps you might consider, inevitable?

Nicholas Soames and Simone Simmons

Now we come to another interesting story: that of the missing landmines dossier. It seems that before her death Diana was compiling an anti-landmine dossier, in which she accused the Secret Intelligence Service of being behind the sale of the British landmines that were causing so much misery around the world. Diana had even persuaded Bill Clinton, the then US President, to assist in achieving a ban. Simone Simmons, a close confidante of Diana's, confirmed that Diana compiled a dossier on this and other matters and she was given a copy by Diana for safekeeping.

Diana later sent her a note, which read: 'If something happens to me then MI5 or MI6 will have done it.' Simmons said she placed the inch-thick dossier and note under her mattress, but later burned it, as she feared for her own safety. To no one's great surprise, Diana's original dossier has never been found.

Simmons also said she was present at Kensington Palace when Diana received a call from Nicholas Soames, the great-grandson of Sir Winston Churchill and Prince Charles's close confidant, who was at the time working as a senior minister in the British Government: Minister for the Army. She testified that Soames threatened Diana with an 'accident' if she didn't stop meddling in matters that didn't concern her.

Soames, of course, denied this in court but it is clear where his loyalties lay. Back in the 1990s, he had appeared twice on BBC television in support of Prince Charles: once on *Panorama* and then on *Newsweek*. On both occasions it was to deny that Charles and Camilla Parker Bowles were an item. To achieve this, he misled the people and caused Diana significant distress since he of all people knew the truth – he had made his own house available on many occasions for the illicit relationship to flourish. Soames even went so far as to accuse Diana falsely of being in the advanced stages of paranoia because she had revealed the affair – an accusation that hurt her enormously. In short, it seems that had Diana been paranoid, she had remarkably good reason.

Rosa Monckton

Let's take a look at the testimony of Rosa Monckton – Diana's self-proclaimed best friend. Monckton stated that Dodi and Diana were not that close; according to her, this was just a summer fling and she believed that Diana wanted to get back with Hasnat Khan, the London-based heart specialist with whom she had had an affair not long before meeting Dodi. When Khan gave evidence he clearly stated this was not true and that Diana had given him the heave-ho not long after spending time with Dodi on board the Al Fayed yacht, the *Jonical*, in the July before her murder (don't forget that Diana knew Dodi because her father and stepmother were both friends of the Al Fayed family) – indeed, he was rather upset by it. (But he had previously said he couldn't handle the celebrity that Diana brought with their relationship.)

Monckton also stated that Diana could not have been pregnant: she said she knew this because her 'friend' had menstruated when they were on holiday together, only weeks before her death. Believe what you will about this, but what must be taken into account is that Rosa Monckton's husband, Dominic Lawson, who is an ex-editor of the *Spectator* and the son of an ex-Tory Chancellor of the Exchequer, Nigel Lawson, worked for MI6 and her brother, Anthony Leopold Colyer Monckton was also an MI6 agent. In court she was forced to admit that Diana didn't know of her connections to MI6, but was aware of her antipathy towards them. Clearly she had deliberately kept this from Diana for it would have meant the end of their friendship. One also wonders why Monckton wanted to maintain a friendship with someone who was much younger and who had entirely different interests. Could there have been another agenda?

Interestingly, Rosa Monckton's grandfather had worked for Edward VIII, another member of the royal family that the Establishment wanted to be rid of, and he reported back to MI6 on all Edward's untoward activities. Could this be a case of history repeating itself?

Part Three

Key Eyewitnesses

General Overview

Witnesses in all criminal matters are crucial but especially so in this case. Following inadvertent revelations by MI6, disclosed through the lawyers' interrogation of the various witnesses and with the State standing against justice, a unique opportunity arises to examine and cross-reference this eyewitness evidence to determine flaws and contradictions. Fortunately these are abundant.

I have personally scrutinised over four million words of evidence produced over a six-month period during and after the inquests. What follows are, in my view, the key and relevant witness observations that focus especially on whether there were vehicles at the tunnel that were 'hindering', 'blocking', 'escaping' or 'loitering'. Also, whether there were any vehicles driving dangerously that all then disappeared before the paparazzi arrived.

Once you have considered this evidence, you will then understand why it is my view that the court couldn't allow the verdict option of 'unlawful killing by persons unknown' because, with such strong evidence, they knew what the jury would find (two jurors refused to concur with the verdict given) and such a verdict would have been a de facto conviction for MI6 and extremely dangerous for the monarchy. Although the coroner, Scott Baker, at least conceded: 'There is some evidence, albeit of doubtful quality, that the crash was staged.'

We now produce maps to assist you with visualising the attack scene and to see where each witness was in relation to the Mercedes as the assassins struck. We position four of these witnesses but please place each of the other witnesses relative to them and then you decide whether all of these people could possibly be mistaken or lying. This is the only possible alternative reason for this event other than a state sponsored, or endorsed, murder.

I ask also that you decide if this evidence was of 'doubtful quality' after you have read the following and whether you think the actions of the authorities were in any way excusable.

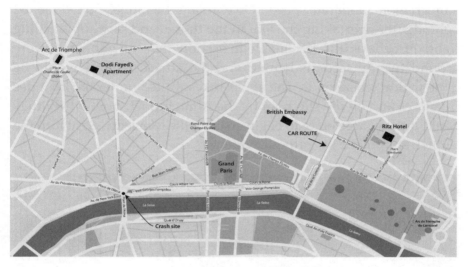

1 The Attack Scenario

The Ritz Hotel to the Alma Tunnel; note the circuitous route being taken by the Mercedes to Dodi's apartment and the close proximity of the British Embassy.

Witness Alain Remy confirms Stephane Darmon's testimony (see Figure 1)

As the Mercedes sped down the freeway and under the Pont Alexandre III, Remy confirmed that a black Mercedes passed him at a speed that he estimated being between 87/94km/hr. At that point no other cars were in sight, either in front of the Mercedes or following it, confirming Darmon's testimony. The attack vehicles lay in wait at the Alma tunnel. So, bearing in mind there were no vehicles near to the Mercedes as it sped towards the Pont des Invalides, where did all the aggressive and pursuing motorbikes that witnesses reported, plus the loitering vehicles at the tunnel's entrance, come from? They were certainly not paparazzi since, at this point, the paparazzi were still travelling from the Ritz. Also, how would they know where the Mercedes intended going?

Following Darmon's supported evidence we may postulate that the paparazzi were some way behind the Mercedes and travelling at a much more moderate speed. (On entering the tunnel, Souad looked behind after overtaking the Fiat in the tunnel and saw approaching lights.) I believe it is reasonable to assume that the paparazzi were around twenty seconds behind and the attack vehicles would be gone within ten seconds. The attack bikes waited under the Pont des Invalides and on the slip road by the Alma tunnel, from where they could quickly accelerate to begin chasing the Mercedes right into the tunnel; supported by witness evidence.

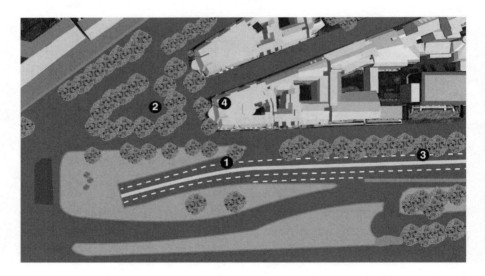

2 The Scene around the Tunnel

An aerial view of the area surrounding the tunnel's entrance that illustrates where vehicles can loiter on the road above, or near the slip road, and then join the freeway at speed.

Position of Eye Witnesses at Tunnel's Entrance
(see Figure 2)

You will observe that vehicles may wait on the road above the freeway. The assassins started moving when they had a signal that the Mercedes was approaching. Once the Mercedes was close, they began the attack with vehicles that had considerable acceleration and were rather like the Turbo Fiat Uno and powerful motorbikes that several witnesses described.

> No. 1: David Laurent and the Blanchards witnessed two cars 'loitering' at the entrance to the Alma; one looked like a Fiat Uno and the other a slightly larger, dark car. Having passed through the tunnel, just ahead of Diana's Mercedes, they all heard a horn that was followed by a loud bang. They then witnessed vehicles fleeing from the tunnel at speed; these people were not hanging around to take photographs, as the paparazzi were in the process of doing when the police arrived.

> No. 2: On the Place de la Reine Astrid (to the right of the approach to the Alma) were the two chauffeurs, Olivier Partouche and Clifford Gooroovadoo. They witnessed motorbikes tailgating the Mercedes at speed and flashes of light coming from inside the tunnel at the moment the Mercedes entered.

> No. 3: As the Mercedes approached the Alma tunnel, American businessman Brian Andersen witnessed motorbikes pursuing the Mercedes 'aggressively and dangerously'; he was approaching the tunnel in a taxi. Andersen also witnessed the flash of light, swiftly followed by a loud bang.

> No. 4: From his hotel bedroom on the rue Jean Goujon, British lawyer Gary Hunter heard the crash and witnessed

the assassins escaping at speed to their hideaway. After passing through the Alma tunnel, the next turn is directly into the rue Débrousse. If, as you will see from the map, the assassins travelled this way and then turned right into Avenue du President Wilson through the Place de l'Alma, right by the Place de la Reine Astrid and then immediately left into rue Jean Goujon, they would not only have passed right below Hunter's bedroom window but would also have taken the shortest and most direct route towards the British Embassy that is less than half a mile from this point. Vehicles could be spirited away in a closed truck and never seen again. Hunter described the vehicles as travelling at 'high speed and bumper to bumper,' saying they looked as if 'they were in a hurry not to be there'. All this was seconds after hearing horrific sounds coming from the Alma tunnel. (Don't forget that Hunter also *died* before the inquest.)

So, we have a Fiat, a slightly larger dark car, a white Mercedes and at least three motorcycles that all vacated the scene and were not there when Darmon arrived. Were these paparazzi that had decided to pass on taking the world's most devastating photographs or is there a more likely scenario? Do not forget that the paparazzi were there later, when the police arrived, in the process of taking photographs. So were these escaping vehicles paparazzi or was it a brutal, state executed murder?

The Mercedes **(see Figure 3)** was travelling at high speed in the left lane and the Fiat, accelerating aggressively from the right, collided with it near the tunnel entrance. You will see the road begins to curve to the right, and there is also a dip in the road at the tunnel's entrance, that caused Henri Paul to collide with the Fiat. At high speed the Mercedes then began to oscillate and had a 'presence in the right lane', so described during the inquests.

Souad Mouffakir and Mohammed Medjhadi had overtaken the Fiat **(see Figure 4)** that was by now in between Souad's car and the Mercedes, just inside the tunnel, driving as though it didn't want to

3 Approach into the Tunnel

This shows the pillars and the tunnel curving towards the right. There is also a dip at the entrance.

4 A Collision at the Entrance

Picture the Mercedes glancing off the wall and striking the Fiat.

overtake them; it was 'much too close'. As the Fiat then overtook them at speed, after the Mercedes crashed, Souad saw the driver's face. Souad also saw lights from approaching vehicles as she looked back at the Mercedes, 'far, far behind'. From witness evidence, these were headlights from Darmon's and Rat's motorbike as they approached the tunnel and who would now be around the Pont des Invalides. Remember, Darmon confirmed that he saw taillights from a vehicle descending into the Alma tunnel when he had just passed under the Pont des Invalides.

François Levistre was travelling through the tunnel at the far end when he heard the crash and, at that moment, witnessed a bright flash of light. He saw people dismount their motorbike, look inside the Mercedes and make a slitting-of-the-throat gesture; they then hastily vacated the tunnel. Levistre described a small white car that the Blanchards, Souad and L'Hostis also saw – and one whose existence the police refused to admit for a further two weeks. When Al Fayed's people found the Fiat a few months later, they were threatened by the French police and told to stop meddling in police 'enquiries' or they would be arrested.

Jean-Pascal and Severine Peyret were also in the tunnel and towards the end of it when they heard a loud noise that was like car hitting another car and then another deeper sound, resembling a car ramming into a truck. A motorcycle rider wearing a white helmet passed them at the end of the tunnel, seconds after they heard these sounds.

Gaëlle L'Hostis & Benoît Boura were together in the opposite lane and saw other vehicles surrounding the Mercedes, including one that was definitely 'hindering' its recovery. They confirmed the colour of the motorcycle driver's helmet as white and the fuel tank yellow, noticing both before it fled the scene.

Grigori Rassinier was also driving under the Pont de l'Alma (in the opposite lane) and saw the motorcycle, confirming it had a yellow tank. He also witnessed the motorbike vacating the scene.

Benoît Boura and Gaëlle l'Hostis

Benoît Boura and his then-girlfriend, Gaëlle l'Hostis (now wife) were approaching the tunnel's entrance in their Renault Super 5 at the same time as the crash. They were travelling in the opposite direction to Diana's Mercedes, in the oncoming lane and on the other side of the pillars, when Boura observed very bright and 'violent flashes' of light ahead which, having been in the army, he immediately thought of as 'radar flashes'.

When he had reached about one third of the way into the tunnel he heard the sound of skidding rubber. 'I heard the noise of the tyres, then an impact,' he said later, thus indicating that these 'very bright' and 'violent flashes' occurred within the tunnel (not from the direction of the river) and only a moment before the Mercedes smashed into the pillars. Between the pillars Boura saw three vehicles approaching: two cars and one motorbike, in addition to the Mercedes. The first car, a dark-coloured saloon, he described as being like a 'Citroën Berlingo Hatch'-type vehicle that was in front of the Mercedes, which suddenly accelerated at the moment when the Mercedes lost control. He saw the Mercedes slide, strike a pillar and then spin around to hit the wall and wind up facing in the opposite direction.

'Thinking about it afterwards, I took it for an impact between two vehicles but bumper-to-bumper, not involving metal,' said Boura before adding that the motorbike rode around the left-hand side of the Mercedes, looked in and then carried on. When asked whether he had seen any other vehicles, in addition to the two cars and one motorbike, he answered: 'Subsequently yes, but at the time no.'

He confirmed that it was 'one or two seconds after' when he saw another motorcycle, coming from behind the Mercedes, which was like a big Piaggio 125 scooter that was rounded at the back. Asked how this motorcycle behaved, he said it also went around the left-hand side of the Mercedes, slowed down, looked into the Mercedes and then accelerated away.

Boura had seen two cars and two motorcycles, all surrounding the Mercedes, which subsequently all departed the scene. There were no other vehicles present, which shows the paparazzi were not the first to arrive at the tunnel. During his summation Scott Baker relied on the fact that 'the difficulty with Mr Boura's evidence is that he says nothing of a white Fiat Uno'. Boura, however, entered the tunnel from the opposite end and was driving his car, so caught only glimpses of the attack vehicles between the pillars; he was less likely to see all the detail than several other witnesses who described the Fiat rather well.

Gaëlle l'Hostis described a similar scene from the passenger seat of Boura's car, although she didn't witness the 'violent flashes' because she was asleep. She was woken when Boura rapidly decelerated. 'Tyres screeching, a car that was apparently braking,' was her description, adding, 'Well, I had the impression that the Mercedes was going towards us and actually, if there had not been pillars, I think we would have collided with it. But as there were pillars, it collided with a pillar.'

She further stated: 'I saw a vehicle of dark colour – a Clio or Super 5 type – that was driving rather slowly. It was "hindering" the Mercedes that was following at a high speed. Behind the big car there was a large motorcycle. I can't be sure how many riders were on it – I knew that it was hindering when I talked to the police officers because where it was in the left-hand lane, it was going at a low speed and even though the driver could hear tyres screeching, he did not do what I would have done – that is, used the right-hand lane instead.'

She then described a large motorbike that was definitely not a Vespa scooter but a much larger machine, so it seems that l'Hostis had seen the motorbike her husband also saw but from a different angle. 'My position when I saw the impact and the other car – the motorcycle was seen just behind,' she confirmed. She also described how this larger bike behaved: 'Well, it slowed down fast, maybe to try and see what had happened with the Mercedes, and then accelerated and left.' L'Hostis said that they parked their car outside the tunnel and, as various vehicles and photographers arrived, 'Some apparent police officers, not wearing uniforms, told the photographers to stop taking photographs.' So, who were these people and how amazing that non-uniformed officers just happened to be there?

Asked about a witness statement she was supposed to have

signed at 2.20am, two hours after the attack, l'Hostis said that it wasn't her signature and not her statement. But surely French police incompetence cannot be the sole reason for so many faux pas? Yet another example of where the police had begun building their 'accident' theory.

David Laurent and the Blanchards

That evening David Laurent was driving his green Volkswagen Polo along the embankment towards the Alma tunnel, accompanied by his girlfriend Nathalie Blanchard and her parents, Lilian and Michelle, together with their son, Gregory. As they approached the Alma tunnel, two cars were travelling very slowly near the tunnel on the right-hand slope. David said: 'I was taken by surprise but even so, I had time to pull the steering wheel to the left to avoid them.'

Laurent described one car as a small, old and light-coloured hatchback like a Fiat Uno. He thought there were 'two figures in the front and, possibly, others in the back'. After Laurent overtook this car and then the second, he didn't notice the people in the second car. The cars didn't seem to be broken down or damaged, he added.

He continued: 'When I came out of the tunnel, just before going down the lane on the right, leading to the Place du Trocadero, I heard an insistent hooting that lasted for about two seconds, then the sound of braking for two or three seconds and a loud crash all coming from behind my car.' Natalie Blanchard mirrored this statement, adding that she believed the car they overtook was an Austin Mini or a Fiat Uno.

David's future father-in-law, Lilian Blanchard, confirms overtaking these two cars and added, 'I remember we overtook these two cars. They were following each other closely and were on the far right-hand lane.' As David exited the tunnel, Lilian turned his head and saw the two cars emerge from the tunnel at speed.

Now let's consider the significance of this evidence. There is no doubt these two cars were ahead of the Mercedes when they approached the tunnel so they were not 'following vehicles' as described at the inquests, but vehicles that had already positioned themselves at the tunnel entrance, clearly having advance notice that the Mercedes would be travelling along this route. The cars were 'following each other closely', which indicates they were 'in it together' and were 'loitering', so had a collective purpose in being there. This was further confirmed by Michelle, David's mother: 'He [David] overtook two cars driving one behind the other.'

The motorbikes seen to be aggressively following the Mercedes by two other witnesses (Thierry Hackett and Brian Andersen) would have been at the entrance to the Alma tunnel very soon after David Laurent entered it, hence the reason why he and his family heard the sound of the crash. These aggressive motorcycles forced Henri Paul into going faster and faster to meet loitering vehicles that all then vacated the scene within seconds and, in the manner that Lilian Blanchard and other witnesses described, just moments after Laurent heard the crash in the tunnel. Does this look like an accident? Let us consider further witness statements.

Jean-Pascal and Severine Peyret

Later on the day of the crash more witnesses came forward. Jean-Pascal Peyret, who had dined with his wife, Severine, in Paris the night before and returned home through the Alma tunnel, realised that what he had heard must have been the attack in the tunnel. He telephoned the Criminal Brigade and the couple returned to Paris for interview.

Peyret said he had passed through the tunnel and was ascending the ramp, almost at the exit, when he heard 'the sound of an impact and then, after that, another sound that was a much heavier, bigger, bigger impact'. He added that he was driving at about fifty mph and must have been at least fifty yards in front of the Mercedes, before saying: 'The first sounded like car against car, but the second was a deeper sound, like a car ramming into a truck.' This second sound was the Mercedes self-destructing against the pillar.

Peyret's wife Severine added that just after the louder crash when they were 'towards the exit', they were passed by a motorcycle mounted by a single rider wearing a white helmet and a dark jacket. It was 'a matter of seconds after the crash'. All this concurs with Benoît

Boura's account of seeing a motorcycle pass the mangled Mercedes just after the attack, before accelerating away.

This is not the action of a paparazzo, who would have lingered to get a photo; in her statement to police later on the Sunday of the attack, Severine said: 'I quickly understood that the motorcycle could have been implicated in the collision and that its rider was trying to get away from the place.'

Peyret also stated that no car passed his Saab after the attack, further enhancing the view that the escape route was the same for these vehicles as it was for the small car and the white Mercedes that another witness, British lawyer Gary Hunter, saw fleeing via la rue Débrousse and down la rue Jean-Goujon, then under his bedroom window (we shall consider Hunter's account in more detail later). Other witnesses saw one bike with two riders and others two bikes, both with one rider, but by all accounts these motorbikes vacated the scene immediately after the crash and they were definitely not paparazzi.

It is of course possible that a pillion rider dismounted in the tunnel and left his driver to flee the scene, when he could then administer the coup de grace and mingle with the gathering throng. Indeed he may be an unidentified face on the photographs MI6 were keen to seize in the Monday morning raid on Lionel Cherruault's London home just twenty-seven hours later.

Mohammed Medjhadi and Souad Mouffakir

Another car had also been in the lane between Jean-Pascal Peyret and the Mercedes. Mohammed Medjhadi and his girlfriend Souad Mouffakir were the closest witnesses to the crash and contacted police the next morning upon learning the identity of the victims.

That night they were driving home to the western Paris suburbs via the Alma tunnel in Medjhadi's light grey Citroën BX when they passed a white Fiat that was travelling slowly, just ahead of them in the left lane, which they overtook as they entered the tunnel. The Fiat was clearly preoccupied with other matters and wanted to maintain its low speed and Mouffakir said that it remained between the Mercedes and their vehicle. She added that the driver was looking for something on the seat next to him and she had noticed the Fiat before hearing the Mercedes' brakes 'because it [the Fiat] was driving much too close to us – it did not want to overtake us. It was really close to us; too close to us.'

She added that, when she turned around on hearing the screeching of tyres, 'I saw a large Mercedes heading sideways across the road onto the island and strike a concrete pillar. Our vehicle was about thirty or forty yards in front of the Mercedes at the moment of the shock. My friend Mohammed immediately accelerated in order not to be hit from behind. After this first contact, the vehicle [the Mercedes] pivoted around and smashed into the other [right] pavement. I could clearly see the chauffeur's body slumped over the wheel.' The Fiat passed them at speed, after the attack had taken place, and Mouffakir saw the driver's face.

She then added, 'I saw other vehicles approaching from behind the Mercedes.' When the court asked how far away they were, she answered, 'Quite far,' and then, on being asked the same question later, she reaffirmed, 'Far, far behind,' again supporting the view that the paparazzi were not close to the Mercedes and weren't there at the time of the attack. By the time they arrived, the assassins had gone.

Mouffakir also confirmed that she saw a flash of light. It was argued in court that this flash of light could have been from the Bateaux Mouches (excursion boats) on the river, but Mouffakir was in the tunnel when she saw this flash so it couldn't have been from a boat. Note too that the flash was again witnessed as being perfectly timed just prior to the crash.

Evidence from Mouffakir, corroborated by Peyret and Hunter, endorses evidence that these attack vehicles vacated the freeway via rue Débrousse after the assault since no vehicles passed them as they continued westward towards the Place du Trocadero. This statement is consistent with the logic that attack vehicles would take the first available exit from the freeway and head towards where the British lawyer, Gary Hunter (now deceased) witnessed these two vehicles driving 'at an inordinate speed, bumper to bumper' towards the Place du President Wilson and in the direction of the British Embassy.

Meanwhile, Mohammed Medjhadi, Souad's then-boyfriend, saw the attack from a different angle through his wing mirror. 'I was driving at about fifty–fifty-five mph,' he told police, 'when I was alerted by a noise of skidding tyres behind me. I was at that moment in the tunnel, on the flat part just before ascending the ramp. The noise was loud because I could hear it over the sound of my radio. I looked in the left-hand wing mirror; I was in the right lane. I saw a big Mercedes in the bottom of the tunnel, moving across the roadway. It was going very fast, I'd say at least ninety km/h [re-affirmed by witness, Alain Remy].

'The Mercedes was sliding in such a way that it formed a forty-five-degree angle with the central island. I remember quite clearly because I saw its headlights illuminate the eastbound lane. I continued to look in the mirror and I saw the Mercedes straighten itself and head back to the right, then immediately, I heard a huge noise and saw a piece of the car go flying as the vehicle smashed into the central pillar. It then bounced off its axis and headed back to the right, but I could no longer see it in my mirror.'

Mouffakir was also asked whether it is true that she had been frightened about mentioning the Fiat to the police and she said, 'Maybe, yes.' When asked what she was scared of, she replied: 'By the whole story.' This is in common with others who realised this was an attack and, when they knew the Princess was involved, the same first thought that Mrs Levistre had of this being a terrorist attack must also have occurred to them. Mouffakir didn't think that this was an accident, nor did any other witness.

Since this information is highly supportive of a murder scenario, one would think the authorities would at least interview her and examine the evidence. Asked whether she had been approached by the British police at any time, her answer was 'no'.

Olivier Partouche and Clifford Gooroovadoo

Chauffeurs Oliver Partouche and Clifford Gooroovadoo also witnessed two cars approaching the tunnel on the night of the crash. They were standing about fifty yards from the tunnel entrance on the Place de la

Reine Astrid, which, ironically, is named after a Belgian queen who died here in a car accident.

Partouche made a statement to police two hours and twenty-five minutes after the crash in which he said: 'The first vehicle was visibly travelling in such a manner as to slow down the Mercedes that was following it. Behind the Mercedes – also tailgating it – was a motorcycle, although I could not see if two people were on it. It was a powerful one. In front of the Mercedes was a dark car, which I could not tell you the make. It was dark in colour and clearly this car was trying to make the Mercedes slow down. The Mercedes was black – I think it was an S-Class 500. The object of this manoeuvre was to make it possible for the paparazzi to take photographs. The Mercedes and *the blocking vehicle* [my italics] were in the right-hand lane and were heading towards Boulogne. The Mercedes driver pulled out to the left. I heard the chauffeur of the Mercedes change gear in order to accelerate and pass the car in its way. Then the Mercedes descended into the tunnel and I heard a huge noise.' So, apart from describing the assassins as paparazzi, this is how the attack would have happened. (I cannot assume witness evidence is other than stated but I just point out that the assassins were hoping that they would be mistaken for paparazzi.)

Partouche was asked about flashes and confirmed that he saw a powerful one coming from the tunnel, not the river, as the Mercedes entered. This is how one would expect assassins to behave and it's clear the motorbikes and cars were working in tandem. It would appear to spectators as though these vehicles tried to slow the Mercedes down but they were forcing Henri Paul to accelerate and overtake this hindering vehicle, thus increasing his speed to improve on the probability of death.

The vehicles knew in advance that the Mercedes was coming, which was information they must have obtained from intelligence sources. Dodi kept this escape route secret from everyone except Rocher and Paul. Partouche had naturally considered that these motorbikes were paparazzi, as the assassins had intended, but everyone confirmed that they didn't hang around after their attack.

Clifford Gooroovadoo (another witness who said he was too

afraid to attend the hearing) gave a similar description prior to the inquests, saying, 'The Mercedes was behind another vehicle; the vehicle in front of it was going at a normal speed. The consequence is that the Mercedes accelerated strongly in order to swing left and pass this car.' He further added that there was a motorcycle about thirty or forty yards behind the Mercedes: 'I can't tell you how many people were on the motorcycle but it was going fast. To reply to your question, I think that I saw flashes before the vehicles disappeared into the underpass. We saw two vehicles on the embankment.'

This latter observation was unusual but reported by others so again very difficult to ignore or sidestep. These could be back-up vehicles, positioned to collect injured personnel and the British lawyer Gary Hunter (of more later) described two cars fleeing under his bedroom window only seconds after he heard the crash. These vehicles were certainly not at the tunnel when other people, including the paparazzi, arrived moments later. Unfortunately, Hunter died before the inquests began and so was unable to reinforce this crucial testimony.

At the beginning of his cross-examination Olivier Partouche remembered he had seen more than one motorcycle travelling behind the Mercedes but when he gave statements to the police, only hours after the crash, he had confirmed seeing only one. Under cross-examination, the question was raised as to whether his memory was more likely to be accurate only a few hours after the crash than after ten years. Of course, MI6 would much prefer that this testimony indicated more than one motorbike because that would be the case if these vehicles were pursuing paparazzi. It would be more likely that there would be only one, or perhaps two, if these were in fact aggressive assassins with a very specific function: one behind to make the Mercedes go faster and one in front to deliver the deadly flash into Paul's eyes from their handheld strobe gun, as described by former MI6 agent, Richard Tomlinson.

Evidence from other witnesses also stated there were only one or two motorbikes and all added that they carried on their way, having first stopped to glance at the crash victims. They didn't remain to take photographs of the wrecked Mercedes, unlike the paparazzi, who were in the process of doing just that when the police arrived.

Partouche's comments on hearing a car change gear and the brutal acceleration described earlier by the witness Boura concur with all rational thinking on exactly what this meant. A Mercedes automatic will not produce a sound such as the one described when changing gear, so although Partouche said this could have been the Mercedes changing to the automatic gearbox sport mode, this sound would more logically be from the smaller car described by several of the witnesses, just at the point where it would have accelerated brutally to get in front of the Mercedes for the attack. This occurred at exactly the point where it would need to accelerate and block the Mercedes' option to turn to the right and avoid the pillars. Paul knew the car was there but was most probably unable to see.

This car accelerated, or rapidly decelerated, after the attack to keep clear of the Mercedes so it would not be involved in the ensuing crash. The reflexes and driving skills of the pilot chauffeur, Henri Paul, nearly denied the assassins their victory but being temporarily blinded, he was disorientated and very possibly trying to steer a disabled car (the Mercedes was not sent to Britain for seven years and the authorities refused offers of help from the Mercedes factory in Germany). Paul reduced speed by braking hard but knowing there was a car to his right made him intuitively turn the wheel in the opposite direction...into the pillars of the Alma tunnel, as intended by the assassins.

François Levistre

Also in the tunnel that night was François Levistre, a harbour pilot from Rouen. He said that as he entered the expressway via the parallel right-hand access road, the Cours Albert Ier, he witnessed the Mercedes approaching the tunnel in his rear-view mirror; two motorcycles were close by and a white car in front. One of the motorcycles swerved in front of the Mercedes and, before it lost control, there was a flash of light.

'But then I was out of the tunnel and heard, but did not see, the impact,' he said. 'I immediately pulled my car over to the kerb,

but my wife said, "Let's get out of here – it's a terrorist attack!"'
In the testimony he gave police, Levistre, concurring with other
eyewitness accounts, said he saw a big motorcycle with two riders
emerge from the tunnel immediately after the crash. He added
that the two men who delivered the flash into Henri Paul's eyes
stopped their bike, when one rider dismounted and walked over
to the car, made a slitting-of-the-throat gesture to his compatriot
and walked back to the bike. Both went past Levistre's stationary
car at the end of the tunnel, looking at him as they did so. Levistre
states there was no interpreting this as anything other than a
murderous attack.

During his summation, Scott Baker's last dismissive words on
Levistre were: 'He has given greatly conflicting accounts; he has a
criminal record in France. You may think his testimony is worthless.'
So, let us examine Levistre's evidence more closely for ourselves
before we decide whether to agree with such a statement.

Forty-three pages of Levistre's testimony were considered
because of the importance of negating and disregarding it (in sharp
contrast to the treatment afforded Paul Burrell after his confession
in a New York hotel room that he hadn't told the whole truth to
the court, which nevertheless did not result in his testimony being
disregarded because, in my view, some of it suited the court's
purpose).

At the commencement of his testimony, Levistre complained
that statements he gave the police, within days of the attack, were
transcribed incorrectly but he was told by the lawyer: 'We shall come
back to that' – which, of course, they never did. He persistently stated
the police were 'trying to put him out of comfort', in common with
other eyewitnesses like American businessman Brian Andersen,
French restaurant worker Erik Petel and Gary Hunter, the British
lawyer, all of whose testimonies we shall consider later.

As for Levistre acquiring a criminal record some twenty or so
years previously, how many people who transgress against society
pay their debt and re-join on a straight course? Surely this is how a
fair and forgiving democratic system is supposed to function. When
a citizen's punishment is fulfilled, they are permitted to begin again

and not have their word presumed irrelevant or suspect, especially where much of the evidence is corroborated.

In any case, the offence referred to was where Levistre had a firearm without a licence for which he served a time in prison twenty years earlier in the late seventies. The other is where his wife offered to act as a surrogate mother for a wealthy German couple. This is illegal in France, though not in the USA or UK. The case never even went to trial. In fact, in light of the attention that Levistre knew this evidence would receive, it's unlikely he would wish to be in the spotlight and ridiculed. He would surely rather not be noticed, which accords with his initial reluctance to come forward.

Levistre said that there wasn't much traffic around on that night because it was holiday season in France, so he was able to travel safely at a greater speed than usual. The traffic lights were synchronised and so provided that one travelled at a fixed speed, it was possible to avoid stopping. As we shall see, this is what Gary Hunter described when he witnessed the assassins escape the murder scene from his bedroom window, when a one-way system allowed them an unimpeded return run to their abode.

One reason for the mystery as to why Henri Paul chose to drive to Dodi's apartment at la rue Arsène Houssaye, via the Alma, was given as to avoid the traffic on the main route back from the Ritz Hotel, the Avenue de Champs-Elysées. But here we have evidence there was very little traffic. Klein had said that no one would travel to Dodi's apartment via Trocadero because the traffic problems tend to be greater. This was supported by other witnesses, so who gave Henri Paul his orders to go that circuitous route and why? (Please satisfy yourselves on the position of the vehicles from the map.)

Levistre also saw several cars parked alongside the service road just before reaching the expressway by the Alma, as did eyewitnesses Hounsfield, Partouche and Gooroovadoo, and also under the Alma Bridge, which was very unusual. They certainly weren't there a few minutes later, when various other people and the police arrived.

The main thrust in court was to convince the jury that Levistre wasn't to be trusted and couldn't even decide on how many vehicles he saw approaching the Alma tunnel as he entered the expressway.

He was badgered as to why he had given conflicting accounts on this number, exactly where cars were and who was overtaking who. This is, in my view, an attempt to destroy his credibility in the jurors' minds. Levistre stated early in his evidence to the inquests that the first accounts he gave to police differed because they took down incorrect, or deliberately misleading, statements (in common with several other witnesses) the day after Diana's murder, but the court chose not to consider this.

The number of approaching headlights that Levistre remembered seeing surely didn't make any material difference – three, four or five? If the inquests had been held several years earlier, perhaps people's memories might have been brighter as stated before, but these vehicles were seen by other witnesses and there was no misinterpreting the flash (as noted by several others) or the gesture of the slitting of a human throat.

The court omitted the elements of Levistre's testimony that were without question, consistent despite a great deal of time having passed since the events took place. Levistre stated all along that the police wanted to 'put him out of comfort' and he described an incident in which French police officer, Lieutenant Isabelle Defez – who transcribed his statement on 1st September 1997 – called him a liar merely for mentioning that he had passed the Brazilian Embassy. She claimed that there wasn't a Brazilian Embassy in that location; she was wrong and two of her colleagues corrected her in Levistre's presence.

Remember this incident occurred the day after Diana's shocking death and the police were already calling people liars when they were merely giving a statement over what would have been a simple error, if incorrect. Surely at this stage they should have collected evidence and, if necessary, dispute any issues with witnesses later if the facts were not corroborated? Why put people 'out of comfort' if they wanted the truth?

The flash that Levistre saw was also witnessed by Brian Andersen, Boura, l'Hostis, Souad, Laurent and family, Petel, Partouche, Gooroovadoo and Brenda Wells, a British secretary and it wasn't the only fact to be corroborated by other witnesses. A few days later,

Levistre checked the tunnel and found car debris, which was a point also made by others, clearly illustrating that the French police were not trying to collect evidence and solve a crime – they already knew the answer. This is, in my view, why they removed the Mercedes from the tunnel with alacrity.

Levistre was questioned by lawyers about a contradictory statement he made when later interviewed by a TV channel, as to what he saw while stationary at the end of the tunnel and looking back. He said a crowd had formed, having previously stated there was none before he left the scene. In fact, the explanation is a simple, understandable and honest one. Levistre was being interviewed and asked questions some days after the murder but not before he read newspapers and spoke with others concerning what happened after he left the murder scene. He quoted other witnesses who arrived after he had left and included his own observations. The lawyer continued to press the point, stating what Levistre said was not true, despite having given a very acceptable explanation. It would appear he is not permitted to do as everybody else and develop an opinion after hearing evidence from others.

The lawyer for the police continued the questioning and now accused Levistre of not mentioning the pillion passenger getting off the bike and making a slitting-of-the-throat gesture with his hands before that day in court. However, the lawyer acting for Mohamed Al Fayed, Michael Mansfield corrected this and proved that the lawyer for the police got it wrong; Levistre had indeed mentioned it. Despite this, Levistre then faced a further onslaught from this lawyer, who said that he wasn't interested in what he had told the TV cameras (why then ask the question?). By this point, all rationality had gone out of the window and Levistre, who had to rely on interpreters, was left to face an extremely hostile court alone.

Not surprisingly, Levistre's wife Valerie refused to give testimony following her husband's maltreatment, but she did say that the police had previously interviewed her and written her words down incorrectly. She said, 'If you say black, they write down white,' and this certainly accorded with her husband's, and other witnesses' experiences.

Brian Andersen

American businessman Brian Andersen said he was riding in a taxi on the expressway towards the Alma tunnel when the Mercedes, closely followed by two motorcycles, passed him. The first motorcycle, mounted by two people, seemed to be heading in a direction to get in front of the car. Making reference to this particular motorcycle, he stated: 'I felt that this motorcycle, certainly without hesitation and any doubt whatsoever, was driving aggressively and dangerously.'

This is precisely how the attack would have been executed prior to the pillion rider delivering the flash into Henri Paul's eyes. On this point Andersen added further dangerous testimony by stating that he saw a powerful flash of light and then heard a loud bang, separated by between half a second and a second. This was just before the Mercedes met with the pillar and is logical because light travels faster than sound so there would be a small lapse between the two, had an explosion rendered the car's steering inoperable, together with a concomitant flash of light to ensure the driver was unable to see. Again, it was suggested in court that the flash was most probably from the bateaux-mouches (excursion boats) area of the river – they had to concede a flash of light occurred because too many people witnessed it. However, much evidence made it clear that it came from within the tunnel.

Astonishingly, Scott Baker told the jury there was serious doubt as to whether Brian Andersen was even present at the murder scene, accepting the testimony of French police commissaire, Eric Gigou, that Andersen didn't even contact them. Andersen asserted that the police didn't want to hear his testimony and even held his passport for a while but Scott Baker dismissed this, despite having criticised the police on several other issues. It would appear that fabricating witness testimony is a recurrent police ploy.

Andersen said that, after having dinner on the evening of 30th August, his friend dropped him off at the taxi rank – he believed at about 11.30pm. Lawyers for the police attempted to say that it didn't correlate with the time that it would take Andersen's taxi to travel to the Alma tunnel, which they believed would be about fifteen to twenty minutes. The attack took place at 12.21pm, so Andersen was made out to be a liar for an understandable uncertainty over a few minutes. (How many people would care what precise time they caught a taxi, if in Paris and close to midnight? I know that I wouldn't!)

Andersen's testimony, together with that of all other potentially dangerous witnesses, was systematically shredded and undermined. The court even tried to cast doubt over telephone calls made from his hotel room at the time of the attack, from automated calls to and from his fax machine to his home in the US, but were unable to offer any evidence that these calls had not been automatically made.

British lawyer Gary Hunter (of more later) also said his deposition wasn't accepted by the French police concerning his having witnessed cars escaping the murder scene and Erik Petel, who witnessed much the same as Andersen, wasn't even called to give evidence, having first been told by the Chief of the Paris Police, Philippe Massoni, not to make his testimony known. Levistre also had his testimony dismissed, in common with several other witnesses (let us not forget the fate of James Andanson). Is it any wonder that witnesses were reluctant to come forward when they knew they would meet with such disdain, or worse?

Christophe Pelât

Another such witness who wished to come forward but was refused was Christophe Pelât. He was the fireman who attended the smouldering BMW car that contained the remains of James Andanson after he had committed 'suicide' near Montpelier in the South of France in May 2000. Pelât saw two bullet holes in Andanson's skull and expressed his desire to attend court and give very damning evidence but the court ruled that Andanson had 'nothing to do with these proceedings'. This was despite the court spending a huge amount of time interviewing several witnesses, including Andanson's own family, concerning his colourful life so it is curious that his death was apparently considered to be of no interest, despite the highly contentious manner of it. There is no doubt that Pelât's testimony would have created serious disquiet in the jurors' minds, had he been allowed to take the stand.

Georges and Sabine Douzonne

Most disturbingly, or perhaps one might by now be thinking inevitably, Pelât was not the only witness who wished to give evidence but whose testimony was ignored or ridiculed. Six days after the crash, Georges and Sabine Douzonne came forward to further confound the authorities in their attempts to deny the existence of the Fiat Uno. They testified that they had crossed the Alma Bridge from the seventh District at about 12.25am and turned west onto the road that parallels the expressway. As they entered the dual carriageway, a white Fiat UNO passed them. The driver was described as a brown-haired 'European type', about forty years old, who behaved nervously by zigzagging and repeatedly looking in his rear view mirror; suddenly he then pulled to the right and parked on the side of the road.

The Douzonnes told police that the Fiat made a loud noise and backfired, as if its exhaust silencer had been damaged. The driver of this car never came forward, so if this wasn't the one involved in the attack, then we have two Fiats in the same place at exactly the same time, both with damaged exhausts and with owners who haven't come forward. In addition, and by a further remarkable coincidence, the Fiat Uno's exhaust that this witness described as damaged was from the same area of the attack vehicle that was damaged in the collision with the Mercedes, as confirmed by the debris collected in the tunnel.

Grigori Rassinier

Professional photographer Grigori Rassinier, who was not involved with the paparazzi on that fateful August night, described what he saw on entering the tunnel in his blue VW Passat from the opposite direction to the Mercedes and just before the attack. Rassinier gave three written statements but didn't attend the hearing, despite offering to do so, because the court said that where, in the case of some witnesses, the evidence they would give is known to be incontrovertible, they need not attend but could offer affidavit evidence instead. Unfortunately, most of these witnesses had significant evidence to impart and they would have made it impossible to render any verdict other than murder if they had attended. In addition to Rassinier these include Dr Dion, Gamblin, Pierre Suu, Remy and Christophe Pelât plus all the French doctors and all the paparazzi.

Here are some excerpts from Rassinier: 'I quickly got into the left-hand lane. The traffic was normal. I was driving at a constant speed of fifty km per hour. As I entered the tunnel under the Alma Bridge going down the slope, I heard an extremely violent crash. I carried on, lifting off the accelerator. I also instinctively put my hazard warning lights on. It was then that I noticed the rear of a large dark car coming to a halt. At that point something important took place that made me decide to give evidence.

'I saw a motorcycle in the same direction of traffic flow as the Mercedes. I do not know whether it was a motorcycle that arrived behind the Mercedes and which swerved in order to avoid the wreckage or if it was somebody who set off very quickly from that place. It was a fairly large motorcycle with a round yellow headlamp. I got an impression of white – I do not know whether it was the helmet or the motorcycle's fuel tank. My clearest recollection of any other vehicle on that side of the tunnel was of the motorcycle, as described. My impression is that it must have been following the Mercedes; it was to my mind relatively close behind the Mercedes, but not so close as to have actually been caught up in the accident because of the fact that it was able to swerve around the crashed car. Although I cannot say for certain, I believe that it continued on its way out of the tunnel rather than stopping in the tunnel after the crash.' (Of course there is additional evidence that this is precisely what this motorcyclist did.)

This description fits in with other testimony, concurring even with the colour of the rider's helmet or tank, thus reinforcing evidence of motorcyclists driving in the manner described. Two further interesting points were then made by Rassinier: 'When I got to the exit, I noticed that some cars had stopped and people were making their way towards the scene of the accident. They did not have cameras.' It could have taken Rassinier just seconds to reach the end of the tunnel and already people were gathering in numbers; vehicles were seen by three or four witnesses who had by now left the scene, not stopping to take photographs.

This shows that this attack was over within seconds and once more concurs with Gary Hunter's testimony, as we shall see, regarding the timing of when he witnessed cars fleeing the scene and passing under his bedroom window, ninety seconds or so after the attack.

As an aside, Scott Baker said in his summation: 'If there was any blocking vehicle or flashing light, he did not see either and you may ask why.' The answer is simple: Rassinier was entering the tunnel from the opposite end to the Mercedes, as did Benoît Boura, of which Scott Baker didn't remind the jury, and the pillars would have prevented him from seeing much detail until he was nearer the end of the tunnel that the Mercedes had entered. He did, however, accept from this 'incontrovertible' evidence that at least one motorbike had been following the Mercedes and continued out of the tunnel, thus confirming there were other vehicles there, as well as the Fiat that didn't stop, and well before the paparazzi arrived.

Rassinier also said Scotland Yard contacted him by letter, in which he was told that they were conducting a new 'investigation' and asked if he was prepared to come to London and give evidence or testimony, if required (you will recall the British police denying they were conducting an investigation but said they were only involved in a role as liaison when excusing their behaviour over the Mishcon note). Rassinier returned the attached form and stated he was prepared to do both. Nothing happened for six months but eventually he was contacted again, this time by telephone: 'They again sought confirmation that I was willing to go to London, whether to make a further statement or to attend the inquests. I again confirmed my willingness. I have not heard anything further since then.'

This is in common with other witnesses including Souad Mouffakir, who was closest when the assault took place. Bear in mind that the

British police were supposed to be seeking justice and this man witnessed at least one of the possible assassins leave the scene. The court added: 'The reason this witness has not been called to give evidence is that his evidence has been agreed to be uncontroversial and can be read to you [the jury] rather than troubling him to come to court.' If so, one presumes the court accepted there were three or four vehicles around the Mercedes at the time of impact, which immediately left the scene, and no paparazzi vehicles were present. If we consider the evidence of Souad Mouffakir from within the tunnel and the second bike seen by Boura that was behind the Mercedes, plus David Laurent and his family describing loitering vehicles, then the whole picture may be seen. With this information, how could the paparazzi be vilified and the jury denied a verdict of unlawful killing by persons unknown if justice was being sought?

Alain Remy

Driving along the expressway in his black Volkswagen Golf under the Pont Alexandre III, Alain Remy was overtaken by the Mercedes travelling at a speed that he estimated to be between eighty-seven to ninety-four km/h. He didn't see any paparazzi vehicles, which is most illuminating because at this point, they would have been tailgating the Mercedes, if they really had pursued it from the Ritz Hotel. The attack cars waited by the Alma entrance, as evidence has already stated, and the attack bikes were at the other side of the Pont des Invalides, which is along the embankment from the Pont Alexandre III and just before the Alma. This was the best position because there would be fewer witnesses if they only entered the fray at the last moment. The paparazzi followed some twenty seconds or so behind.

Dr Elizabeth Dion

The issue of Diana's embalming is one of the main examples of a vital question being side-lined; something that we have seen repeatedly throughout this narrative. Therefore we now need to consider the situation of Dr Elizabeth Dion, the French radiologist, who told friends she had seen a foetus in Diana's womb but who didn't attend court, although her affidavit evidence was accepted.

Dr Dion gave a brief statement that didn't tell the court anything because it left out the crucial parts. Sue Reid, a reporter from the British *Daily Mail* newspaper, discovered Dr Dion's whereabouts, which made it necessary for the court to respond to this evidence. In her article, she wrote that Dr Dion was deeply concerned about what she saw on an X-ray of Diana's crushed body and on a later sonogram, which examined her internal organs. She added: 'The radiologist has told friends that a small foetus of perhaps between six to ten weeks was clearly visible in the Princess's womb.'

Isn't it strange that the police were unable to find Dr Dion, given the resources at their disposal (compared to those of a British newspaper journalist)? The reason she wasn't 'found' earlier is more logically because her evidence was extremely dangerous, as it established a motive for murder and explained Diana's illegal and speedy embalming; this was sidestepped by the court despite Dr Dion's evidence being stated as 'incontrovertible'.

After the initial newspaper article, Reid spoke with Dr Dion's friends but couldn't locate her a second time and so she informed Detective Sergeant Easton of Scotland Yard's Paget inquiry team, who managed to locate and speak with Dr Dion on 2nd June and again on 12th June 2006. After all this time, however, all Dr Dion offered was an affidavit that went as follows: 'I, Elizabeth Dion, solemnly declare that on the 30 and 31 August 1997, I was living in San Francisco, California, and working as a visiting Professor at the University in San Francisco California.' That is the whole statement!

Dr Dion didn't say in her statement where she was on the night of Diana's death but only that she was resident in San Francisco. Was she visiting family or friends in Paris during August 1997? Nor was there any explanation as to how she could see a foetus in Diana's womb, if she wasn't in Paris. Dr Dion couldn't be cross-examined but Scott Baker still felt able to say there was no foundation whatsoever to the embalming theories, adding, 'There remains little, if any, substance in some of the allegations, such as pregnancy and embalming.' He continued: 'You may think, having heard so many witnesses on the topic, that there is really no doubt at all that the embalming was entirely innocent.'

Yet another attempt to strip away motive, despite Commander Mules, the French police officer in charge of this investigative charade, having inadvertently admitted that the decision to embalm was taken at 'a diplomatic level'. Is anyone able to imagine an 'innocent' diplomatic decision with regard to this particular case, especially considering that the British policeman who was liaising the French investigation, David Veness, said that he appointed Jeffrey Rees, a police colleague, 'to collate all the information coming in from France because there would be the need for a post mortem in England". After the embalming there couldn't be a meaningful post mortem but how would the jury respond, had Dr Dion given her 'incontrovertible evidence' to the court and explained her remarks about seeing a foetus in Diana's womb?

It would certainly have been useful to ask Dr Dion the questions raised here but it seemed the court was prepared to accept her sworn affidavit statement despite so many questions again remaining unanswered. I ask that you please decide whether you find this acceptable.

Erik Petel

Twenty-six-year-old restaurant worker Erik Petel was riding his motorbike home from work via the Alma tunnel when a black Mercedes overtook him, going very fast. When he approached the Alma tunnel, he saw flashing lights coming from within, which he presumed were car headlights, but could have been the strobe gun. As he entered the incline at the beginning of the tunnel, Petel heard what he described as an implosion. His first reaction was to think he had a problem with his bike and he remembered checking it to ensure all was well. By the time he entered the tunnel, he saw the Mercedes settling against the wall in its final movement and, dismounting, ran over to the car to see what he could do. Immediately, he recognised Diana.

Panicked, he rushed to a public telephone to call the police, going the wrong way out of the tunnel, but the operator refused to take him seriously and so he went to the police station in Avenue Mozart. There, Petel told police officers that Diana was lying injured within the Alma tunnel but again he was disbelieved and the police took him to one of the Paris Police's more secret locations, close to the Alma. Petel was once more kept waiting before he gave a statement.

Some hours later, another officer came to discuss the implications of Petel's statement regarding his memory of flashing lights, an implosion and the fact that there were no paparazzi near the car when it crashed. The police did not wish to hear this because it meant that they couldn't then focus on the paparazzi, seize their photographs (which they didn't want in the public domain), or sustain the excuse for blaming them for the whole affair, as well as denying the Fiat's existence. It would be extremely difficult to explain all this testimony away and maintain any pretence of an accident.

The new police officer therefore advised Petel that it would be better if he didn't make his testimony known. Already it seemed the political machinery had swung into action. Petel was then released, but he later saw this man again. He was Philippe Massoni, Chief of the Paris Police, who was known to be in the Alma tunnel with Monsieur Chevènement, Minister for the Interior, within an hour of the attack and at the time Petel was at the station.

It must be stated that many people have singled out Petel for special criticism because what he described as happening was claimed to be impossible but, had the court permitted his testimony, surely this could have been determined, one way or another? After all, this was the supposed purpose of these proceedings and the intended purpose of a democratically appointed jury. If the jury were not to be permitted their democratic role, then why bother appointing one. It's strange that neither Petel nor Massoni were called to give evidence (an old statement from Massoni was read out in court).

The police made strenuous efforts to maintain that Petel was a junkie and not to be believed without any evidence whatsoever to support this assertion, which is reminiscent of their attitude towards several other potentially dangerous witnesses. But, consider what could induce the Chief of the Paris Police to leave his place at the side of his political boss, the Minister for the Interior, in the Alma tunnel just to attend the interrogation of a 'junkie'?

Genuine questions have been raised over some witnesses and Petel was especially vilified, but it appears that the greater the threat that the testimony produced, the more inventive the accusations became. It's interesting the police should make such an effort to insinuate that Petel was a junkie, if his testimony was physically impossible. Perhaps if he had been allowed his time in court, the jury could have made a democratic decision and forever removed this uncertainty.

Gary Hunter

Now we come to the damning testimony of British lawyer Gary Hunter, who was in his third-floor room (No. 304) of the Royal Alma Hotel in the rue Jean-Goujon, about one hundred yards from the Place de l'Alma, at the time of the attack.

Hunter had just been out to dinner with his wife Teresa. On returning to his room, they went to bed and Gary watched television while his wife slept. Here are some excerpts from his written testimony, which were read out to the jury:

'At 12.25am I heard the noise of an almighty crash, followed immediately by the sound of skidding tyres and then immediately a further, very loud crash. I took the time from the clock on the television. I jumped out of bed and it was one pace to the open window. I looked to my immediate left, from where the sound had come. From the same direction, there was the continuing sound of a car horn. I saw people running from the junction at the bottom of the road, rue Jean Goujon, across the grass area towards the direction of the tunnel, where I believed the noise was emanating. I continued to watch for approximately a minute; I could not see what had happened. My wife remained asleep and I did not wake her. I returned to the bed and lay down for what felt like a minute; it may have been less. I was then alerted by car noise in the form of tyres screeching at the bottom of the road from where the crash sound had originally emanated.

'I immediately returned to the window and looked left to see that a small dark vehicle had completed its turn into rue Jean Goujon, immediately followed by a larger, white vehicle. I believe this second vehicle to have been a white Mercedes. The Mercedes completed its turn immediately behind the smaller, dark vehicle. The two vehicles then preceded in tandem along the rue Jean Goujon, passing under my bedroom window towards the junction in the rue Jean Goujon, which comprised a roundabout formed by an ornamental fountain, which was lit. Both vehicles were travelling at inordinate speed; the white vehicle was almost touching the rear bumper of the smaller, dark vehicle. I thought the white car was shielding the small black car from behind. At the junction with the roundabout, with wheels screeching, they turned right and out of my sight. Whilst all of this was happening, and from my position – the street lighting was good and it was a dry, humid night – I noticed that the Mercedes was not manoeuvring or signalling to pass the smaller, dark car. It was this that makes me believe that the Mercedes was shielding the rear of the small car.'

It is strange that the police didn't seem at all interested in following up on this evidence since, together with other testimony, it strongly supports a murder scenario. However, the police were unable to dismiss Hunter's dangerous testimony – being a lawyer, his evidence would have carried significant weight – so instead they simply refused to accept his deposition. But let us consider the implications of two cars both travelling at high speed less than two minutes after an attack on Diana's car in the tunnel and then decide on the probability that this was a random coincidence.

This account also gives good reason why Peyret and others didn't see any cars pass them as they continued on their journeys, because the murderers had already turned off the road and were escaping via la rue Débrousse, from where a right turn takes one into the Place de l'Alma. Then, via rue Goujon, they continued to the Avenue du President Wilson when, within a minute or so, they could reach the British Embassy. But they also needed to pass under Gary Hunter's bedroom window. Perhaps it's not unreasonable to question why several vehicles would leave the expressway together after an assassination and head in the same direction at speed, 'bumper to bumper'. Hunter said it looked 'very sinister'.

Hunter contacted Mohamed Al Fayed's security chief John McNamara, who was heading Al Fayed's own investigation, and was asked to return and tell his story to the French. He did so on 7th September, but the French judicial authorities declined to consider his evidence, in common with most of the other witnesses who gave valuable and damning information. The French police should be required to explain their reasoning because Hunter's testimony, according to one French judicial source not involved in this case, was something to be 'handled with extreme care'. But why should useful evidence need to be 'handled with extreme care'? Why would the truth need to be handled with extreme care?

Hunter's evidence was largely dismissed because it was said he couldn't see anything of the attack scene from his bedroom window or even the tunnel. Yet he stated as much in his written testimony, as you have just read, so this is irrelevant. The point is that the exit from the expressway that the assassins would have taken after the attack would logically be the next one after they had emerged from the Alma tunnel: rue Débrousse. Witnesses ahead of the assassins on the expressway confirmed no vehicles had overtaken them, which leaves this exit as the most probable route.

From Hunter's testimony, it's beyond doubt that several vehicles, which either escaped or failed to come forward after the attack, were involved. It's interesting how several witnesses describe the same or very similar events, even down to the colour of motorcycle fuel tanks or riders' helmets. However, we must consider why some witnesses refer to a dark vehicle while others refer to the same one as being white. The lighting in this area can give a false perception of colour because of the varying light intensity. Some vehicles will look white or black from one position and then as they move, their colour appears to change so these witness descriptions of colour cannot be considered reliable. The same caution should be applied to Gary Hunter's description of colour when he described two cars fleeing under his bedroom window.

It is very possible the fleeing Mercedes was black, not white and that the Fiat, or smaller car, was white and not black. However, from this evidence it is incontrovertible that they did exit via the rue Débrousse, the Mercedes was following the smaller car 'bumper-to-bumper', they were travelling at 'an inordinate speed' and, as Hunter stated, they looked as though 'they were in a hurry not to be there'.

Three of the first four witnesses spoke of motorcycles near the Mercedes and Benoît Boura stated that a motorcycle rode around the Mercedes after the impact and then disappeared. Jean-Pascal Peyret, who was ahead of the attack scene, spoke of being passed by a motorcycle, seconds after the impact, and all confirmed that several vehicles had left the scene before the paparazzi arrived.

It was a few weeks before the authorities were forced into even admitting there was a Fiat Uno and a collision – or collisions – between this car and the Mercedes. By 12th September, the police had no option other than to admit they had fragments of a rear light found in the tunnel, collected from the collision with the Mercedes. It was confirmed that this was from the turbo model Fiat Uno made between May 1983 and September 1989 – the only one capable of out-accelerating a Mercedes 280.

Stephane Darmon

The paparazzi didn't attend court (prevented by proven political intervention), so proving whether they arrived at the tunnel concomitantly with the Mercedes crashing, or after the crash when others had already left the scene could only be explored by checking witness evidence. However, one paparazzo rider, Stephane Darmon, gave his testimony via video link from Paris. Darmon was a rider for Rommauld Rat, one of the paparazzi, and both stated that they were the first to arrive after the Mercedes had crashed. They said there was no one else there at first but their colleagues arrived soon afterwards.

Perhaps the reason Darmon was allowed to give his testimony at the hearing was due to a comment he had made on another point. Darmon said: 'On a very personal note, I have to say that my father was an alcoholic, and when I saw Mr Paul he reminded me of my father – his eyes, the way he acted.' Of course this was a gift for those seeking to confirm Diana's death was caused by Henri Paul's incapacity. However, there are other interpretations of the way Paul acted that night. He was euphoric and enjoying his game with the press; he had also received a significant payment for the night's work and was the centre of attention. (It must also be remembered it was proven that the police had emphatically stated Paul was drunk before they even had the results of his blood tests and that Inspector Scotchbrook of the British Paget inquiry said that Paul had only had two drinks that night.)

Darmon said that while they were outside the Ritz Hotel before Diana and Dodi left, Paul came outside and goaded them that the couple would be coming out in ten minutes in order to retain their interest. He then employed a diversionary manoeuvre by having a Mercedes drive around to the front of the Ritz to stir up anticipation, saying to the press, '1 versus 0,' meaning he had scored a point. This strongly suggested that Paul considered it all a game. Later, he ensured the paparazzi didn't leave by telling them that Diana and Dodi would be out in five minutes.

Diana's Mercedes left from the rear of the hotel at around 12.20am and headed towards the Place de la Concorde. This manoeuvre had now become a standard ploy, having twice been used in the past. First when the couple were at the Ritz the previous month, but also that same afternoon when they left the hotel at around 7pm to return to Dodi's apartment at the rue Arsène Houssaye. Perhaps the paparazzi shouldn't have been so surprised but, because of these two recent and similar ploys by Diana and Dodi, maybe the assassins expected the paparazzi to realise quickly what was happening. This would ensure the paparazzi arrived on site at the Alma for their unwitting scapegoat duties, now only minutes away.

Darmon said that when they were told the Mercedes had left from the rear of the Ritz, they rushed down the rue de Castiglione (on the other side of the Ritz) to the rue de Rivoli, where the hotel's rear exit is located. They saw the Mercedes stationary and surrounded by cars at the traffic light intersection between the Champs-Elysées and the Place de la Concorde. According to Darmon, when the lights changed, Henri Paul accelerated brutally and 'took off like a plane' as soon as a clear space became available. Darmon was also at these lights behind other vehicles and tried to follow the Mercedes, but by the time he had cleared the traffic it was out of sight. When he reached the curve in the expressway, he had a clear line of vision to the Pont Alexandre III but the Mercedes was by then gone. It would have only seconds remaining before reaching the Alma.

Every driver knows that a one half-minute head start at full throttle takes a good deal of catching up, since at ninety miles per hour the Mercedes would travel three-quarters of a mile in thirty seconds, which is about the distance to the Alma tunnel from these traffic lights and the freeway is only a few hundred metres away. The Mercedes could have been travelling faster, in which case it would have reached the Pont Alexandre III within seconds. There was no obstruction after the traffic lights to prevent it from reaching a very high speed as the assassins required and it is important to understand that the attack was also over in seconds. It was a further few seconds before Darmon and Rat passed under the Pont des Invalides and arrived at the Alma. These were most probably the lights seen by Souad Mouffakir approaching the tunnel 'far, far behind'.

Darmon said this was his first assignment for the paparazzi and he wasn't prepared to ride dangerously just to get a scoop, so his speed was around sixty to seventy km/h. When the lights changed, he managed to get ahead of the vehicles waiting at the traffic lights but, on emerging from under the Pont Alexandre III, there were no vehicles in sight. When he reached the Pont des Invalides, however, he saw red lights from a vehicle descending under the Pont de l'Alma. He couldn't describe the vehicle (it is necessary to reach the Pont de Invalides before the Alma becomes visible).

Darmon said he didn't see any other vehicles around him on the freeway (confirmed by Alain Remy), so the paparazzi would need to be inside the Alma tunnel with the Mercedes, together with the soon-to-be-escaping vehicles when the incident took place, if they were indeed ahead. But we know this wasn't the case. Furthermore, the paparazzi would have told the police and also their employers – the press – about these escaping vehicles if they had indeed been there. After all, they were not in the pay of the Security Services. They didn't do this because, quite simply, they were not there.

But we know there were other 'loitering', 'escaping' and 'blocking' vehicles around and in the tunnel that all then fled the scene – a significant amount of other evidence confirms this crucial point. When Darmon reached the tunnel, the Mercedes was against the right wall with the horn blaring, so he rode past and parked his bike about fifteen metres away. Rat dismounted and went over to the Mercedes. Moments later the paparazzi (later arrested as a smokescreen) began to arrive.

The police tried to establish that there were other vehicles and paparazzi present when Darmon arrived at the tunnel so they must have been ahead of him on the freeway. Therefore they wrote down the following statement, purportedly from Darmon and presented to the court: 'I was going at about sixty km/h at the top of the slope down into the underpass. The whole group was there, four or five cars mingling with the traffic, about three motorbikes and two scooters'.

Darmon emphatically refuted saying this or giving any such statement to a Captain Nouvion. Instead he responded to the court, 'No, there was nobody – nobody at all.' He continued: 'There was nobody in front of me or alongside me – these people got there at a later stage. [Later] I was joined by a group of photographers, who I saw in my rear-view mirror.' Of course it was important for the police to prevent testimony being recorded that would destroy an accident theory. This would prevent the paparazzi being used as scapegoats since, if these escaping vehicles were not paparazzi, then they could be nothing other than assassins.

You will recall several other situations where the interviewee disagreed with police transcriptions of the evidence so one must wonder why the police would incorrectly transcribe witness statements from those with crucial evidence to give after such an event. In addition to Darmon, these include Benoît, Levistre, Mrs Levistre, Andersen, Hunter, Rassinier and L'Hostis. The police presented statements that these witnesses said they had neither given nor signed so their signatures must have been forged. (Remember also the evidence of Gary Hunter where the police wouldn't accept his deposition.) It was Mrs Levistre who made the uncompromising remark, when being interviewed by French police, that 'if you say white, they write down black'.

Scott Baker said that the police 'had shown carelessness at the very least' in their taking of evidence. He even acknowledged the possibility that police planted evidence in Henri Paul's apartment when a packed of Ayotal tablets was found that everyone knew did not belong to Paul. But perhaps the drug had been taken by the man lying next to Paul in the mortuary – you will remember that he had committed suicide by gassing himself with his car exhaust fumes that would account for very high levels of carbon monoxide in blood and solve one of the mysteries surrounding Henri Paul's apparent blood samples. But can anyone explain what reason the police could have for doing this?

Taken together, these witnesses described a vicious attack on Diana's Mercedes, since there is too much evidence of escaping, blocking and loitering vehicles to have any innocent interpretation. Look especially at the evidence of Alain Remy, who confirmed that the Mercedes overtook him along the freeway near the Pont Alexandre III, unaccompanied by other motor vehicles. This confirms that paparazzi were nowhere near the Mercedes as it approached the tunnel, as Darmon also stated. Other vehicles awaited the vehicle's arrival at the Alma tunnel.

Part Four

Deliberation

Rationalising the Evidence

As stated at the beginning of this narrative I am required by lawyers to repeat that I am expressing my 'honest opinion' and exercising my rights of 'qualified privilege' under rules of English Law. You will discern the points that are proven and, rest assured, my perception is not given to exaggeration or fancy but is based on the facts.

★

Lord Justice Scott Baker received a poisoned chalice when he accepted the role of coroner in the case of Diana, Princess of Wales. A guilty verdict would jeopardise the monarchy and the whole Establishment since it would then be clear that either the Palace or the British Government was responsible for this most brutal of crimes, whether or not supported by the incumbent Prime Minister, Tony Blair. It would also raise serious questions as to who had the motive and power to give this order; there wouldn't be many names in the hat.

If, however, a verdict could be delivered that exculpated the State by claiming it was the work of over-zealous paparazzi, together with a delinquent driver, then the whole matter could be ended, the risk to the monarchy removed and the British Government would not be burdened with an issue that could topple it. The judiciary could reason that nothing would be gained by revealing the truth since Diana was dead and the position fait accompli. Those taking such a line of reasoning would believe that the problem within MI6 had, hopefully, been resolved and the appropriate people chastised, so what was now more important: the continuance of a wayward and undemocratic, albeit well-embedded system, or the truth?

Yet by deciding whether to support this venture and debase their honour, the involved protagonists knew that they stood against justice and everything decent so needed convincing that the risk to their country far outweighed any later conscience they might endure. They must also accept an eternal tarnishing of the Establishment's integrity, should there be a subsequent disclosure. The judiciary, therefore, needed strong guarantees from the Security Services and the government that no similar act could ever recur, along with a conviction that the perpetrators were just a few people who ran ahead of their remit but without support from the Secret Service hierarchy. (You will recall Lord Justice Scott Baker's constant reference to rogue officers.) This is, in my view, untrue – MI6 just messed up.

The risk that this deception posed to the British state was gargantuan since it needed compliance from the government and police for any hope of success. Failure to deceive the electorate would mean an end to the people's current loose acceptance that Britain is a democracy since all powers used in this process could never be described as democratic.

Certain actions were essential. There mustn't be any possibility of a murder verdict since this would, essentially, convict MI6 and greatly damage the monarchy so witnesses whose testimony would jeopardise this must not attend the hearing. If this could not be prevented, they must be vilified, their testimony eviscerated and the whole process obfuscated.

Three coroners withdrew from the hearing before Lord Scott Baker's arrival. John Burton, the Royal coroner, retired through stated ill health. (One wonders why the royal coroner was involved in the first place since Diana had already been stripped of her HRH and had left the royal family when her divorce from Charles Windsor was made Absolute on 29th August, just hours before she was murdered. The fact that Diana was no longer royal is the very reason why the Queen objected to Diana's body being returned from France on a *royal* flight.)

The second coroner was Michael Burgess who cited a large workload for standing down. He had also said after his appointment in 2003 that, 'In time, as the law requires, there will be inquests into the deaths of Dodi Fayed and Diana, Princess of Wales,' adding, 'It would be premature to say when the inquests would be held.' Burgess resigned because he was 'too busy' but there was a report that he considered the whole affair 'suspicious'. (It was he who asked Lord Stevens, the then Scotland Yard chief, to look into whether MI6 were in any way responsible for these deaths.)

The penultimate coroner, Dame Butler-Sloss, even endeavoured to break the law by having the jury comprise members of the royal family, thus evading the people's court. She eventually stood down citing her inexperience at dealing with juries. (So why did she accept the role? Did she never intend having a jury?) In fact Butler Sloss only stood down when her attempt to hold court without a jury was declared illegal by the high court after pressure from Mohamed Al Fayed. If Al Fayed had not pursued justice for his murdered son, does anyone believe there would even have been a public inquest?

The purpose of this chapter is to summarise the evidence and ask that you, the ultimate jury, make your final judgment. So imagine you are in a court of law weighing up the evidence. You hear the police and security services repeatedly refuse to answer crucial questions. It is then demonstrated that a former boss of MI6, Sir Richard Dearlove, denies any knowledge of a previous MI6 betrayal in a Cayman Islands court of law. He then immediately responds that the lawyers had 'dug this one out' when confronted with proof of this treachery and the court appeared to be unconcerned he had just confirmed such a revelation. One wonders what else could be 'dug out'.

So one questions why, especially when the purpose of the hearing is finally to clear the air and establish whether this was a mere accident. Why are those in whom the people have placed their trust now obviously masking the truth instead of achieving the hearing's supposed purpose of seeking it? You might well wonder what reason there could be for such corruption and perversion of the people's justice; how could this help the establishment's cause?

But then there is the realisation that there is no option because the cracks are appearing and MI6 are crumbling under the truth onslaught so a continuous subterfuge is necessary, especially with the world watching. But what could be so important that they must hide it at all costs? What else could there be other than the truth concerning their brutal murder of Diana Spencer? So I must say that I wonder why the judiciary didn't respond to this abuse; why there was no sanction applied and why this corruption was not even acknowledged in court.

The examples chosen to summarise this unacceptable process focus on the central issues to prove murder beyond any reasonable doubt: Henri Paul's drunkenness, which vehicles arrived first to the tunnel, Diana's pregnancy and the position taken by MI6.

It's my view that these points illustrate we are not reflecting on a few minor errors in law or fact but instead describing a deliberate stratagem established for the sole purpose of preserving the status quo. A central point you must decide on is whether, in your view, the hearing delivered a fair and balanced review of the facts or was grossly slanted in favour of ensuring a suitable verdict.

Certainly there was no mistaking Lord Justice Scott Baker's gratitude for MI6 bothering to attend the hearing and his persistence that, if MI6 had been responsible, then it could only have been rogue officers. This stance was undermined when Richard Dearlove (the ex-MI6 boss and operations director at the time of Diana's murder) intuitively proclaimed it couldn't have been rogue officers: 'That was impossible.'

When Scott Baker pressed home the possibility of rogue officers being responsible, despite Sir Richard Dearlove's opinion being in sharp contrast, he didn't clarify an important point. Since the option for 'unlawful killing by persons unknown' had been excluded from the jury, if it was shown that the culprits were indeed rogue officers, how did Scott Baker intend that justice would be meted out? There was no suitable verdict available to the court because he had excluded this option.

But Dearlove realised that by giving his forthright and spontaneous evidence that rogue officers were an impossible option, he had endangered MI6. This is the reason why, in my view, he offered the jury alternative, possible culprits to shield MI6 from blame since some jurors were bound to realise this was murder, which two clearly did.

So Dearlove now effectively reversed his 'evidence' by stating that it would be difficult but possible for rogue agents to be responsible; otherwise it could only be MI6. (A doubt was therefore created in the minds of the jury and, provided they didn't realise that these putative rogue officers remained MI6 officers irrespective of their specific remit, MI6 could be off the hook. In any event Dearlove survived this without needing to explain why his opinion had changed.)

If Dearlove had maintained his spontaneous response that 'it couldn't have been rogue officers without the knowledge of the Service, that was impossible', then we accept that he would have been foolish to investigate an event that he had already stated could not possibly happen. But these rogue officers had now become possible with Dearlove's complete reversal of 'evidence' so there was no longer any excuse for him not having investigated who they were.

Note: This pretence is in similar vein to Dearlove saying that he interviewed Witness 'A' over his 'dreadful' assassination proposal for Slobodan Milosevic that had been 'strangled at birth' when 'A' denied that he was interviewed by Dearlove at all – another of Dearlove's dalliance's with the truth and proven through slips in evidence from his own, current MI6 officers and the lawyers' forceful interrogation.

If Dearlove truly believed there was a possibility that rogue officers could have carried out this attack, you must first consider why he initially stated, unambiguously and intuitively, that this was impossible. Then you must also try to understand why he didn't immediately seek their identities if he was convinced they might be responsible and he genuinely sought justice.

But Dearlove's unexpected proclamation and utterly banal contradiction that it would be 'difficult but possible' for rogue officers to have committed this crime, though gifting MI6 an escape route, placed the pressure squarely on the shoulders of the judge who now needed to establish exactly what Dearlove did to discover these rogue officers' identities. If Scott Baker truly believed this new 'evidence', then he needed to ask Dearlove this crucial question. So you might wonder why Dearlove was never asked this question.

Dearlove's mainstay position was that it was impossible for rogue officers to be responsible so it was either impossible or it wasn't, but evidence cannot just be changed without considering his previously held reason for not investigating. So, what was Dearlove's reason for not investigating, or was he lying to the court? Again, ask yourself these questions.

It cannot be that Dearlove was confused over rogue officers for he would have needed to be completely wrong about this issue during his whole time in the Service. Having reached the pinnacle of power in MI6, he was no rookie and had already stated in court that he knew the workings of the Service extremely well. The concept that rogue officers could be responsible was a fundamental opinion when he would instinctively know whether or not this was possible and he unambiguously stated that they were an impossible option.

Also, do not forget that without the nod from someone in a position of significant power, there could never have been an attack and so if designated rogue, it was clearly MI6's chosen route to assist their 'deniability'. The only alternative is that this influential person dealt directly with these putative rogue officers but without the knowledge of, or assistance from, their friends in the MI6 hierarchy. Did Dearlove instinctively know this wasn't credible?

During his summation, Scott Baker mentioned crucial evidence from several witnesses concerning a powerful flash of light just as the Mercedes entered the Alma tunnel when he said 'was a flashing light of this kind, a technique used by MI6 and could rogue officers have decided to use it here?' Even at the end of these proceedings he continued to proclaim that it could have been rogue officers but not MI6 proper, greatly assisted by Dearlove's somewhat ridiculous and contradictory reversal of 'evidence'.

It would also be interesting to ask Scott Baker what he believed several senior MI6 officers were doing in Paris during the attack on Diana – would they also be assisting rogue officers? If not, they would certainly be aware of their presence and that included Dearlove, who was in Paris and the then operations director of MI6. During proceedings, Dearlove had also admitted that all proposals for murder went through him.

This convoluted nonsense greatly strengthens our view that these inquests were intended to be a stage-managed catharsis to satisfy the people and bury the truth of Diana's murder for eternity, in defence of MI6 and the monarchy.

But to find for murder we must be satisfied on the central issues concerning activity around the tunnel. Were any speeding, aggressive cars and motorbikes near the Mercedes when it crashed, which all fled before the paparazzi arrived? Was there a concomitant flash of light inside the tunnel and were vehicles seen to be escaping the scene? Did some first drive slowly around the crashed Mercedes and peer through its windows?

This activity is the most telling because, ignoring all other evidence, if you are content that this is proven then it is evident the paparazzi were not involved so this cannot be anything other than murder. Prove this to a jury and six months of court debate should be superfluous, yet although clearly shown, it was ignored. Nonetheless, the paparazzi were immediately incarcerated as part of the smokescreen and this is why the police called Levistre a liar before they had even finished incorrectly transcribing his statement. Someone needed to be blamed and credible evidence neutralised before everyone started to ask difficult questions.

Unfortunately for the police, there were several witnesses who gave similar incriminating statements. Many stayed away from court but when those in attendance were asked why they didn't come forward and give their observations to the police sooner, a common reply was that they were scared. François Levistre's wife, who attended the video link in Paris, decided not to give evidence despite Scott Baker's entreaties because of how her husband was treated during his cross-examination – in the same manner as all witnesses who knew, or had seen, too much.

The main value in discussing the paparazzi is to show that in common with Henri Paul, they were no more than convenient scapegoats. Also, since none of them attended court and few even gave affidavit evidence, the court couldn't test their version of events.

This is particularly interesting since Scott Baker admitted during the inquest proceedings, under pressure from the lawyers, that the French *political machinery* had prevented the paparazzi from attending court and you might wonder why, especially when it had also been admitted by the French policeman in charge of the 'investigation' – Jean-Claude Mules – that the decision to embalm Diana was taken at *a diplomatic level*.

At this juncture it will be helpful to show you some dialogue between Michael Mansfield QC, Diana's and Mohamed Al Fayed's lawyer and Scott Baker where it's proven that the decision not to permit the paparazzi to attend court and give evidence was through 'political intervention'.

This is a substantial exchange and you may read it all yourselves since the transcripts are available to all but I insert interesting pieces that have great relevance to the whole purpose of this book. The extract refers to the paparazzi but if there was *political intervention* here don't you agree with me that it's highly probable there was such intervention with all dangerous witnesses, as I believe this book shows.

This is the most relevant part that is worthwhile describing in some detail. Mr Mansfield QC makes the point that French witnesses can be required to attend at court hearings. In brief he says:

'Failure to appear, to take oath or to give a deposition, without any excuse or justification, before the investigating judge or before a judicial police officer pursuant to letters rogatory, on the part of a person who has been summoned by him to be heard as a witness is *punishable...*'

so suggesting that failure to comply with the court's requirement to attend has consequences for the witness. Then he asks the coroner Lord Scott Baker,

'My only request is that a further dialogue takes place between yourself and the French authorities so that publically a very clear basis may be stated to the French and the British public as to the basis on which French witnesses are not going to be compelled under the same article by the French authorities to attend.'

At the next session Lord Scott Baker's reply is;

'My information from the British liaison magistrate resident in Paris is as follows. The decision to respond to my international letter of request in the terms that I have received and disclosed to you was taken in the minister's office at a very high level and appears to have been a *political decision* (my italics). Despite repeated efforts by the liaison magistrate to obtain a more detailed explanation, I am told that there is nothing to be added to the response to my international letter of request. There will be no change of position.'

Michael Mansfield response is, in brief, and having thanked Lord Scott Baker,

'…one is that we are concerned obviously that it is *a political decision* (my italics). Plainly, if that is the level at which matters are being considered then plainly in response you might consider similarly whether there should be a political response to this.'

To continue;

'…so to have this matter relatively resolved at this stage, in other words, if there are to be no revelations by the French as to the basis upon which this *political decision* (my italics) has been taken…and the reasoning is not transparent and we say, on the face of the reasoning at the moment, it does not add up at all and it is a *subterfuge* (my italics) in the sense that is being used for other reasons; namely we are concerned that witnesses are being protected in one way or another by the use of reference to public order and so forth. So we would ask that not only you make further representations, if you would be minded to do so, but those who have as it were judicial and political office may also consider…since this is a unique proceeding and has been recognised as such from the beginning, the point we would wish to emphasize is that if this was going to be the position, and it could not have been something which was never on the horizon and not anticipated, why is it that it is only now that this matter is being raised when these proceedings have been on the cards practically for the whole of the year. So we would say this needs a great deal more probing before we resort to a paper inquest.'

Another lawyer, Mr Croxford, then takes this point up by saying;

'Perhaps I can put it this way: if I was standing here addressing you as my Lord, seeking to justify political intervention in a process which is governed by international obligations of law, I suspect I would have quite a difficult time. Our initial reaction is that it is very surprising that something that is governed by international obligations and, in particular, obligations within the union, should be interfered with, if that is what it is, by a *political process* (my italics). Sir, that is a matter we and others will have to look at over the adjournment.'

Nothing was done. Justice continued to be ignored. All fine so long as the monarchy is well. As stated many times before, if the paparazzi persuaded the jury that they were not first to the tunnel, then the verdict must be murder so their cross-examination was avoided.

Rommauld Rat and his rider, Stephane Darmon, were the first paparazzi to arrive at the tunnel after the Mercedes had crashed and Darmon gave evidence over a video link. This was useful to those who wished to exculpate MI6 because initially, he had intimated that Henri Paul looked inebriated.

We now know through evidence educed during the inquests'

proceedings that the police had deliberately misled the people by issuing false statements concerning Henri Paul's alcohol levels before confirmation of Paul's blood results were received by them but Darmon's comment assisted this subterfuge. (Why did the police pretend they knew Paul was drunk. What reason could there be?) Darmon made other less useful remarks, however, that didn't help these people by offering convincing testimony that the paparazzi were not the first to the tunnel, supported by several other witnesses.

The paparazzi were held to account for the whole affair and their opinions considered valueless, yet still none of them were ever convicted of anything that endured. For some reason the court still decided that the opinion of another paparazzo – Pierre Suu – was perfectly acceptable. Suu said that the man believed to be driving the white Fiat Uno in the tunnel – James Andanson – couldn't have been in Paris at the time because he (Suu) would have known about it (despite Suu's later proclamation that he wasn't there when Diana's car was attacked).

It was reason enough, from an unknown paparazzo who didn't even attend the hearing, for the court to decree that Andanson therefore couldn't have been in Paris. As Scott Baker announced, 'If he wasn't in Paris, then he couldn't have done the deed.' Andanson not only said that he had chased Diana's car into the tunnel but was also bragging to friends that he had photographs that would be 'Un Baum'; they would rock the world. These would be some of the photographs that thugs were looking for when they raided Cherruault's house in London and also on another raid in Paris when a guard was shot in the foot.

We have seen on numerous occasions where the facts have been misinterpreted and false information recorded. The paparazzi arrested after the crash were told by the police to sign statements, but when they later saw those statements, most complained that the signatures were not theirs; their statements had been forged. This also applied to several other witnesses.

One must also remember that in France, people are considered guilty until proven innocent (the reverse of the USA and the UK) and there are also no 'Miranda rights'. (This is where, in democracies, people are granted the option to not incriminate themselves and the police are required to inform them of this when the suspect is arrested.) The French police may also confine anyone for twenty hours before permitting them access to a lawyer, so police powers are considerable. Most useful if one wishes to conduct a political murder.

People were horrified to learn that the paparazzi were taking photographs of the Mercedes on arrival at the crash scene. But since the paparazzi were still on site doing this when large numbers of the public arrived, where did these loitering, aggressive and blocking vehicles, witnessed leaving the Alma tunnel by several competent witnesses, go?

The paparazzi may have displayed shocking taste by taking photographs in these dreadful circumstances but that's not to say they had anything to do with the Mercedes crashing into the pillars. How absurd it was to consider they were in any way responsible for the crash since these aggressive vehicles that witnesses saw leaving the scene were long gone by the time the paparazzi arrived. Indeed, would you remain in the tunnel if responsible for this incident with malevolent intent? But the paparazzi were still there when the police arrived.

So, several paparazzi are blamed, abused, incarcerated and then held to account for the whole event. For years, they are kept in the limelight just to divert attention from the real cause of the incident and when the authorities are forced into holding an inquest, the same paparazzi are then prevented from being questioned in court through proven *political intervention* (my italics).

Let us imagine that you witness a crime; you do your duty by informing the police and give your opinion of what happened. But in addition to others who witnessed very similar events, you are then mistreated when the police decide, for no perceptible reason and before testing any evidence, that you must be suffering from a flight of fancy and that you are a liar, drunkard or criminal to boot. By contrast, when others offer anything that might be interpreted as being conducive to an accident, the police listen and follow that line of inquiry. Would the police behave in this way without good reason?

The court alleged that Mohamed Al Fayed had withdrawn his claims, stating: 'The benefit of these last six months is that various propositions that were being asserted have been shown to be so demonstrably without foundation that they are no longer being pursued by Mohamed Al Fayed's lawyers, even if he still carries the belief of their truth in his own mind. They are not being pursued because there is not a shred of evidence to support them.'

The only reason why no further claims were pursued by Al Fayed's lawyers during the inquests is because of the futility of further legal endeavour in a matter where the truth will never be permitted and whatever is necessary done to preserve the Establishment. But not much further on in the summation, to balance this comment, Scott Baker said: 'This does not mean, however, that all the suggestions you have heard about the possibility of a staged crash are irrelevant because there is evidence, albeit limited and of doubtful quality, that the crash was staged.' Surely this alone is worthy of consideration as a 'shred of evidence'?

Scott Baker also says in his summation that he can't permit the jury the option of finding for unlawful killing by persons unknown because he couldn't *be sure* there was sufficient evidence; not, you will note, that there is no evidence. (At this juncture, remember the evidence of David Veness, the policeman in charge of this whole debacle. He admitted that he didn't investigate any of these vehicles around the Alma tunnel; he didn't believe any of this detail was relevant.) But the court conceded during the inquests that this is not so. So here is evidence that Veness didn't investigate valuable evidence when it was presented to him and you must ask why.

How, when Scott Baker accepted there was evidence of a staged accident, could he presume the jury was incapable of doing the job for which they were appointed and draw their own conclusions as to the doubtful quality of the evidence? Their democratic role was supposedly to determine whether, on the balance of probabilities, it was an accident or murder. No wonder the jurors found themselves unable to concur. It is my view that Scott Baker thought there was an unacceptable risk the jury would find for murder and that would bring the whole Establishment crashing to its knees; otherwise why else would this verdict option be excluded?

We have considered evidence from witnesses who described vehicles being involved in the 'crash' that then fled. Vehicles were driving around the Mercedes, looking inside and then continuing on their journey; loitering cars were ahead of the Mercedes and flashes of light seen inside the tunnel. These flashes were even witnessed by those who entered the tunnel entrance from the other side of the freeway and in the oncoming lane (discounting the court's reasoning that the flash of light came from the Bateaux Mouches excursion boats since it was impossible to see river lights from here). There were also people in the tunnel not in possession of cameras who prevented onlookers from encroaching.

Benoît Boura, an army man, described the flash as being like a military strobe gun and he corroborated other witness evidence of the escaping vehicles, as did a British lawyer, Gary Hunter. Souad Mouffakir was within the tunnel and just ahead of the Mercedes when she observed a flash of light, while Olivier Partouche was outside the tunnel with Clifford Gooroovadoo when they observed the flash coming from within. François Levistre saw two motorcycles and a white car; one motorcycle swerved in front of the Mercedes and delivered a flash of light, but Levistre was by now at the far end of the long Alma tunnel so again the light could not have originated from the river.

Levistre's wife Valerie had instinctively described the whole event as a terrorist attack. Remember, Levistre also witnessed the rider dismount his bike and approach the Mercedes before making a slitting-of-the-throat gesture. His wife also witnessed a motorcycle with two riders on board that rode right past her as it exited the tunnel.

Brenda Wells, a British secretary, witnessed the attack and saw the flash coming from the direction of the tunnel, but in common with other difficult witnesses she was also advised, as was Erik Petel, not to make her observations of the crash known. In fact, she has completely disappeared and one wonders why! What other evidence might she have been able to give?

Jean-Pascal Peyret witnessed two cars exiting the tunnel and Peyret's wife Severine saw a motorbike exit the tunnel immediately after the crash, which the couple confirmed did not continue past them, thereby indicating these vehicles quickly left the expressway. Brian Andersen saw two motorcycles pass him, driving 'aggressively and dangerously' as he approached the tunnel and then a flash of light was followed almost immediately by a loud bang.

Grigori Rassinier saw, as did Benoît Boura from the opposite lane, a large car coming to a halt and a motorcycle with a large yellow headlamp and white helmet or fuel tank following closely behind the Mercedes, which accelerated out of the tunnel. Scotland Yard ignored him when he tried to give evidence yet he even corroborated detail of the attack bikes. Alain Remy saw the Mercedes speeding along the freeway by the Pont Alexandre III and there were no paparazzi in sight. He was ridiculed, but evidence confirmed that loitering vehicles waited ahead.

As Scott Baker said: 'You will remember from photographs taken in the tunnel that wheel tracks in the debris do show that a number of vehicles must have driven past the crashed Mercedes,' thus accepting that other vehicles passed through the tunnel, most of which were never identified. We also have a description from the testimony of several witnesses who described these cars and motorbikes that all passed the crashed Mercedes, which had been loitering, hindering and blocking its path, then carried on their way never to be seen again. The police initially denied this but two years after the murder there was confirmation from the police that several vehicles were indeed present. They had vacated the scene but apparently 'nobody could adequately describe them'. Once more, why not permit the jury the option of a suitable verdict?

Darmon said that when he arrived at the tunnel, nobody else was there and the Mercedes was already smashed against the tunnel wall, its horn blaring. The assassins were gone; the paparazzi were not in sight and, since we know the vehicles that had already passed through the tunnel were not paparazzi, who were they?

Typically, the police tried to establish that there were several paparazzi present when Darmon arrived by fabricating his evidence, but of course if no one was there, then those vehicles later described by many witnesses as having already left the scene could be nothing other than assassins. So, why did the police fabricate this and much other witness evidence; who was responsible for this abuse of the people's justice?

The motorbikes and cars that were aggressively pursuing Diana's Mercedes were witnessed by Boura, who saw two cars and one motorbike that rode around and looked into the Mercedes before hurriedly accelerating away. His passenger, Gaëlle l'Hostis, saw a dark car driving slowly and 'hindering' the Mercedes, together with a large motorcycle just behind it.

David Laurent said that when he reached the tunnel just before the attack, there were two cars loitering near the entrance; one he described as being a small, old hatchback car, rather like the Fiat Uno, and the other one a larger, darker saloon. Laurent said he avoided them by swerving, which his passengers confirmed and then, towards the end of the tunnel, they heard a loud bang and witnessed these vehicles exit the tunnel at speed.

Souad Mouffakir and Mohammed Medjhadi saw a white Fiat Uno ahead of them as they entered the tunnel, which they overtook. So the Fiat was behind them and just ahead of the Mercedes. Souad described the Fiat as 'driving much too close to us; it did not want to overtake us, it was really close to us. Too close to us.' Medjhadi also reaffirmed that after the attack that the Fiat then exited the tunnel at speed and Souad saw the driver's face.

Souad also saw the lights from approaching vehicles 'far, far behind' the Mercedes. So, since the 'interfering' or 'blocking' vehicles that were involved in the attack had hurriedly departed, it follows that they could not be the paparazzi arrested later in the tunnel. The lights seen by Souad would have been from paparazzi (probably Rat and Darmon) that had not yet reached the tunnel but who were now only seconds away and who were still there when police arrived – they did not hurry away.

Olivier Partouche and Clifford Gooroovadoo gave supportive evidence when they said that a powerful motorbike was tailgating the Mercedes, together with a dark car in front that was 'visibly slowing it down', which they described as a 'blocking vehicle'; they also heard a noise that sounded like a car changing gear.

Gary Hunter, the British lawyer who is now deceased, confirmed how only seconds after hearing a loud crash coming from the direction of the Alma tunnel, he had witnessed two cars tailgating each other 'bumper to bumper' and travelling at 'an inordinate speed' below his bedroom window; he described them as being in 'a hurry not to be there'. They were heading in the direction of the British Embassy. Hunter said it looked 'very sinister'.

Witness evidence stated that the Mercedes was seen to straighten out after the initial collision, hence the need for further intervention by the Fiat, to ensure a collision, was evident – and had witness support. Add a concomitant flash of light and high speed and, as the police expert witness Anthony Read said, here was a fatal scenario.

Scott Baker said that 'the only reason there were deaths was because of the speed at which the Mercedes struck the pillar', but the assassins would also know that and this is why they not only forced the Mercedes to go faster along the expressway but planned for the blocking vehicles to do as police expert witness Read had described and cause Henri Paul 'a major problem' at the tunnel's entrance. The Fiat blocked its path so that Paul didn't have the choice of going elsewhere.

Scott Baker added that this was worsened because those in the car were not wearing seatbelts but one can hardly accept his description of this as being merely 'unfortunate'. Why do you think that the Mercedes HQ in Stuttgart offered to inspect the Mercedes, on two occasions, and were turned down for no apparent reason? The Mercedes also wasn't allowed into the UK for seven years after the murder and was by then no longer intact. It is my view that tampering would have been discovered with both the brakes and seatbelts, had the Mercedes factory been permitted to inspect it.

Scott Baker also stressed that only Souad Mouffakir saw the Fiat during the attack, with the implication being that others didn't or that there are so many differing opinions of what happened that it's not possible to determine what did. My view is that this is typically disingenuous. Several witnesses saw two cars and one or two motorbikes and Laurent even mentioned an old white hatchback at the tunnel entrance, as did Levistre. In fact a few witnesses described James Andanson's Fiat rather well.

There was also similar evidence of motorbikes with yellow lights and white helmets or fuel tanks so, since we know the Fiat was there, this surely only serves to indicate that much goes unobserved in crime scene situations as police and judiciary are both well aware.

But even the court was forced into accepting that the Fiat was there and this despite attempts by the police to keep knowledge of its existence from the public for two weeks after the murder. In addition MI5 (British homeland security) were engaging in vigorous activities with Monsieur Cherruault, where his house was 'burgled' in London the day after Diana's murder and this had been clearly described by both the policeman Kemp and Cherruault.

During summation the coroner described the exchange between Cherruault and Kemp, who made the comment about grey men breaking into Cherruault's house, as some 'misunderstanding between them'. In my view it is a pity the jury were not reminded of what precisely was said between these two men when they first met. The policeman, Kemp, clearly said that Cherruault had been targeted by the security services; this evidence was avoided in court.

Sometimes the situation became surreal with Scott Baker at one juncture even raising a point over whether the Fiat, on entering the main carriageway from a slip road, had the right of way. Did the court seriously believe that the SAS were concerned about breaking motoring regulations? But the slip road was the logical place for assassins to lay in wait and Laurent described swerving to avoid vehicles on the slip road.

Where the Fiat came from, however, is surely less relevant than where it was and what it was doing when the Mercedes arrived at the tunnel. Scott Baker should have remembered the evidence from witnesses such as David Laurent, whose integrity he had no reason to question. Laurent considered that these vehicles were 'together', 'loitering' near the tunnel's entrance. 'Were the following vehicles in it, together with those near the tunnel?' inquired Scott

Baker. From the evidence of several witnesses, it appears certain that they were.

Scott Baker said, 'The Fiat was going at a maximum of forty mph,' and then he added, 'It could, of course, have been travelling less than forty mph,' again supported by Laurent's testimony ('loitering' vehicles would be travelling very slowly but they began to move as the Mercedes approached). So what did he think this Fiat was doing at the tunnel's entrance, 'loitering' in tandem with another larger, dark vehicle?

Scott Baker also said that the theories about the Fiat Uno failed to grapple with how anyone knew that the Mercedes would be travelling along the expressway, still ignoring any possible MI6 involvement. Yet with Henri Paul at the wheel and working for MI6, the assassins would have known the Mercedes' exact whereabouts and time of arrival at the Alma to within seconds. They would also have spotters en route to alert the assassins of the Mercedes' position.

It is the perennial contention of those who know the Princess of Wales was murdered that Paul was persuaded that the task ahead was to assist Dodi by raising his macho image with Diana.

There is also the suggestion that it wasn't necessary to force Henri Paul into the tunnel because the Mercedes could have been prevented from exiting the freeway before the tunnel by using a blocking vehicle. That, however, misses another crucial point.

The reason why the assassins drove fast behind the Mercedes was to force it to maintain a high speed on entering the tunnel and ensure a fatal impact. If the assassins had relied on vehicles to block the Mercedes' possible exit just before the Alma, the Mercedes would need to reduce speed before reaching this exit and, on realising it was blocked, couldn't regain sufficient speed for the assassins' purpose as the tunnel entrance is very close. This is why the assassins needed to force Paul into overtaking the blocking vehicle – to increase speed for the impact.

Another interesting point arises here. Philippe Dourneau, Dodi's regular driver, was available to drive that night, so why didn't he? Dourneau said this was the only time since he had worked for Dodi that someone else had driven him so what an amazing coincidence that Henri Paul should be chosen to drive solely on this occasion. Dourneau would have accepted this task and Paul could have remained outside the Ritz, goading the paparazzi, but lucky for him, Dourneau wasn't in the Security Service's pay and couldn't be relied on to follow the desired path.

Henri Paul placed a doorman, Didier Gamblin, at Dodi's apartment before the couple returned there from the Ritz at around 7.00pm on the Saturday evening. Gamblin gave his 'incontrovertible' affidavit evidence that he knew the couple would be in Paris from the previous Thursday so this evidence confirms that a specially selected team of military assassins had at least four days to prepare. Does anyone think they would need more than four days? These people were already on hand and there is logic, and some evidence, to indicate MI6 would have at least twelve full days' notice, through covert eavesdropping, to plan and prepare for this murder.

In addition, Alain Guizard, editor of the Angeli agency, told how he had witnessed Diana's arrival at the airport and then before they left the Ritz via the rear entrance, Martinez (one of the paparazzi) had telephoned him to say that Diana and Dodi would be leaving from the rear of the hotel. Clearly detailed information was available to Rocher and Martinez. It also appeared many others knew – except, if you are to believe the court, the British Security Services.

Scott Baker stated, 'Where evidence is incontrovertible, it makes sense to read the evidence rather than bring the witness to court,' and, as Gamblin's evidence was considered incontrovertible, presumably this meant the court was satisfied that his evidence was accurate. Why didn't Scott Baker accept that this incontrovertible evidence clearly shows MI6 had at least four days to prepare and say so during his summation?

Why then did Scott Baker continue to stress that they wouldn't have had time? Why ask for advice from experts in their field, such as police and Sir Richard Dearlove, and then discard it? But all incontrovertible evidence, such as Gamblin, Dr Dion and other eyewitnesses, was evidence that collectively could bring the curtain down and, in my view, needed to be curtailed. It was certainly undesirable to have the evidence from these people questioned in court.

Gamblin's evidence was given during the morning session on 23rd January but it didn't prevent Scott Baker from reiterating, during his April summation finale that if this was a murder plan by MI6, they would have had only hours in which to prepare. 'What motive would any individual in the Service have for murdering Dodi and Diana and, practically, how could it have been arranged at short notice in Paris on 30th August 1997?' Scott Baker re-stated. He once more flatly refused to accept the evidence of several people, including those whose evidence he had already declared to be 'incontrovertible', that MI6 had ample time to prepare.

Motive resides at the heart of this issue because it is true that MI6 officers would not have motive without exhortation from very senior figures; they would certainly never 'go it alone'. But perhaps the jury could have been reminded that the Security Services have a history of secret machinations within their organisation. For example, it is proven that MI5 engaged in careful and illicit scrutiny of a serving prime minister – Harold Wilson – and kept this knowledge to a select few within the Service.

In a similar vein of accepting evidence only when useful to direct the jury's conclusions (as I believe happened throughout the inquests), remember the testimony of Richard Tomlinson, where he stated that in his view it was unlikely the MI6 hierarchy would have implemented this crime, but that it was more likely a cabal of single-minded agents. (But even if so, these agents could have been another MI6 deniability ploy.) During summation, Scott Baker latched onto this when he said: 'So, no support for Mohamed Al Fayed's allegation that Prince Philip got MI6 to set up the crash is to be found in Tomlinson's evidence. He suggested that one or more members of MI6 could have arranged it unbeknown to the Service.'

This was, according to Dearlove's initial and autonomic opinion, impossible. There is, however, much evidence to suggest the presence of several senior MI6 personnel in Paris that weekend and even if you discount this amazing coincidence, you would still need to believe that a cabal of rogue agents executed this murder in the presence of a large contingent of their colleagues and without the nod from someone in a very senior position. But whether the hierarchy knew is irrelevant to any verdict because these people were serving agents, whoever initiated the order and so remained the government's responsibility.

The most credible route was for someone close to the royal family, who knew the machinations of MI6 and the military, to act as a go-between with senior people they knew within the Service. In this instance all participants could be considered rogue because this act would not have been officially approved by the Service hierarchy despite the majority of their senior personnel being aware. This would assist with the possible problem of keeping information from decent MI6 officers.

During the inquests, the police and Security Services both repeatedly insisted they had no interest in monitoring the Princess of Wales's whereabouts during the summer of 1997 but after the Paris incident both parties even denied knowing that Diana was in Paris at the end of August. Yet it was proven the authorities had been engaged in an illicit surveillance of Diana for several years and knew she was in the South of France with Mohamed Al Fayed in July 1997. More importantly, they had prior intelligence that she intended going there. Does anyone believe that MI6 would suddenly cease watching Diana when she travelled to Paris?

It was also shown that the Queen was informed of these intentions by very senior police officers and/or the Security Services. So, why didn't Her Majesty make these false police and MI6 statements known to her people, without waiting for lawyers to reveal this truth?

We also know that the then Chief of Police – Lord Condon – had received advice from his officers, who were watching Diana, that 'it was unwise for the holiday to take place at all'. The police passed on this advice to the Queen although Diana was leaving the royal family within weeks and this indicates, in my view that the royals still intended to control her movements and continued to abuse her civil liberties.

Evidence was forthcoming that the Security Services speak directly with the monarch, who has the power to seek redress on issues that cause her concern. In British so-called democracy, it's not acceptable for the monarch to be permitted dealings with those who are granted uncontrolled and unlimited powers over the people given that Britain has an elected government to make its executive decisions and that the monarch's democratic role, as head of state, is titular. I believe this could lead people into thinking that the monarch possesses unlimited powers also since, if MI6 possesses them and the Queen in turn gives them active directions, then she clearly possesses absolute powers.

Sir David Veness said he was making arrangements for the 'post mortem requirements that would be needed' when Diana's body was returned to the UK; also, that 'all appropriate samples and forensic exhibits should be properly collated and recorded'. He explained that he chose Jeffrey Rees over the duty officer to lead this process because he needed a man 'who could be relied on to collate all this evidence' but, since a proven 'diplomatic decision' was taken to embalm Diana in France, there was no remaining evidence to collate.

Do you believe that the reason given for Jeffrey Rees's appointment needed further explanation; why was he preferred? Veness headed up the repatriation so he would have known what was happening to Diana's remains and even a lawyer, who questioned John Macnamara in court, repeated on three occasions that there was 'an obvious need for a post mortem when Diana's body was returned to England'.

You may also recall the journalist Peter Allen saying he had been told by Madame Coujard that the order to embalm came from the top of the British Establishment. Allen, of course, was not invited to attend court.

David Veness appears as the common denominator in police scrutiny of Diana, both prior to and post the Paris incident. He admitted to not doing anything about her privacy being infiltrated during the 'Squigygate tape' incident and also to not investigating obvious leads or irregularities in the supposed police 'investigation' or as the police prefer to say, 'liaison', into her murder. (If the police were proven to be investigating then they were guilty of perverting the course of justice by withholding the Mishcon Note.)

Veness was the policeman responsible for Diana for over ten years but claimed he was unable to remember why he ignored any intrusion into her private life. Does anyone believe this is acceptable in a democratic society; again, what of Diana's civil liberties? He also admitted that his behaviour towards the Queen would have been different in these same circumstances but was unable to explain why.

Veness then confirmed that he knew of Diana's phone being tapped but did nothing about it, adding what proved to be his usual response: 'I cannot recall what action, if any, was taken.' This applied to all his dealings concerning Diana, none of which he claimed to remember (rather like MI6), which makes it hard to consider anything other than Veness's job was to ensure Diana was unable to do anything without the Palace knowing about it. So this is the man who was put in charge of Diana's murder 'investigation' (liaison?).

Scott Baker admitted there was some evidence 'that the crash was staged' with reference to the blocking, loitering, aggressive and hindering vehicles at the tunnel entrance but Veness admitted that he didn't even look into this transparent information. In my view this is de facto proof that he must have had another reason for not doing his job. Can anyone imagine any justifiable reason for the police not looking into such evidence? Why didn't the court question this omission? Veness also claimed that he had never heard of James Andanson and later dismissed him as being of no relevance; he just ignored him. (But remember how much time the court spent interviewing Andanson's wife and son and also the family of his friends, the Dards.)

The 'Mishcon note' – so-named because Diana gave it to her lawyer Lord Mishcon – in which she described her husband's intention to kill her in a car 'accident' was disgracefully kept hidden and the police feebly claimed they intended releasing it when 'they considered it appropriate'. But it's proven they only released it when they had no other choice. Following the note's forced disclosure as a result of Paul Burrell giving his note from Diana to the press, Lord Mishcon visited the police and the inquests were opened within weeks.

Does this not show that if the note had been released much earlier, then the inquests would have opened earlier and witness memories would have been brighter? More witnesses might have been alive, too. Don't forget the deaths of Gary Hunter, Frederic Dard, James Andanson and Lord Mishcon, any of whom could have brought the curtain down. (Also remember the politically high principled British Foreign Secretary, Robin Cook, the MI6 political boss when

Diana was murdered. He died under very strange circumstances on Ministry of Defence property a few months before the inquests opened; what, perhaps, had he discovered? This is my postulation. I have no evidence on this point.) But how could any police force justify holding back what they admitted was *'potentially relevant* [my italics] information' from a genuine investigation unless to hide a crime?

In addition, and despite Stephens having described Lord Mishcon as a 'very, very honourable man', Veness still tried to persuade the court that Mishcon agreed to break the law by withholding this note. In any event, this point is irrelevant because the decision was a police responsibility irrespective of Mishcon's preferences. Veness also stated that he had laid out his stall with two 'building blocks' (here we go again) for determining whether to release this note. These were that there must be some relevant suspicion concerning the deaths and that authority must be obtained from Lord Mishcon or his firm to release it.

I leave the question of suspicion to you but as for the other building block, no one sought Mishcon's permission as Lord Stevens confirmed in his own words: 'No one did it – it was not done at that stage.' In fact, it wasn't done at any stage, as the police later confirmed. Had the police approached Mishcon he would have agreed but then the inquest would have needed to be opened.

Lord Stevens let slip that Sir David Veness was the police linchpin who controlled the Diana 'problem', both prior to and post the Paris incident but since we know Veness worked with the Security Services and that his descriptions and opinions were taken as sacrosanct by the police, what hope was there of a fair and balanced view ever being taken of whether MI6 were in any way responsible?

Stevens also confirmed his lack of interest when he said with regard to the Mishcon note that, 'David Veness has the overall responsibility of liaising so I *suppose* (my italics) he would have been reviewing it as to when it should be disclosed.' He was neither aware of what Veness had done with regard to the Mishcon note, nor was he concerned.

Stevens fell further into the mire when questioned about comments he is reputed to have made in France to the parents of Henri Paul that, 'If this was an assassination, the repercussions in England would be great and incalculable.' This comment indicates serious doubts about whether this was an accident and, if Stevens did say this, then it also posed an inadvertent insight into the reasons for Diana's sham murder 'investigation'. Stevens denied saying this, despite witness evidence that he did, and said this comment was made by Sergeant Philip Easton.

A flustered Stevens spluttered that there was no evidence he made this remark but clearly didn't deny its utterance. So, do we presume he checked prior to attending court whether there was any further evidence of his having made this remark? But, if so, he only needed to check if he knew he had made it (since there would be no need to check if he knew he hadn't) and to ensure his denial couldn't be exposed in court. It didn't help his cause when he admitted having discussed his proposed evidence with Easton to, 'get their stories straight'.

Let us now look at Scott Baker's comments regarding Gerald Postner, an American journalist whom he ridiculed as being with the 'so-called Trusted Intelligence Sources'. Postner gave evidence that he had information from a source in the DGSE, the French equivalent of the CIA or MI6, but had received it from other contacts. Despite being ridiculed, his evidence was accepted because he stated that he didn't believe MI6 could have anything to do with this attack. However, Postner also said that Henri Paul was a paid informant of the DGSE and was with them during the Saturday afternoon but he believed it was pure coincidence this was the day before the attack, although he didn't explain why.

Henri Paul had apparently met with the DGSE to discuss other matters when some money was passed over. Dodi and Diana were discussed, though only in passing and this despite stating earlier that they discussed various things at the meeting 'that did not include Diana'. But 'Postner was told there was no suggestion of any relationship with either the American or British agencies' and the meeting was part business and part social (in other words, again stressing his opinion that MI6 were not involved).

Postner promised to contact his source and obtain further information, which did not materialise. Scott Baker did not endorse this testimony but it didn't prevent him from stressing: 'It is not related to any plot to kill or harm Diana.' However, the point concerning Paul's contact with the DGSE was ignored.

Also remember John Macnamara's visit to the USA where he approached high-level people in the US government at the Pentagon with Senator Mitchell of Northern Ireland fame for information on Diana that it was known they possessed. First it was granted and then the judge's directions were reversed, clearly following a request from London for the records to remain secluded. A further request was made by Senator Mitchell for the files to be released for his perusal but the reason for denial was that national security could be threatened; does this ring any bells? Who believes Senator Mitchell would threaten US national security?

Scott Baker declared James Andanson's bizarre suicide was 'inappropriate to these proceedings' and said, 'If he wasn't in Paris, then he couldn't have done the deed.' You will recall that this assumption was made simply because of Pierre Suu's proclamation that he would have known if Andanson had been in Paris and Andanson would have been noticed. This opinion was accepted in sharp contrast to the court's stated view of all other paparazzi, where they were dismissed as having 'an axe to grind'. Suu didn't attend court.

As we have seen, Andanson went on a 200km round trip on the Saturday morning to spend seven minutes in a town called Vierzon that happens to have a railway transportation system to Paris. Despite being only 100km from Paris, he then apparently went home to Lignières and returned again to Paris the next morning, travelling on to Corsica. This is despite a major event that he has pursued for years being about to unfold and having just joined a major paparazzi organisation specialising in this kind of work.

He owned a white Fiat Uno car, which happened to be the same type of car that we know crashed into Diana's Mercedes. Andanson's car was damaged in exactly the same place as the attack Fiat had been damaged. We know this from debris found in the tunnel (despite the police keeping these details – and the Fiat – hidden from the public for two whole weeks after the crash).

Andanson gave conflicting alibis and didn't sell any photographs of his 'assignment' to Corsica so, do we believe he went there? The court conceded that Andanson had lied to police about his whereabouts (and therefore his alibi) but said Andanson had apologised, so this statement was accepted without further question. The police didn't tell the court whether Andanson was asked if he was in Paris when Diana was murdered nor why Andanson lied to them and there was no explanation as to why they were so relaxed about these disclosures. Of course Andanson could have told them everything, yet, for some reason, this evidence wasn't made available to the court.

We have seen the evidence of Mrs Andanson, where she states that her husband was at home that night despite her son saying (later contradicted) that he wasn't. But it was proven that James Andanson wasn't home because his son reaffirmed that when he returned home that evening, having borrowed one of the family's two BMW cars, the other car wasn't in the garage; his mother confirmed that she was at home, so clearly his father was not.

We were told Mrs Andanson initially believed MI6 had murdered her husband (later denied), but one must wonder why she would think the British Security Services had any reason to kill him in the first place. After all, he was merely a photographer!

Mrs Andanson was uneasy when asked about a phone call she received from a Monsieur Poincloux on the morning of her husband's disappearance but said she didn't know who this man was – the call was for her son. When asked, her son had never heard of him. We are told that James Andanson was known to be indiscreet and had been bragging about being in the tunnel when Diana was murdered; he said that he had photographs to prove it and claimed they would be '*un Baum*' – in other words, they would rock the world.

We then migrate to his mysterious death, some thirty-three months later during which he shot himself twice in the head before self-cremation in his locked BMW car. Christophe Pelât, the fireman from Montpelier who witnessed the two holes in Andanson's skull, wasn't even called despite expressing a desire to attend. Andanson's car keys were never found.

Another enormous coincidence is that Frédéric Dard, a famous crime writer and friend of Andanson, died five weeks after

Andanson's 'suicide'. Dard's daughter gave evidence that some weeks before her father's death he had discussed co-writing a book with Andanson on the attack on Diana in the tunnel. Dard would, therefore, at the time of his death, have held some very dangerous information on that attack. Strange that Dard and Andanson should specifically talk of an attack in the tunnel.

Elizabeth Dion, the French radiologist, said she had seen a radiogram of Diana womb in Paris and there were clear signs of an early developing pregnancy. Dr Dion did not give evidence in person and so she could not be cross-examined, but she sent a sworn affidavit into court, saying merely that at the time of the attack she was working as a visiting professor in San Francisco, with no mention of her previously stated observations on Diana's pregnancy.

Whereas we do not doubt Dr Dion's new appointment in San Francisco, what she omitted to do was confirm her whereabouts on the night of 30th August 1997, or say how she could have read the radiogram and observed a foetus in Diana's womb if she was in the USA. Her previous observation of having a clear picture of an early pregnancy cannot just be ignored without satisfactory comment. People do go home for a holiday and August is a popular time for many – surely Dr Dion was in Paris that night?

It is strange that Detective Sergeant Philip Easton from the British police wasn't able to find Dr Dion; it fell to a British *Daily Mail* newspaper reporter, Sue Reid, to do so and then Easton contacted Dr Dion on 2nd and then 12th June 2006, by telephone. Either Dr Dion, in common with other dangerous witnesses, wasn't asked to give evidence or she refused and instead sent a written sworn statement so couldn't be questioned in court. (One might be somewhat suspicious that Dr Dion didn't attend and the police were unable to find her when a reporter did.)

This was fortunate for those seeking to confound justice because scrutiny of her evidence would elicit a reason why French medics, who gave written evidence on Henri Paul's blood samples, elected not to attend the hearing and were not required to do so by the authorities. But since Diana's embalming was a diplomatic decision, then perhaps this explains the authorities' reluctance to have Dr Dion testify in court. Confirmation of Diana's pregnancy would greatly accentuate the motive for murder.

Scott Baker said that 'the Fiat was a poor choice to knock the Mercedes off its path'. But this is based on his assumption that this was the assassin's intent. He should have remembered the evidence from expert police witness Anthony Read, who said that if there had been a blocking vehicle in the left-hand lane and a slow-moving vehicle in the right-hand lane, both affirmed as happening by eyewitness evidence, there should be no need for the Fiat to crash into the Mercedes. The vehicle's mere presence would have caused any driver 'a serious problem'.

Scott Baker repeated the crash would have been 'a hit-and-miss' affair for assassins but we again refer to Read's evidence, in which he added that a presence in the right-hand lane was sufficient to cause a major problem and in these circumstances, the pillars were the probable outcome. Also remember when lawyers showed that MI6 had lied about Richard Tomlinson's evidence to the French authorities concerning their plan to assassinate Slobodan Milosevic in a Geneva tunnel using the same method that they used to murder Diana? You must first consider whether MI6 would lie to the French about something trivial and then decide whether they would ask the SAS to use this plan if it was a 'hit and miss' affair, especially considering the consequences to MI6 of discovery.

Scott Baker then asked the jury to put themselves in the place of Henri Paul and, separately, to consider whether 'the following vehicles' were in it together as a joint enterprise: he would hardly make this suggestion, if illogical. Indeed several witnesses described that this is precisely what happened.

The reason Scott Baker gave for ridiculing the notion that an assassin would deliberately crash into the Mercedes was because the Fiat was considerably smaller than the Mercedes and the assassin himself could have been killed. This is not unreasonable but remember that the Fiat's primary goal was to prevent the Mercedes achieving recovery after the strobe flash into Paul's eyes and to ensure it struck the pillars. It did not intend to make contact with the Mercedes since a collision would leave evidence (which it did), and that is the last thing these killers wanted.

Scott Baker did, however, follow this by saying if it was an attack, then the intent to frighten and not kill was nonsense (I agree). He accepted that in a murderous attack these people wouldn't want any of the car's occupants giving evidence against them. (You will recall one of the bodyguards, Trevor Rees-Jones, having said to Al Fayed's cleaning lady, 'If I remember, they will kill me.') It's also interesting to note that Scott Baker intimated assassins could only know details of the route in advance with Security Services intelligence. It's one of the reasons why the truth must never be known because he is right; this attack could only have been directed by a Security Services organisation.

Since Scott Baker gave consideration to this possibility, doesn't it stretch disbelief that he did not consider how the Mercedes would be directed towards the tunnel, Henri Paul's whereabouts on the Saturday afternoon and where his cash deposits came from? These are explained by the same theory. The reason for the collision is that the Mercedes had escaped the first attack so the Fiat needed to pursue it and block it again, where it would have no alternative other than to veer towards the tunnel's pillars (again, remember police evidence that blocking by the Fiat alone would have caused it a major problem). Without this second manoeuvre, the attack could have failed.

The court advised the jury that substantive proof was needed before they could draw the conclusion that Henri Paul and the paparazzi were responsible for the manslaughter of Diana, Dodi and Henri Paul. Scott Baker summed up these requirements as follows:

> 'It is not sufficient to prove mere negligence, which only gives rise to damages claims: manslaughter requires gross negligence.' He also said, 'The conduct of the driver must be so bad in all circumstances to amount to the criminal act or omission; it must be proved to have been reckless.'

The next comment further illustrates the obstacles faced when he said, 'It must be clear the driver actually foresaw the risk of death but ran it nonetheless.' Scott Baker then added: 'The jury must *be sure* (my italics) what was going on at the critical time and whether the various vehicles that surrounded Diana's car were working in tandem. Were they in it together?' But several witnesses had remarked that these vehicles were working 'in tandem' and also 'following each other very closely'. You must decide whether these people were paparazzi or assassins.

Another interesting thought is that if the court was so convinced it was paparazzi that were following the Mercedes, why then were they not described as 'the paparazzi' instead of 'the following vehicles' throughout these inquests and why permit jury inculcation during summation by then referring to them as 'the paparazzi'?

Surely it follows that the reason they were called 'the following vehicles' was because even the court couldn't presume it was paparazzi so this obviously shows that Henri Paul couldn't have known who was 'aggressively and dangerously' pursuing him either? Again, Scott Baker's conditions were not met and the jury couldn't be sure of gross negligence or recklessness to any standard, let alone the one purportedly required by the court.

The jury couldn't know what Paul was thinking: he might have been driving fast through safety fears from speeding paparazzi or assassins, so it's reasonable to presume that he simply saw the need to escape from this aggressive driving, showing that his behaviour should have been entirely vindicated. Either way, Scott Baker's conditions to prove manslaughter by showing Paul was 'reckless' or that he could see 'he risked death but ran it nonetheless' were not met. This meant his actions did not reflect gross negligence but that Paul acted reasonably and in good faith.

To find for manslaughter the jury also needed to believe that those proven to be at the tunnel and around the Mercedes and before the paparazzi arrived were innocent bystanders despite several witnesses having described the vehicles as 'aggressive', 'together', 'loitering' and acting as 'blocking' vehicles with flashes of light being delivered towards the Mercedes' driver.

More doubt was thrown on whether Henri Paul had consumed

excessive amounts of alcohol by the crash expert Dr John Searle, who said that although alcohol impairs nearly all driving abilities, he was not persuaded this had any relevance, even if the driver was twice over the limit; a view echoed by Professor Forrest.

Also, the police didn't have any blood results from Paul when they made their statement to the world that he was drunk so this completely negated the police view. Even if he had, there was no certainty that it would have made any difference without consideration being given to Paul's alcohol tolerance.

We also remind you of Inspector Scotchbrook's comment (one of Scotland Yard's Paget team) that Henri Paul had had only 'a few drinks and no more'. Stevens interdicted that this isn't what Scotchbrook meant to say. He didn't clarify what she *did* mean. In fact, details concerning Henri Paul's apparent drunkenness should never have been admitted into evidence. It's clear from the coroner's own words that there is the probability of switched samples and a huge question mark over the excessive carbon monoxide in his blood; it was impossible for his blood to contain this amount of CO and for him to be still standing, let alone driving a car.

(The police tried to claim that this carbon monoxide came from the Mercedes' airbags upon impact with the pillars. When asked, Mercedes said their airbags don't contain carbon monoxide. Also, the fire-fighters that arrived on site have equipment that detects various gases; none were present. Remember the poor soul that had committed suicide by using his car's exhaust fumes and whose body lay next to Henri Paul's in the mortuary. Where do you think the blood samples came from?)

DNA tests were not carried out on Paul's blood samples when they were supposed to be, and when called for, these samples had gone missing. In the morgue, the number of Paul's body was incorrectly recorded and two medicines that he was supposed to have taken even prompted the coroner to suggest that the police may have planted evidence. Scott Baker then said that the blood source was very much in doubt and questioned whether there had even been 'a deliberate mix-up', later adding, 'Is this Paul's blood?'

But following this comment from Scott Baker, even 'Accident

theorists' surely cannot have any remaining doubts that the blood evidence should never have been permitted to stand. Scott Baker told the jury, 'Even if you were satisfied that the 31st August sample had come from Henri Paul you would want to consider whether this *inexplicable reading causes you to have doubts about the whole process of analysis. If the carbon monoxide readings must be wrong, what about the alcohol readings, the Prozac readings, the Tiapride readings?'* (My italics.)

Scott Baker had no confidence in these results and even considered police corruption. Why didn't he reject this evidence and refuse to permit the court to find Paul responsible for the crash?

Another extraordinary occurrence is that Scott Baker had established eight building blocks at the commencement of proceedings that he must address during the hearing. One of these was that he was to discover where the money in Paul's bank accounts came from, since it was generally believed that this was payment from MI6 for the night's work. But during the hearing, and for some inexplicable reason, Scott Baker switched to this comment (with reference to Paul's unexplained amounts of cash), 'In any event, are these mysteries relevant to any verdict?' How could a judge make the specific comment that this was one of his main building blocks only to change his mind completely and without explanation?

We once more repeat a major point. Scott Baker was content to accept a verdict from the jury that Henri Paul was responsible for this crash, so long as the jury were satisfied of the above criteria where as you can see, and Scott Baker concurred, there was enormous room for doubt. Also remember that the police said Paul was drunk before they had even received his blood results and there is much evidence to suggest that Paul wasn't drunk at all; reference the Paget inquiries' Inspector Scotchbrook's comments.

But, despite accepting the above, Scott Baker wasn't prepared to permit the jury the option of doing their democratic duty by finding for unlawful killing by persons unknown because, in his words:

'...I explained to you at the start of my summing-up why I had decided that there was insufficient evidence for you *to be sure* (my italics) that this was "Unlawful Killing by Staged Accident".'

Scott Baker clearly acknowledged here that there is 'some evidence, albeit of doubtful quality, that the crash was staged'. But it's all right to accept a verdict on extremely dubious evidence such as Henri Paul's results based on Scott Baker's view of 'any alcohol he *may* (my italics) have consumed' when it's known the police didn't have Paul's blood results when they proclaimed to the world that he was drunk.

And then it's all right to presume Paul's unknown thought processes when confronted by these aggressive vehicles; this wasn't sufficient to satisfy the court's grounds for a manslaughter verdict. (Remember Scott Baker's instruction to the jury that they must *be sure* [my italics] that Paul saw the risk of death but ran it nonetheless when, from the evidence, it's clear Paul couldn't know whether he was being pursued by paparazzi or assassins).

But it's unacceptable to find for unlawful killing by persons unknown because the coroner couldn't *be sure* (my italics) that these aggressive, loitering, hindering and blocking vehicles were assassins, despite substantial evidence to the contrary. So the jury were denied the option of finding for a verdict that would bring the curtain down on the monarchy and, now, many British officials.

Don't forget that two of the eleven jurors were clearly not prepared to bow down to pressure and so, although Scott Baker had said that the verdicts 'must be unanimous'; they were not. Also, these two jurors were most probably not the only ones that would have opted for a verdict of unlawful killing by persons unknown if they had had the option. But since this verdict, as Scott Baker intimated, would have meant that MI6 were responsible, I believe that the two dissenting jurors shared my view and believed that MI6 had committed this vile crime.

The court also stressed that the reason for the deaths was in part because of the speed at which the Mercedes hit the pillar and the fact that seatbelts were not worn: 'Failure to wear seatbelts cannot have caused this crash but it may have contributed to their deaths. There was also evidence that the fact of striking the pillar rather than, for example, the opposite wall increased the forces involved and the likelihood of death.' All along, we have stated that it is a probability the seatbelts were rendered useless before the journey for this express purpose and since the court was able to reason this would greatly contribute to the deaths, isn't it obvious that so too would the assassins?

When discussing evidence from the witnesses Searle, Jennings and Read, the court did not remind the jury that the Mercedes wasn't delivered to the UK for seven years and in bits. It was not possible to determine whether the seatbelts had been rendered useless and the court didn't question why the authorities refused to accept several offers of assistance from the Mercedes factory in Germany. It's true that the pillars increased the chances of death and this is why the murderers used the plan that Richard Tomlinson had seen while in MI6, where a similar technique was planned for Slobodan Milosevic's demise where the pillars were specifically mentioned as being necessary to increase the probability of death and speed was obviously crucial to this ploy.

One witness, James Huth, gave evidence that, having lived near the tunnel for twenty years, he couldn't see why a car would apply the brakes so violently unless there was something in its way, offering further confirmation of blocking vehicles. You will recall also the very important witness, Alain Remy, whose offer to attend the hearing was declined. He said that he was driving his black VW Golf on the freeway when, after emerging from under the Pont Alexandre III (the one just before the Pont des Invalides), he was overtaken by a large black car travelling at around eighty-seven to ninety-four km/h. At this point there were no other vehicles, including paparazzi, in sight.

This crucial testimony was vigorously challenged and it is worth repeating here. If there were no following vehicles near the Mercedes at this point of the journey, clearly the paparazzi couldn't have been involved. But where did the loitering vehicles at the Alma, and also the pursuing motorbikes that chased the Mercedes into the tunnel, come from?

These loitering and aggressive vehicles began the assault upon the arrival of the Mercedes. Some were waiting at the tunnel's entrance, as witness evidence confirmed, while the bikes were probably under the Pont des Invalides and rapidly accelerated as the Mercedes approached. We know that other vehicles were on the slip road before the Alma tunnel (Laurent entered from the slip road and described the loitering vehicles that he swerved to avoid) and Gooroovadoo mentioned vehicles parked on the verge by the side of the tunnel.

The court proceeded to question whether Remy was even there and challenged his integrity by suggesting that it couldn't have been Diana's Mercedes. It was suggested his memory of timing was in question because this testimony was fundamentally crucial. There was only one crashed Mercedes in the Alma that night, however, so do we really believe a man would deliberately lie about such an issue? Remember, he had offered to come to England and give testimony to the British police but they didn't even bother to telephone him, having 'lost' his initial letter; also, his statement 'wasn't received' by the police.

Scott Baker asked whether it was likely Dodi would have played an active role in wanting to leave from the rear of the hotel because he had been upset by the paparazzi when he and Diana returned from their abandoned Chez Benoît supper. He says that one would think Dodi would be 'anxious to ensure that the arrangements went more smoothly thereafter'. Does this suggest the likelihood of some input on his part into what was to happen?'

Well yes, of course, because Dodi intended that those arrangements should go smoothly. He wanted to ensure his earlier experience at the front of the Ritz would not be repeated, so he used the same ploy that he and Diana had adopted only five weeks earlier when they left from the rear of the Ritz; successfully on that occasion.

Scott Baker repeated the question of how Henri Paul could arrange the rear exit plan, saying, 'He only knew about it minutes before departure,' before adding, 'There is no basis for saying that he had any idea of the third car plan until he was told by M Thierry Rocher at about half past ten.' But it had already been proven that Paul orchestrated this ploy and gave the order. Also, again remember the 'uncontroversial' evidence of Gamblin where he confirmed that MI6 knew at least four days before the murder took place. I believe they knew at least twelve days before the attack; after the engagement ring was purchased.

Scott Baker considered there was no evidence that MI6 gave Paul instructions, despite evidence given in court that it was Henri Paul who gave the order to leave by the back door. He initially rejected the MI6 connection and dismissed any idea that Paul could have been in a guiltless alliance with them. It is palpable Paul knew of the rear escape plan a long time before his conversation with Rocher; evidence proved some of the paparazzi did!

Scott Baker later contradicted this previous observation, in my view, because of the strength of the evidence and said, 'It may have been a decision made by Henri Paul himself on the assumption that that was what Dodi wanted. Either way, it is apparent that Dodi expected Henri Paul to organise it and that is what he did.' So, from this it's clear that the court now accepted that Paul was associated with the rear-exit plan.

Referring to evidence from the Ritz's assistant manager, Rocher, Scott Baker then said: 'So, here is clear evidence, if you accept it, that the initiative to depart from the normal practice of having a car and back-up vehicle leaving from the front came from Dodi (as opposed to the bodyguards). But for that decision, you may think that any staged accident could not really have happened.'

Perhaps we could consider this the alternative way. Since it was accepted by the court that the order did come from Dodi, then this is further evidence that, at the very least, a 'staged accident' could have taken place, especially since Scott Baker had already intimated this and also conceded that there was some evidence of a staged attack. Why then preclude the option of a verdict that reflected this and why take MI6 and the royals out of consideration for any guilt since the court intimated that only a security services organisation could have conducted this attack?

I believe it to be incredulous that a judge could be so contradictory by accepting that assassination was possible and then not permitting any consideration that MI6 and the royals could have been behind it. This was the entire, purported reason for the hearing.

Scott Baker also alluded to a short period when Paul was out of sight of the CCTV cameras, saying, 'There is a short period of about eight minutes when Henri Paul is out of view of the CCTV cameras at the front of the Ritz, so it must have been in that period that he made the necessary arrangements.'

It's my view that this comment is sardonic and grotesquely insulting to people's intelligence. It's absurd to suggest that such preparations would be left to an off-chance conversation with Henri Paul during a snatched eight-minute interlude. But this is yet a further indication that Scott Baker wasn't prepared to allow even the thought of MI6 involvement.

I believe the final review of this plan, as Richard Tomlinson suggested, was during the Saturday afternoon when Henri Paul's whereabouts for a three-hour period remain unknown. Scott Baker said the jury might think there is no evidence or no reason why Paul should have contacted people away from the hotel, but conceded: 'It is theoretically possible for Henri Paul to have contacted people away from the hotel after the plan was made to leave from the rear. But you may think that there is no evidence that he did, and no evidence of any reason why he should have done so,' thus continuing to downplay Paul's association with MI6.

Add to this Scott Baker's change of heart regarding the source of Paul's money when he questioned whether this was 'relevant to any verdict', despite this point being one of the eight initial building blocks that he set out to address at the start of the inquests and one can only wonder how the jury coped with all the perverse reasoning that abounded in court.

Scott Baker says with reference to claims that Philip, Duke of Edinburgh (Her Majesty, Queen Elizabeth II's husband) was the mastermind behind Diana's murder,

> 'The benefit of these last six months is that various propositions that were being asserted have been shown to be without foundation that they are not being pursued by Mohamed Al Fayed's lawyers, even if he carries the belief of their truth in his own mind. They are not being pursued because there is not a shred of evidence to support them.

Foremost among them is the proposition that Diana was assassinated by the Secret Intelligence Service [MI6] on the orders of the Duke of Edinburgh. There is no evidence that the Duke of Edinburgh ordered Diana's execution and there is no evidence that the Secret Intelligence Service or any other government agency organised it.'

You will all by now be aware that I take great issue with that proclamation and would you really expect much evidence, unless dug out of them, especially when it was proven during proceedings that MI6 shredded many documents. I presume this means evidence.

Scott Baker also gave his view that accusations against the Duke of Edinburgh had become muted and then made perhaps the most illuminating comment in support of MI6:

'One reason, perhaps *the* reason, (my italics) why the conspiracy has shifted from the original allegation that the Duke of Edinburgh was its mastermind is the unprecedented manner in which the Secret Intelligence Service and indeed others have been prepared to open their doors and give evidence about their inner workings. No longer can it be said, as Mohamed Al Fayed has frequently complained, that there was a steel wall that it was completely impossible to penetrate.'

Let us consider this. Having read the dissertation on MI6 in this book and their earlier 'evidence', I believe you will agree that this wall flourishes as nuclear proof.

So, if Scott Baker is right and this is the main reason why any consideration of conspiracy had shifted away from Edinburgh (Although I take issue that it did), then you would need to believe that MI6 opened their doors and freely gave unbiased evidence.

But, if you do not accept that MI6 gave unbiased evidence and instead accept this book's reasoning that they only turned up because they were required to clear the air finally and that their 'evidence' was worthless, then Scott Baker's main reason for exculpating MI6 goes up in smoke. MI6 answered as few questions as possible, prevaricated on many and refused to answer those that they didn't wish to answer so we know they had a great deal to hide.

Accusations against Edinburgh may have appeared muted because it is almost impossible to pursue the truth when MI6 is involved. (Don't forget the Way Ahead Group where MI6 agents and Edinburgh used to discuss, presumably, the way ahead; from their perspective, of course.)

Remember, MI6 is an organisation that doesn't issue books on assassination techniques, only handouts and when asked why an 'abhorrent' proposal that they initially denied ever existed wasn't destroyed, they said it was because 'they might go back to it'.

Of course the most blatant example of perverse MI6 behaviour during the inquests was when Richard Dearlove, ex-boss 'C' of MI6, immediately conceded that the lawyers had 'dug this one out' with reference to the Cayman Islands' incident (where MI6 had been criticised by a judge and was proven to have perverted the course of justice in a court of law).

When asked about this, just moments before its revelation in court, Dearlove had denied knowing of any such criminal behaviour. Whether he had just committed perjury in this court would be determined by whether he remembered this incident before answering the lawyer's question. We cannot say he did know but he spontaneously knew of this incident when it was put to him. His memory didn't need jogging which is amazing for MI6; most have appalling memories. So you must decide whether or not Dearlove committed perjury.

Add the tacit admission by MI6 that they deliberately deceived the French police about Richard Tomlinson's evidence on MI6 plans for an intended attack on Slobodan Milosevic, President of Serbia, (because it was almost identical to the plan used to murder Diana) which Tomlinson confirmed having seen and the picture continues to grow (The Cayman felony that MI6 were proven guilty of was on Dearlove's watch as 'C', the MI6 chief) but you will now appreciate that, although difficult to seek justice with these wretched people, it is worth continuing to seek slips in their 'evidence'.

Lawyers showed that MI6 do indeed murder people as part of

their remit, which was at first vigorously denied until they were forced to admit that they do sometimes, 'but only with a minister's approval'. (Robin Cook would certainly not have given his approval to murder Diana but more likely arrested those who mooted such a crime.) When asked about the use of white and pink paper in their reporting, they were caught out concerning why a file had been shredded but shouldn't have been. They described that situation as where 'white, treated as pink' (also proven as yet another untruth during proceedings by Witness X) and Tomlinson confirmed that this couldn't happen under MI6 rules for it would be 'a hanging offence'.

If in difficulty during questioning, MI6 said they could not answer for reasons of national security, but Witness I refused to answer virtually everything asked without intercession by the court. His name was not, of course, revealed but could it be Richard Spearman? According to Richard Tomlinson, Spearman was in Paris a few weeks before and during the attack on Diana and was also the MI6, SAS liaison officer. Perhaps one can understand why such a person would be reluctant to be interrogated.

Then we remember Witness 'X', the official contact for Lord Stephens' Scotland Yard inquiry team, who was granted 'God's access' to all files within the Service. Clearly a very senior officer whose modesty mustn't be allowed to mask her station, she claimed to have given Lord Stevens all that he had asked for. But she didn't give him valuable evidence that the lawyers needed to educe in court, such as the confidential write-up of agent 'A's' assassination proposal report, which she claimed not to have remembered. (Would any of you fail to remember if you had read a proposal that described the need to assassinate a head of state?) MI6 obviously planned their responses to the court for the existence of this document was only revealed the previous week during Dearlove's interrogation by lawyers so what else didn't she reveal?

The excuse for not revealing this evidence to the police inquiry was that 'X' 'didn't want to lead police in certain directions'. But here more untruths were apparent because she had just given evidence that she couldn't remember this file. Therefore how could she have consciously decided not to lead the police by giving it to them when she cannot remember it?

Richard Dearlove said it would not have been possible for rogue officers to execute this attack, which Scott Baker ignores. He continues to insist that it could have been rogue officers. But having said it could be rogue officers seemed to allow the court to presume that this somehow let MI6 off the hook. However, we have shown there would have been no possibility of bringing these people to book, thanks to a suitable verdict being unavailable, and so, even here, justice would, once more, have gone unrequited. (Also, why didn't the court pursue these rogue officers or request that the police do so if they genuinely believed this could be the case? Why didn't the court ask Dearlove why he didn't pursue them? My belief is that Dearlove changed his evidence to suit the court and assist MI6.)

MI6 initially denied that Richard Tomlinson saw a plan for the assassination of Slobodan Milosevic despite Tomlinson describing the plans he saw from one of his close colleagues, Witness 'A', as being entitled 'The need to assassinate Slobodan Milosevic'. Scott Baker said that Tomlinson's evidence was flawed because of his antipathy towards his former employers MI6 with reference to his dangerous evidence on having been trained in the use of strobe guns while training with the SAS and SBS military during his MI6 induction program (Tomlinson was in the SAS before joining MI6). MI6 categorically denied this, but the court had already accepted Tomlinson's testimony in support of a point where he agreed with Scott Baker on rogue officers.

Tomlinson stated that, in his view, 'It was unlikely MI6 would have implemented this crime but that a cabal of single-minded agents might.' The court appeared to allow this evidence from Tomlinson whereas they disputed it when he talked of strobe guns and of his training with MI6. Surely Tomlinson's testimony is either flawed or it isn't? One cannot pick and choose evidence that suits a particular purpose and take a different view of the witness when it does not, as this court did on more than one occasion.

Remember, Dearlove was asked whether MI6 permits murder and he initially stated, unequivocally, it does not. But he was later forced into confessing that all Section 7 proposals seeking authorisation for murdering people went through him as operations director (He didn't say who authorised these murders but may I speculate, following Dearlove's above admission that he did.)

So, MI6 do kill people but apparently only under 'special circumstances', which is in contradiction to the previous MI6 statement that they do not murder people. Add Dearlove's admission that '...all these proposals (for murdering people) went through him as Operations Director' during the period in which Diana was murdered and all you need to decide upon is whether Diana could be considered a 'special circumstance' when you then have an admission – straight from the lips of a former MI6 boss – that she was, at least, most definitely a potential target.

The MI6 operations director travels to Paris just before the incident, together with the MI6 SAS liaison officer. They prevaricate about having given all their evidence to the Lord Stevens' inquiry; also about their use of heads of security at major hotels since this was confirmed as a main target for MI6 officers to recruit, so Henri Paul would have been of routine interest to them.

They were also equivocal about the use of strobe guns and on several other occasions throughout the proceedings. What was their reasoning? Even more interestingly, why did they attend court knowing they would have to be economical with the truth and under full public gaze? From what imperative truth did they need to divert people's minds that justified them taking such a risk?

Remember also that we show MI6 and the police were watching Diana's every move during her last summer, contrary to their evidence. We are shown that the results of any tests concerning the alcohol levels in Henri Paul's blood were not available to police when the world was told he was drunk, so we hope your verdict is building, and remember, the judge at these inquests neither arrested nor even admonished any of these MI6 witnesses for avoiding lawyers' questions in court and he was certainly aware of all the truths herein described. So we ask that you decide why MI6 were permitted to be equivocal throughout these inquests, as it is proven they were.

The public will not tolerate such an abuse of their hoped for democracy ad infinitum and murdering the few people whom they adore is a certain way of ensuring MI6's proscription. The motive for this murder also raises serious questions over the continuance of the monarchy. If illicit actions from the Security Services are required for this system's continuance, it will soon lose the support of the people and so its nemesis would be nigh. Already we have made the point that since the royal family has strong links to MI6, the assassination route to circumvent the government would be a few select officers accompanying their 'Increment' team as a so-called 'black operation'. But from whom would MI6 accept such an order?

We know of Richard Dearlove's visit to Paris a few weeks before the murder and of Richard Spearman, whom we believe was Witness 'I', who was with Dearlove and had been stationed there two weeks before the attack. An undocumented 'black op' would restrict its knowledge to a small number of agents since it's unlikely all MI6 agents would be prepared to countenance such criminal behaviour. But, if performed without the consent of either the MI6 hierarchy or the government, what was the operations director (and soon to be boss of MI6) doing with the MI6 SAS liaison officer in Paris that night together with a large number of MI6 agents?

Surely it's more logical that the murder was executed by MI6 and knowledge kept from the main body of agents and that the rogue officers' option was an MI6 'deniability' ploy? Otherwise you must believe that a cabal of officers did this without the nod from someone at the pinnacle of power, which surely most people will agree is extremely naïve. And why didn't Scott Baker ask the police to immediately begin looking for these rogue officers? I believe we all know.

It was confirmed the Service have a team of military hard men known as the 'Increment' and Dearlove did not deny this but also admitted 'having other capabilities about which we all know nothing'. So since we are told by Richard Tomlinson that this 'Increment' is made up from the SBS and SAS military services and are required to be 'ethically flexible', what do you think they do for a living? MI6 had the motive, the means and the opportunity; they were there in numbers and they also stayed silent. The French and British police were operating at the highest political level and the British police were ordered to stand down. Does anyone need further proof of bias or conspiracy?

(Certainly it is true that MI6 attended court, but consider the alternative: an inquest held without them would be meaningless and so to bring this matter to a close, they needed to persuade people of their benign intent and so fool them again. They were required to show they had nothing to hide, but were extremely disappointed by the lawyers' torrid questioning, although they managed to avoid answering most pertinent questions.)

The court refused to allow either HM Queen Elizabeth II or her husband Prince Philip, Duke of Edinburgh, to be called to give evidence on the basis that there was insufficient evidence to justify it, nor would they permit a verdict to be returned against the Duke of Edinburgh because:

'The coroner's rules prohibit any verdict that appears to determine civil liability generally or criminal liability of a named person. Parliament has decided that inquest verdicts should not appear to determine the question of criminal liability of a named person. An unlawful killing verdict amounts to a finding that a crime has been committed, even though it may be obvious who the jury believe have committed the crime.'

Unless my reasoning has betrayed me then this means it is perfectly acceptable for the common citizen to be labelled a criminal but those in one particular family should be excused such an affront – even when they are, in essence, the ones in the dock. If so, then it follows that the court never intended to permit their scrutiny and had already decided on a verdict before the commencement of proceedings. (Such a verdict wouldn't necessarily involve Edinburgh since it could have been someone else actually liaising with MI6, although I do believe that Scott Baker got this right by thinking that most people would assume Edinburgh gave the order.)

You will note, however, that everyone in court – indeed the whole world – knew Henri Paul's name and all the paparazzi were also individually named, so how does this square with Parliament and the people's democracy? The court didn't seem concerned about allowing these people to be vilified and blamed for the whole event, even when innocent.

Of the verdicts available to the jury, the only permitted one that could cause any embarrassment to the British State or the monarchy was the open verdict. Scott Baker laid this out clearly. The jury were permitted to return a verdict against Henri Paul, or the following vehicles or both. An open verdict would mean a lingering and festering wound in the British psyche since, from the establishment's view, there would then be no closure. (Note that the following vehicles refer to either paparazzi or, of course, assassins so you might be surprised that Scott Baker at one point referred to them during summation not as the following vehicles but as the paparazzi. Was this a slip or deliberate to inculcate the jury's thinking?)

But note that since the jury were not permitted the option of the verdict 'unlawful killing by persons unknown' they were effectively prevented from returning any verdict that could cause a serious problem to the state and the monarchy. I once more repeat the important point during his summation when Scott Baker was trying to clarify why he wasn't permitting this verdict;

'...I had decided that there was insufficient evidence for you *to be sure* that this was unlawful killing by a staged accident.'

But we know Scott Baker was aware that some evidence existed when he said in court that '...there was evidence, albeit of limited quality, that the crash was staged' but he decided there wasn't sufficient. I thought that that is what juries are for in a democratic society. But I repeat that it was perfectly OK to accept a verdict against Henri Paul even when the jury were told that for a manslaughter verdict they had *to be sure* (my italics) that Paul saw the risk of death but ran it nonetheless. It is clear he could not have done and don't forget that the blood evidence against him was clearly flawed and severely criticised in court; by Scott Baker.

Also remember that neither Queen Elizabeth, her husband the Duke of Edinburgh nor MI6 were ever going to be considered in these proceedings, as stated by Scott Baker at the commencement of proceedings. So with the main parties being excluded from consideration and with such a restrictive choice of verdict, together with proof that one of the most important witness groups, the paparazzi, were prevented from attending court through *political intervention* plus that the decision to embalm Diana was taken at a *diplomatic level,* you might again ask what the point of this hearing was other than to protect the monarchy and administer catharsis to the people?

While deliberating your findings, consider the following. Since most of the evidence you have read in this book is proven, can anyone really believe that it could all be coincidental or, as Scott Baker said during proceedings with regard to seatbelts not being worn, unfortunate? Sitting in any court throughout the world, could you hear this evidence and return any verdict other than murder – if, of course, you resided in a democracy and were permitted such a verdict? But, if you take this view, consider the consequences.

Murder means that state agents planned and executed this vile crime for the benefit of one family. But for this to have success they needed subsequently to coerce the support of the police in their nefarious purpose and, because MI6 messed up, the government also needed to collude later. It was a dark day for British 'democracy', even if it originally existed. What was the reason for this perversion of the people's justice? – The protection of one family?

But the court's democratic duty is to the people and not one family or group of public servants that are all supposed to have the people's interests at heart. These issues are central to democracy and bring into question whether the gulf between monarchy and the people's democracy has reached such proportions that they can no longer co-reside. It also raises extremely disturbing questions over the police and the government of the day when all will have been culpable in committing a murderous and treasonous act against the British people simply to protect this family.

The USA is the best example of a democracy since here the people are the law and the most important part of their society; Americans may even remove their head of state if they so choose. But in Britain the whole process is engaged in the defence of one family at the expense of the people and democracy, and those who seek justice are liable to legal suppression and, in some cases, far worse reprisals. How much does this differ from the burning of books and curtailing the freedom of the press that various regimes such as the Nazis and KGB used to ensure that the people remained suppressed so that the states' chosen systems could continue?

The judge also claimed during proceedings that the Duke of Edinburgh could no longer be considered a murderer because the lawyers were now only accusing him of having created a hostile environment towards Diana. But this is untrue: the only reason for the softening of the approach towards Edinburgh was that the lawyers were trying to overturn the court's decision not to call him to court and a lesser accusation was the one remaining ploy.

It follows from this position there was never going to be an examination of the royal family or the security services since these two main parties that should have been under scrutiny for this crime were taken out of the equation from the outset. It would also be impossible to protect these people if witnesses gave evidence that brought the curtain down. As already stated, a murder verdict alone is a de facto conviction for MI6.

To consider that the paparazzi were responsible for this crime is beyond reason since evidence inescapably supports the view that they arrived after the crash. If there were only one or two inexplicable incidents that aroused suspicion, then we might retain some doubt and be persuaded there was insufficient evidence to permit our questioning this whole debacle. But there is substantial eyewitness evidence that, together with equivocation from the authorities, confirms this as a murderous attack.

If, therefore, you are satisfied the detail described in this book has no innocent interpretation and that important eyewitness testimony was circumvented, you must return a verdict of murder and state compliance in a perversion of justice, if not high treason. Two jurors refused to be bludgeoned into allowing the British state to wriggle out of this obscenity despite Scott Baker first saying the verdict must be unanimous (which it was not) and this hearing has convinced very few people, if anyone.

The vehicles at the tunnel were palpably attack vehicles and the obvious truth is that 'loitering' vehicles waited at the entrance to the Alma tunnel for a Mercedes, which, from their behaviour, they clearly knew was soon to arrive. This Mercedes was being 'tailgated' by motorbikes in hot pursuit, driving 'aggressively and dangerously'; when they then commenced 'hindering' or 'blocking' it on arrival at one of the most dangerous spots for motor accidents in Paris, where there had been eight fatal crashes during the fifteen years prior to Diana's murder and another eight people had also been seriously injured during this same period.

The Alma just happens to be close to the Ritz Hotel where Diana and Dodi were staying, and also to Dodi's apartment and the British Embassy. A 'flash of light' appeared just prior to the moment when the Mercedes impacted with the pillars, at which point all vehicles fled in the direction of the British Embassy, 'closely following one another' in tandem and were never seen again.

How a court could sidestep all unambiguous evidence from witnesses and use procedure to pass off the incident as being an accident is arguably the worst abuse of justice the British people have ever had to endure and the court's direction that the paparazzi and Henri Paul were culpable is derisory.

We are expected to be grateful for the effort spent in perfecting one of the biggest ever confidence tricks in British history and to consider this process was fairly executed, then deem the matter closed, as we observe a supposed democracy slide into the eternal abyss and accept the findings of, but forever ignore, this carefully orchestrated affront to justice.

Epilogue

Had the British police refused to bury this crime and placed their integrity above a perceived need to bow to political pressure, I would not have been driven to write this book. But despite strenuous efforts by police and security services to expunge all evidence of murder and so remove any threat to the monarchy, this grotesque abuse of the people's justice failed to persuade thinking people and too much evidence remained available for discovery.

Had the police retained their integrity, an appropriate headline might have been 'Executed for High Treason', or 'Murdered by the Establishment', or even 'The Monarchy is Finished'. Perhaps we would all have been queuing to observe justice being done to those responsible in the manner then still available to the British courts; that is until the death penalty for high treason – introduced in 1351 under King Edward III – was abolished 646 years later under Section 36 of the Crime and Disorder Act 1998, just months after Diana's murder.

The press would pay large sums for photographs of necks being stretched on the gallows to the tumultuous acclaim of many millions of civilised people throughout the world, with everyone contemplating significant changes to the structure of the British establishment, not to mention a new government. But if the authorities had succeeded with this obscene cover-up, there would have been insufficient evidence for critical scrutiny so, no book. Diana would have become but a fading footnote of history.

Evidence for murder doesn't need to be of the smokin' gun variety and often the police investigate crimes without much initial evidence, but here, the evidence was abundant. However, most police forces do at least investigate unless prevented from doing do by political forces. What should concern us most is that this crime was not properly investigated at all and very clearly for political reasons.

Having read this book, you now know there is substantial evidence in this case, especially when one adds the number of mistakes, leaks and proven misrepresentations by the British police and MI6, together with proven corruption of the French police that have all been exposed. We apply a sardonic thought that is highlighted by our star turn, Commander Mules, who first makes decisions about what happened and then discards everything else that steers him away from his God-given theory. Perhaps over time this will become known as 'Mules' Law'? One has to believe this is how Commander Mules conducts his business, which should seriously alarm the French people, or – viewing his actions in a kinder light – perhaps he was unable to carry out certain instructions adequately from high office. Personally, I am unable to think of any possible alternative reason for his otherwise inexplicable remarks.

Over a five-year period (2000–05), the British Government felt the need to increase the numbers of their spin doctors by nearly 500 per cent. So, what are spin doctors? They are people who are employed to lie to the public, presumably because their employers are insufficiently competent to do the job for which they were elected: otherwise why anyone would pay a person to lie about what they have been up to is a mystery. Why not just show what has been achieved? – Unless, of course, the answer is nothing; or worse?

These people can only be necessary when levels of incompetence must be masked and a different reason for a failure put forward, or indeed the need is perceived for us to be told that what we wanted isn't what we thought we wanted all along but is nearer to what has inadvertently happened and aren't they wonderful for achieving it?

This is similar to what happened with the Paris attack. The British Government tells us what they want us to believe and hope that after years of deceiving people and sending former police officers on trips for photo calls in France, plus holding a belated and dubious inquest, they can dispense with a proper criminal investigation and expect us to accept that Diana died in a tragic accident.

What is tragic for MI6 is that people have perceived the spin put on Diana's death and are discontented at the government's continued deception. The Establishment will do their utmost to prevent the truth from emerging, so anyone who holds evidence of Diana's murder will be dealt with either by misuse of the British court system or by any other obscenity perceived as necessary.

Charles Windsor has also benefited from the effects of spin and appears to need a team of image builders in order to stay afloat. Many years ago in Australia, a bathing beauty came rushing up to him in the surf, with all the cameras on standby; this is known to have been a set-up in an effort to enhance his image. It was considered necessary even then. For many years, the Palace has needed to portray Charles as 'Action Man' to try and interest the people in someone whom they clearly didn't perceive as being a suitable king, otherwise why put out spins about him on a regular basis to try and improve his image? When did anyone last feel the need to put out a spin on Prince William?

During the last few years there have been more suppressed scandals about Charles Windsor, one involving his activities with a male servant that was naturally denied by the Palace but not before the very person responsible for dealing with such matters on their behalf had been reported to ask whether his boss, Charles Windsor, is homosexual. 'Risible' came the answer from this very same man who had asked the question of Charles's sexuality when confronted, but how is one to call something risible if the same thought had crossed one's own mind? If the person who works for Prince Charles takes this view, then no one else can be blamed for thinking similarly.

Diana had serious doubts about her husband's fitness to be king and said that he himself had questioned whether he was capable. Even the gentleman's club, Whites of London (of which Charles was a member) had voted him 'Shit of the Year'. I doubt even the sturdiest of sycophants would say he is ideal as head of the Church of England either, so this role should be reconsidered, should Charles sneak through the net to become king.

Surely the days should be past when we are required to accept whomever we are given with regard to the succession? If the system doesn't allow for this, Parliament could enable it. Should the people be forced to accept an accidental order of birth? Surely it would be preferable to choose the future monarch from a royal list, thus ending the random selection process of first-born male that is the current method? Why should the people be forced to accept an accidental order of birth; why first born, why male? This argument reinforces the idea that the monarchy exists for the people (and not the reverse) and on this, the people must therefore decide.

One must also remember that the motive for Diana's murder was solely because of her relationship with the monarchy, irrespective of from where the order for her murder emanated. The prime reason was her husband's behaviour and Diana's subsequent, and understandable, response to this that put the monarchy in grave danger. Prince Charles swore to love and honour his wife till death did them part, though not in the unacceptable manner of it. By marrying Diana, he could do his duty for the production of offspring in order to keep the 'Firm' going, but not his duty before God by sacrificing his love for a married woman to serve the Crown and honour his marriage vows to Diana.

Diana's father-in-law, Prince Philip, Duke of Edinburgh, knew that Charles didn't want to marry Diana and it was a duty purely for the production of offspring. Diana was certainly clear that Philip told his son that he could leave her within five years to be with his mistress; this was at the beginning of the 'marriage'. Charles, of course, didn't wait because, as he admitted, he never did love Diana. But the monarchy must have known that by the time this point was reached, Diana's life would be destroyed.

As this evil unfolded, Diana needed to be labelled paranoid and deliberate lies put out to the people through various royal sycophants about her having 'lost all reason', simply to enable Charles to continue in his illicit relationship. Soon, the Palace would have no control over Diana and so there had to be another solution to prevent the monarchy from disintegrating. It was known that Diana would ensure justice was done for the abuse she had suffered.

Diana was totally deceived as to where her marriage was going, which was for her either to conform to Palace dictates and turn a blind eye on her husband's infidelity for eternity, or to head for the divorce courts. If Diana were still alive, I have no doubt that criticism of Charles Windsor would not be to the forefront of the people's minds because not many of them care what he is up to. Most would have been interested in Diana and, until that night in Paris, therein lay one of the monarchy's main issues.

When the Princess of Wales had her HRH title removed, the Palace believed that the Diana phenomenon would disappear but with public knowledge of this it was now even more dangerous because with rapidly diminishing control, Diana could do as she pleased – especially when she had established her relationship with Dodi Fayed, when her position became significantly more dangerous. For her, the central issue was to retain custody of her children and that accentuated her problems because of the tactics she was forced into using. She prepared a dossier of royal skeletons – powerful stuff that could help her anticipated custody battle – but one that also endangered the monarchy.

Diana knew too much about the royal family to be in this position and swore publicly that she would 'fight to the bitter end and not go quietly'. She planned to take her children with her to whatever country she selected, where they would grow up out of the monarchy's control so who knows what the future would have held with regard to the ultimate succession? This could have signalled the end of the monarchy but it would almost certainly have destroyed Charles Windsor's chances of becoming king.

Diana met Dodi as people all over the world meet, largely by chance and circumstance. She didn't know that her decision to go to the South of France would briefly change misery into complete bliss and make her world light up once more; that all the treachery and deception of the past fifteen years would begin to fade. It's not uncommon for couples to meet and then discover a bond so strong that it develops into something special in a very short space of time. There is no doubt in my mind that the relationship between Diana and Dodi was leading to marriage within weeks.

It's proven that MI6 continually watched the Princess's every move and had a history of engaging in electronic eavesdropping surveillance on her, so what are the chances that they did not know exactly what Diana and Dodi were planning and when they intended to marry? They denied it, of course but then as has been proved elsewhere in this book, they prevaricated and delivered a flurry of untruths concerning virtually everything else and remained untouched by the court.

The method that Diana and Dodi used to inform the people was to use a well-known society photographer, not considered one of the usual paparazzi pack, to take discreet but meaningful photos that would leave the world in no doubt of their intentions. To this end, Mario Brenna was told where they would be during the first week in August. It was on this assignment that he shot the famous 'KISS' photograph of the couple while they frolicked on board Al Fayed's yacht, the *Jonical*, on 7th August 1997. The whole flow of events left us with no doubt that marriage was their intention, despite the subsequent failure of both MI6 and a futile government non-investigative, procrastination programme designed to deny it: Diana was not hiding her love under a bushel.

In addition, why would the Secret Service apparently show no interest when, not only was it their job to observe and watch Diana, but they knew their greatest fear was about to unfold at the end of August 1997? Is it an unbelievable coincidence that a huge number of MI6 officers, including several senior ones, had concomitantly decided to descend on Paris together with Diana and Dodi? Are we expected to believe that, despite this, they were not even aware that she was in Paris?

There might have been a semblance of credibility, if MI6 had made a statement concerning their activities that night and explained why they were in Paris, especially knowing what people would be thinking. Surely they would wish to correct this 'misunderstanding'? However, they obviously decided that saying anything would open the floodgates for more and more questions they would be unable to answer so, to avoid self-incrimination, they stayed silent. Besides, there was no demand from the then British Prime Minister – Tony Blair – for them to do otherwise.

Now let us consider the MI6 ploy of different coloured paper that they used to try and confuse the jurors. Imagine you are a company CEO and one of your executives puts an idea down on paper – pink, white or whatever colour – suggesting that you murder the head of one of your competitors. Do you just shrug your shoulders and throw it in the bin, having first sent it round your company directors for consideration as it is proven MI6 did, or do you make a citizen's arrest and call the police?

The whole MI6 evidence charade was either a pack of untruths, complete and utter nonsense, or they simply refused to answer any difficult questions. This is unacceptable behaviour for public servants and will leave all except the totally naïve amazed at how these people could be entrusted with the defence of any realm. They must have a wonderful record system or they would be completely lost, but no, they have a system that relies on white and pink paper that may, according to some, be shredded, while others declare this to be a 'hanging offence'. According to others, however, many are shredded as a matter of routine.

When caught out over a proposal that Agent 'A' had put forward on formal white paper, having claimed it was on pink, 'A' gave ridiculous 'evidence' that it was a case of 'white treat as pink' – once more proven as untrue by Witness X. Some denied having any interest in the Paris Ritz Hotel, while others admitted to having held covert meetings there and another said that MI6 held several meetings there on one project alone. They don't murder people but they do, however, only with a minister's approval; and they don't have textbooks on murdering people, only handouts.

It's incredible that the British police didn't take action since they were supposed to be seeking out the murderers. Ultimately, they were forced into admitting 'they cannot rule out murder' when everybody else knew this several years before. They admitted to this possibility because of the loss of public confidence and the attendant risk of chaos. Why didn't they join the French before seven years had lapsed and then why did the 'investigation' take nearly a decade?

Imagine that Her Majesty the Queen was assassinated – does anyone expect us to believe the British police would do nothing for seven years and then use one retired police officer, Lord Stevens, to look into the crime. All that Stevens then did was conduct a forty-minute interview with one of the chief suspects? You could, of course, take the view that the police didn't interview Charles at all because Stevens was retired so he was no longer with the police.

The policeman in charge of the Diana investigative debacle in France, Sir David Veness, admitted that if this had been the Queen this situation would have been handled differently without clarifying why. Of course had the police properly investigated, they would have found copious evidence of murder and MI6 would have been under intense scrutiny – everything the Security Services were trying to avoid. But this admission from Veness at least shows something very sinister was going on. The police were controlled by political dictates, which explains the elaborate smokescreen and their assent only to what the public already knew. It looked like murder, they proclaimed, but of course it was an accident – an example of 'Mules Law' in action.

The British police had a letter handed to them, written by Diana two years before she was murdered and given to her lawyer, Lord Mishcon, in case of an attack on her life. The letter expressed fears that her husband was planning to kill her in a car crash. Diana also wrote a similar letter to Paul Burrell, her former butler. The first letter, the Mishcon note, was handed to police on 18th September 1997 but kept hidden by police for six years until Paul Burrell's letter forced its release into the public domain, when within weeks, the inquests were opened. No one can possibly justify such a criminal act.

The Burrell letter wasn't handed to the police; it was first handed to the press to ensure that it saw the light of day otherwise we would almost certainly have heard nothing of it. In this event it is also unlikely that the inquests would have ever been held in such a reasonably open forum. More likely, the previous failed attempts to hold illegal inquests would have fared much better. Can you perceive any other country tolerating this behaviour without a plausible explanation or accepting that the police may be used as a political pawn?

Since the police deemed it necessary to admit that they 'cannot rule out murder', they inadvertently conceded an investigation ought to have immediately commenced and so instead of taking day trips to France for photo calls, perhaps they should have answered our questions. Why didn't you investigate this crime and who stopped you from doing so? If political forces didn't prevent you from going to France immediately after the attack, why didn't former British Prime Minister – Tony Blair – insist that you did?

The British nation has fought wars to ensure that it didn't need to succumb to a politically controlled police state yet from the beginning, nothing was ever done because of 'political intervention'. (Don't forget that during the inquests it was proven that the paparazzi were prevented from attending court through 'political intervention' and that the decision to embalm Diana in France was taken at a 'diplomatic level'.)

But the police were in a difficult position: they couldn't investigate something controlled and perverted by the British Government since their success would mean the government's own demise and no government would order its own nemesis. However, it is my belief that the continuing disquiet and the government's failed attempts to pervert the course of justice will now come back to bite some of their number.

Is anyone able to give one example where such a situation would be allowed to occur anywhere else in the world (except in dictatorships) without redress from the people? Are the people now going to question whether they can trust the police, if they can be bought and directed by politicians, even with reference to murder, and then subsequently keep silent?

Are we entering a period of chaos and anarchy, where centuries of law and order for which the British have been admired and proclaimed around the world shall now sink into the abyss because of the arrogance and stupidity of some people who actually believe murder was justified, or by some politicians who believe that lying to the people and compromising the integrity of the police by forcing them to pervert the course of justice is permissible?

When Richard Tomlinson, one of MI6's highest qualified, but disenchanted former MI6 agents, attempted to assist in the search for the truth in identifying Diana's murderers, he was incarcerated in

December 1997 by a British judge, who said that it was in the national interest. Tomlinson had tried to see the French judge, Stephan, just after Diana's murder but was prevented from doing so. He then tried to return to France but was again prevented this time through incarceration. (He served six months of a twelve-month sentence.) There were forces afoot that feared he would reveal too much and cause an insurrection in Britain.

Tomlinson persisted with seeking the truth. He went to New York at the invitation of NBC to give a TV interview in September 1998 but was frogmarched off the plane in New York by customs officials and kept in isolation for several hours before being turned back. American customs officials didn't attempt to hide the fact that he had been detained on orders from the CIA. Who do you think requested the CIA's intervention? Also remember the amazing and extremely sad death of 229 people aboard Swissair flight 111 from New York that Tomlinson was booked to return on; an almost unbelievable coincidence; perhaps.

We know of these two Security Services people, Richard Tomlinson and David Shayler, who both made us proud by refusing to follow orders that they knew the people would find unacceptable and for standing their ground against evil. It is inevitable that the establishment would seek to undermine such behaviour and say that both are disgraceful for breaching the code of their previous office by stating some unpalatable truths.

Consider, however, the Second World War, when the Allies executed German officers for war crimes on the basis that those officers should have refused orders that were considered to be outside acceptable human behaviour. Now consider the courage of Tomlinson and Shayler, who both took that decision. Their treatment attests to the justifiable fears expressed by those German officers and whose executions appear more of a political show than having anything to do with justice.

Have Tomlinson and Shayler been well treated? And have the people come out in their support, thus preventing the Services from running roughshod over their liberty? What category do you think Diana's murder fits into? Was this act acceptable to you? If we are not to descend from disgust and shame into utter hypocrisy, then we must also understand what these Services are all about and whether they are needed. If so, do they need the degree of autonomy currently enjoyed?

If MI6 were more accountable, the 'deniability' they rely on would significantly diminish so, if they committed a crime 'in the interests of the state' (but usually in the interests of a select few) and it became public knowledge, the Prime Minister would have to accept responsibility – not an option. So, for this reason, MI6 activities remain secret, details about them are obfuscated and we must accept behaviour that decent souls find abhorrent. This is one reason why principled MI6 operatives, who joined the service to protect the nation, like Richard Tomlinson, have become disillusioned.

Imagine how any decent agent could deal with this situation from within the ranks of MI6. He cannot openly talk to anyone since there is no one to listen. If he talks to the police, they refer him back to the Security Services, or if he approaches a judge then he will be sentenced to imprisonment for attempting to breach the Official Secrets Act. If he seeks redress using the political route, spineless politicians say they are unable to answer questions on matters affecting the national interest. This is British democracy, twenty-first-century style.

Do you believe that the former British Prime Minister, Tony Blair, doesn't know Diana was murdered? Do you think he doesn't know who was responsible? As that great sage of French investigative procedures, Commander Mules, said in his TV interview: 'Think a little bit.'

It was deemed necessary to convene inquests because British law required them and the people would never allow the establishment to forego one, but if Mohamed Al Fayed had not successfully challenged the process, especially the issue concerning one of the coroners' illegal attempts to sit without a jury, then clearly the matter would have been brought to an end behind closed doors. In fact, it took three Law Lords to decide that this was illegal. Following this Law Lords' ruling, the culpable coroner – Dame Elizabeth Butler-Sloss (who is personally known to the royal family) – resigned.

A complete analysis of what happened during that fateful night in Paris can only be determined through a full and proper criminal investigation conducted by those who wish to divine the truth. This murder is a simple story: Diana was a threat to the monarchy and, for this reason, was murdered by the British Security Services, along with – at the least – a nod from the Palace.

There is no other explanation for the prevarication, lies and illogical behaviour; substantial evidence points to it. Who other than the British Prime Minister would wield the power to exert the necessary influence over the MI6 boss in consideration of Diana's death? Who else had the connections and motive, if it wasn't Tony Blair?

Although you may now fear that the courts are corrupt, we also know that many suppressed truths throughout history have been proven and there are many honest judges (proven by the Law Lords' ruling) who spend their entire lives defending justice. You, the public, are the ones whom the government and the Security Services fear, since you are the law and are therefore Diana's only hope. You are millions, the miscreants are few, and they dare not abuse you too often since history shows the outcome of such folly. It is up to you, the world grand jury, to decide on your verdict.

You will note throughout that all who were ridiculed at the inquests were those who had given evidence that supported murder whereas all those who supported an accident did not, on any occasion, receive any insults or ridicule or even have their evidence questioned. Some witnesses were even challenged when their evidence didn't suit the court and then the same witness would later have his evidence extolled when it did.

Why, when it was clearly shown that MI6 were sidestepping most pertinent questions in court, didn't the judge admonish them or even require that they answer the questions? Why wasn't Lord Condon, the former London police commissioner, pursued by the court to explain his claims that he had informed Diana's sister, Lady Sarah McCorqodale about the Mishcon note (a claim that she has denied)? Why didn't the court insist that Dr Dion, representatives from the medical profession, the paparazzi and Christophe Pelât attend and confirm what the court expected the jury to believe in their absence – because this is evidence that would expose the authorities' subterfuge and why there was proven political intervention to prevent their attendance? Why didn't Tony Blair insist MI6 files were released and order an immediate investigation?

As a member of our jury I trust you have considered this book with a critical mind to judge what you might regard as the probability of murder. The law works this way, so it is not unreasonable for you to do this and decide what you think. Had there been one or two irregularities or even several, one might take the view that, well, it looks rather sinister but we cannot be certain of murder. But I believe that the number of incidents and unanswered questions, together with the authorities' behaviour, leave no doubt whatsoever of murder.

The monarchy may now suffer through discovery of the truth and you may consider that the attraction of a republic is that a president is accountable to the people whereas the monarchy never will be. But provided the monarchical system enjoys an acceptable structure with those who command the love and respect of the people, some may believe there is an advantage of greater stability, provided the monarch doesn't interfere in the nation's political life.

But no monarchy should be allowed to survive by standing above the democratic will of the people or by disposing of some people because it suits their purpose. A system that endorses this behaviour should never receive a vote of confidence from the people and if changes are required, Parliament needs to do the job for which it is elected or the people must seek an alternative.

The authorities must be suffering from some delusion that they acted in the interests of the British people either by committing this crime, or suppressing knowledge of it. Consider the situation with Diana's former butlers, Harold Brown in November 2000 and Paul Burrell in January 2001: both were arrested within weeks of one another and apparently on unrelated matters. Add to that the fact that the police were looking for Diana's tapes, dossiers or written memoirs concerning the royals, and the British soul heads further towards the abyss. 'Not in my name!' the universal cry goes and I dare say a good majority of you feel like making that same cry now.

We piece together fragments and raise issues that receive a deathly silence from those whom we have elected to rule us but they rule with our consent and we shall not tolerate any government displaying complete contempt for the law, which is the same as contempt for the people who are the law. This they must never be allowed to forget; only the people can end this evil.

Diana's son William has married and I know that he and his brother Harry will want justice for their beloved mother. (You will remember that heart-wrenching note of the top of Diana's coffin as she was being taken on her last journey down the Mall in London that merely said 'Mummy'). All those murdered on that fateful night must now have justice and find peace but, if the current British Government doesn't lend its support to this venture, we may still expect a major battle in pursuing justice.

Prince Charles remarried in 2005 and much has now changed, but the government must resist the inclination to let matters lie. They may consider there are no loose ends that can now arise and none of the Alma victims can give testimony. James Andanson has also been silenced in what was clearly a French political cover-up by falsely passing off his death as a suicide.

It seems improbable that anyone will further challenge the blood results of Henri Paul after all this time and Trevor Rees-Jones has fortuitous amnesia. (I know of no attempt to see whether he still has amnesia after all this time. I have no doubt the authorities won't want to know. He made a good recovery and was back on light duties at Harrods by 2nd March 1998, just seven months after the crash.) Unless more officers from MI6 reveal further evidence to the people, there is no one left to challenge the lies put out by the previous British Government. Even if any MI6 officers were so inclined, then they would no doubt face a well-chosen British judge, who would imprison them in the so-called national interest. Richard Tomlinson serves as a stark reminder to all MI6 operatives of conscience.

It's also highly improbable that any decent serving MI6 officer would feel inclined to commit professional, or actual, suicide by disclosing the truth even though there will be those whose minds it may have crossed. If the new British Government were to ensure that honest officials are in office and order MI6 to release its files to a new chief of police, who would be impartial by not allowing political intervention to sway his judgment and abuse the people's democracy, then we could have testimony from MI6 personnel, who would come forward to end this evil.

This would need the Prime Minister, David Cameron (2013), to demand that MI6 cooperate with a new police chief. What about appointing John Yates, ex of Scotland Yard, as the head of a new investigative force (provided he is prepared to). Here is a man that the British people might well trust. He certainly ignored the rantings of politicians, Tony Blair in particular, in the interests of doing his duty so perhaps he should be declared 'the people's policeman'.

Let us re-establish the pride that could once be justly felt towards the UK instead of suffering the current shame, disgust and dishonour that the establishment has brought on their nation.

★

June 1997. Diana's marriage was over, with the Decree Absolute soon to be declared on 29th August. She had no plans for the summer holidays with her children. Life had become intolerable and options limited, which is clear from her comment: 'Who will take me on, with all the baggage I am carrying?' School would soon be out and all her friends were going on holiday with their families. Diana, meanwhile, felt completely alone. She returned home to an empty palace and cried herself to sleep, wondering what fate could have in store: perhaps a new life awaited somewhere. Maybe someone could take on the 'baggage' and shoulder the consequences of giving happiness to a woman who loved nothing more than to give it. She was the world's most adored woman, yet paradoxically one of the loneliest souls on earth.

On 3rd June 1997, Diana was invited to a rendition of *Swan Lake*, her favourite ballet, at London's National Theatre. She sat near to Mohamed Al Fayed, a man she knew through her father, who invited her to join him on a holiday at his home in St Tropez, South of France. It was a blessing sent from heaven! She would be able to take her children on holiday, away from prying eyes, in absolute security and in a beautiful part of France adored by the world's rich and famous, with yachts, swimming, sunshine, security, no press and the one thing

Diana craved most of all: privacy. This would allow her to regroup, enjoy the summer with her family and once more take on the world in search of that elusive happiness.

Nothing was going to keep her from this brief idyll, but on accepting, Diana had taken an irrevocable step towards the scrutiny and harassment from the Security Services that would inevitably ensue. A confident and rich Diana, burning with vengeance for her years of abuse by the royals and knowing most of the skeletons in their cupboards, was a dangerous combination. This, together with the additional power and support of Al Fayed, resulted in the emergence of a lethal cocktail that the Palace and the British Security Services could not endure.

Diana pondered her decision and duly wrote to Mohamed Al Fayed on 11th June, accepting his kind offer. The Security Services, who continued to watch and assess this on-going and growing problem, knew this. Diana was a problem to all those who wished to maintain the status quo and protect the heir to the British throne, Prince Charles, even when that entailed terrifying, ruining and murdering people. There appeared to be no obscenity too great to contemplate in the preservation of that position.

How many people will think this system is an asset now that the facts are known; for how long will it be permitted to continue? It stretches credulity to believe that the people want to retain a system that can only remain in power by such means without first an admission of the truth and significant changes being made.

To the few who might still be wavering, consider this: imagine you are on a Grand Jury and hearing a case. You have to decide not whether specific people are guilty but whether you consider that the evidence before you at least justified a full and immediate investigation. Presented with the facts, you then deliberate with your colleagues. The evidence before you is what you have read in this book: please now decide whether this could be anything other than murder.

If, after reading this book, you decide that an investigation should have taken place and consider there is a huge amount of unacceptable and proven criminal behaviour that has been sidestepped and left unexplained by the authorities, then also ask yourself why the British police didn't investigate this crime but went to such elaborate lengths to do so several years later? They needed to be seen doing something before they made their pronouncement, both pre- and post- inquests, of an 'accident'.

Do you find this acceptable? Why didn't the former British Prime Minister insist that they investigate? Is all the evidence before you 'conspiracy theorist' nonsense or has your soul been awakened to a 'terrible secret' that clearly hangs over this affair? What is your verdict and what will you do? Walk away and say, let's not bother?

Diana stood for truth against evil and had the courage to live by it. Remember, before you have justice there must first be a government in power to seek it. Once the wrath of the people is kindled, nothing will extinguish it other than the breath of truth.

THE BEGINNING

Index

D

F